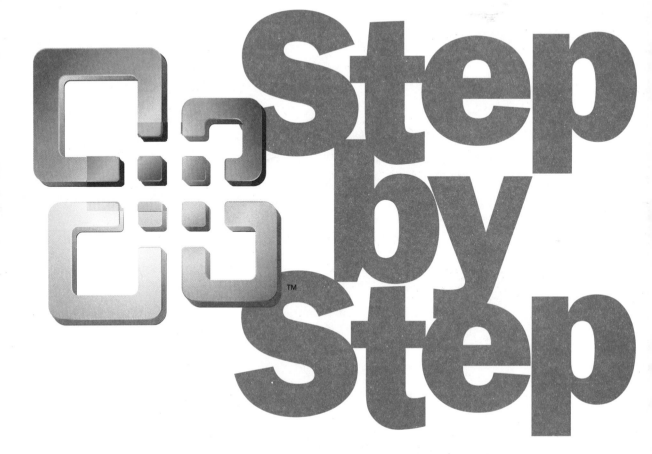

Step by Step™

Microsoft® Office
FrontPage® 2003

Online Training Solutions, Inc.

PUBLISHED BY
Microsoft Press
A Division of Microsoft Corporation
One Microsoft Way
Redmond, Washington 98052-6399

Library of Congress Cataloging-in-Publication Data
Microsoft Office FrontPage 2003 Step by Step / Online Training Solutions, Inc.
      p. cm.
    Includes index.
    ISBN 0-7356-1519-5
    1. Microsoft FrontPage. 2. Web sites--Design. 3. Web publishing I. Online Training Solutions (Firm)

HF5548.4.M525M527   2003
005.7'2--dc21   2003052674

Printed and bound in the United States of America.

8 9   QWE   8 7 6 5

Distributed in Canada by H.B. Fenn and Company Ltd.

A CIP catalogue record for this book is available from the British Library.

Microsoft Press books are available through booksellers and distributors worldwide. For further information about international editions, contact your local Microsoft Corporation office or contact Microsoft Press International directly at fax (425) 936-7329. Visit our Web site at www.microsoft.com/mspress. Send comments to *mspinput@microsoft.com*.

Acquisitions Editor: Alex Blanton
Project Editor: Aileen Wrothwell

Body Part No. X09-71440

Contents

1   Understanding How FrontPage Works   1

What's New in Microsoft Office FrontPage 2003

You'll notice some changes as soon as you start Microsoft Office FrontPage 2003. Many of the familiar program elements have been reorganized to give you better access to the features you use most, and many new features have been added to make it easier to create excellent functional Web sites.

New in Office 2003

Many of the features that are new or improved in this version of FrontPage won't be apparent to you until you start using the program. To help you quickly identify features that are new or improved with this version, this book uses the icon in the margin the first time those features are discussed or shown.

The following table lists the new features that you might be interested in, as well as the chapters in which those features are discussed.

To learn how to	Using this feature	See
Easily publish entire Web sites or specific files to a local folder or Web server	Remote Web Site view	Chapter 1 Chapter 10
Reduce the size of a page file when publishing it, by removing extraneous white space and unnecessary formatting	Optimize HTML	Chapter 1 Chapter 10
Switch between page views and site views	Web Site tab	Chapter 1
Work with Web pages in Design view, Code view, Split view, and Preview view	Web page views	Chapter 1
Simultaneously view the layout and HTML code of your Web page	Split view	Chapter 1
Check your Web site against standard guidelines for accessibility	Accessibility checking	Chapter 2
See how your Web site will look in different Web browsers or at various screen resolutions	Browser and resolution reconciliation	Chapter 2
Apply new cascading style sheet-based themes	Improved themes	Chapter 5
Control the layout of your Web page	Layout tables and cells	Chapter 6

To learn how to	Using this feature	See
Add professionally designed buttons to your Web page	Interactive Buttons	Chapter 7
Add Macromedia Flash content to your FrontPage Web site	Macromedia Flash support	Chapter 7
Use ready-made scripting options to add functionality to your Web page	Behaviors	Chapter 7
Quickly select the contents of any HTML tag in your Web page, from Design view, Code view, or Split view	Quick Tag Selector	Chapter 7
Provide feedback on your FrontPage usage to Microsoft	Improving quality for the customer	Chapter 11
Save frequently used code snippets for easy retrieval	Code snippets	Chapter 11
Customize the ruler and grid options	Page rulers and layout grid	Chapter 11
Automatically complete or insert code elements	IntelliSense	Chapter 11

Getting Help

Every effort has been made to ensure the accuracy of this book and the contents of its CD-ROM. If you do run into problems, please contact the appropriate source for help and assistance.

Getting Help with This Book and Its CD-ROM

If your question or issue concerns the content of this book or its companion CD-ROM, please first search the online Microsoft Press Knowledge Base, which provides support information for known errors in or corrections to this book, at the following Web site:

www.microsoft.com/mspress/support/search.asp

If you do not find your answer at the online Knowledge Base, send your comments or questions to Microsoft Press Technical Support at:

mspinput@microsoft.com

Getting Help with Microsoft Office FrontPage 2003

If your question is about Microsoft Office FrontPage 2003, and not about the content of this Microsoft Press book, your first recourse is FrontPage's Help system. This system is a combination of help tools and files stored on your computer when you installed The Microsoft Office System 2003 and, if your computer is connected to the Internet, help files available from Microsoft Office Online.

To find out about different items on the screen, you can display a *ScreenTip*. To display a ScreenTip for a toolbar button, for example, point to the button without clicking it. Its ScreenTip appears, telling you its name. In some dialog boxes, you can click a question mark icon to the left of the Close button in the title bar to display the Microsoft Office FrontPage Help window with information related to the dialog box.

When you have a question about using FrontPage, you can type it in the "Type a question for help" box at the right end of the program window's menu bar. Then press Enter to display a list of Help topics from which you can select the one that most closely relates to your question.

Another way to get help is to display the Office Assistant, which provides help as you work in the form of helpful information or a tip. If the Office Assistant is hidden when a tip is available, a light bulb appears. Clicking the light bulb displays the tip, and provides other options.

If you want to practice getting help, you can work through this exercise, which demonstrates two ways to get help.

1 At the right end of the menu bar, click the **Type a question for help** box.

2 Type How do I get help?, and press `Enter`.

A list of topics that relate to your question appears in the Search Results task pane.

You can click any of the help topics to get more information or instructions.

3 In the **Search Results** task pane, scroll down the results list, and click **About getting help while you work**.

The Microsoft Office FrontPage Help window opens, displaying information about that topic.

Maximize

4 At the right end of the Microsoft Office FrontPage Help window's title bar, click the **Maximize** button, and then click **Show All**.

The topic content expands to provide in-depth information about getting help while you work.

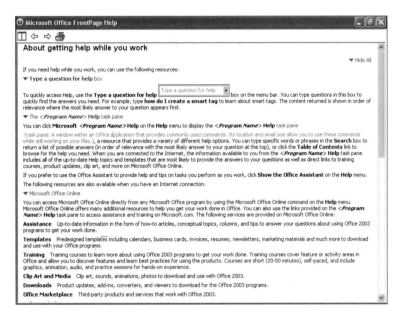

Close

5 At the right end of the Microsoft Office FrontPage Help window's title bar, click the **Close** button, to close the window.

6 On the **Help** menu, click **Microsoft Office FrontPage Help**.

The FrontPage Help task pane opens.

7 In the task pane, click **Table of Contents**.

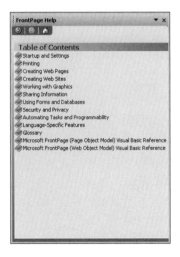

The task pane now displays a list of help topics organized by category, like the table of contents in a book.

Back

8   On the toolbar at the top of the task pane, click the **Back** button.

Notice the categories of information that are available from the Microsoft Office Online Web site. You can also reach this Web site by clicking Microsoft Office Online on the Help menu.

More Information

If your question is about a Microsoft software product, including FrontPage 2003, and not about the content of this Microsoft Press book, please search the appropriate product support center or the Microsoft Knowledge Base at:

support.microsoft.com

In the United States, Microsoft software product support issues not covered by the Microsoft Knowledge Base are addressed by Microsoft Product Support Services. The Microsoft software support options available from Microsoft Product Support Services are listed at:

support.microsoft.com

Outside the United States, for support information specific to your location, please refer to the Worldwide Support menu on the Microsoft Product Support Services Web site for the site specific to your country:

support.microsoft.com

Using the Book's CD-ROM

The CD-ROM included with this book contains all the practice files you'll use as you work through the exercises in this book. By using practice files, you won't waste time creating sample content with which to experiment—instead, you can jump right in and concentrate on learning how to use Microsoft Office FrontPage 2003.

What's on the CD-ROM?

In addition to the practice files, the CD-ROM contains some exciting resources that will really enhance your ability to get the most out of using this book and FrontPage 2003, including the following:

- *Microsoft Office FrontPage 2003 Step by Step* in e-book format.

- *Insider's Guide to Microsoft Office OneNote 2003* in e-book format.

- *Microsoft Office System Quick Reference* in e-book format.

- *Introducing the Tablet PC* in e-book format.

- *Microsoft Computer Dictionary, Fifth Edition* in e-book format.

- 25 business-oriented templates for use with programs in The Microsoft Office System.

- 100 pieces of clip art.

 Important   The CD-ROM for this book does not contain the FrontPage 2003 software. You should purchase and install that program before using this book.

Minimum System Requirements

To use this book, you will need:

- **Computer/Processor**

  Computer with a Pentium 133-megahertz (MHz) or higher processor; Pentium III recommended

- **Memory**

  64MB of RAM (128 MB recommended) plus an additional 8 MB of RAM for each program in The Microsoft Office System (such as FrontPage) running simultaneously

- **Hard disk**

  - 245 MB of available hard disk space with 115 MB on the hard disk where the operating system is installed

■ An additional 20 MB of hard disk space is required for installing the practice files

Hard disk requirements will vary depending on configuration; custom installation choices might require more or less hard disk space.

■ **Operating System**

Microsoft Windows 2000 with Service Pack 3 (SP3) or Microsoft Windows XP or later

■ **Drive**

CD-ROM drive

■ **Display**

Super VGA (800 × 600) or higher-resolution monitor with 256 colors

■ **Peripherals**

Microsoft Mouse, Microsoft IntelliMouse, or compatible pointing device

■ **Software**

Microsoft Office FrontPage 2003, Microsoft Office Word 2003 and Microsoft Internet Explorer 5 or later

Installing the Practice Files

You need to install the practice files on your hard disk before you use them in the chapters' exercises. Follow these steps to prepare the CD's files for your use:

1 Insert the CD-ROM into the CD-ROM drive of your computer.

The Step by Step Companion CD End User License Agreement appears. Follow the on-screen directions. It is necessary to accept the terms of the license agreement in order to use the practice files. After you accept the license agreement, a menu screen appears.

Important If the menu screen does not appear, start Windows Explorer. In the left pane, locate the icon for your CD-ROM drive and click this icon. In the right pane, double-click the StartCD executable file.

2 Click **Install Practice Files**.

3 Click **Next** on the first screen, and then click **Yes** to accept the license agreement on the next screen.

4 If you want to install the practice files to a location other than the default folder (My Documents\Microsoft Press\FrontPage 2003 SBS), click the **Browse** button, select the new drive and path, and then click **OK**.

5   Click **Next** on the **Choose Destination Location** screen, click **Next** on the **Select Features** screen, and then click **Next** on the **Start Copying Files** screen to install the selected practice files.

6   After the practice files have been installed, click **Finish**.

7   Close the Step by Step Companion CD window, remove the CD-ROM from the CD-ROM drive, and return it to the envelope at the back of the book.

Using the Practice Files

Each exercise is preceded by a paragraph or paragraphs that list the files needed for that exercise and explains any file preparation you need to take care of before you start working through the exercise.

The following table lists each chapter's practice files.

Chapter	Folder	Subfolder	Files
Chapter 1: Understanding How FrontPage Works	Understanding		GardenCo
Chapter 2: Creating a Web Site to Promote Yourself or Your Company	CreateWeb	InsertText	GardenCo
		InsertExist	PR1, PR2, Classes
		FormatText	GardenCo
		InsertHype	GardenCo, PR
		Preview	GardenCo
Chapter 3: Presenting Information in Lists and Tables	ListsTables	CreateList	GardenCo
		CreateTable	GardenCo
		TableText	GardenCo
		TableStruct	GardenCo
		FormatTable	GardenCo
		TableInTable	GardenCo
Chapter 4: Enhancing Your Web Site with Graphics	Pictures	AddPicture	GardenCo
		CropPicture	GardenView
		Thumbnail	Pictures
		PhotoGallery	plant1 *through* plant12
Chapter 5: Creating a Web Site from Scratch	FromScratch	NewPage	GardenCo
		PageTitle	GardenCo
		Backgrounds	GardenCo, tgc_bkgrnd, bgimage
		Borders	GardenCo
		Banners	GardenCo
		Themes	GardenCo, bgimage_small

Chapter	Folder	Subfolder	Files
Chapter 6: Changing Web Page Layout	PageLayout	Template	table_template
		Assembly	table_template
		Frames	tgclogo_sm
		LayOutFrame	GardenCo
Chapter 7: Enhancing the Capabilities of Your Web Site	Capabilities	Organize	GardenCo
		Subweb	GardenCo
		LinkPages	GardenCo
		LinkSites	GardenCo
		Components	GardenCo
		Effects	GardenCo, tada
Chapter 8: Communicating with Your Visitors	Communicate	AutoUpdate	GardenCo
		VisitorInput	GardenCo
		FindInfo	GardenCo
Chapter 9: Creating a Web Site to Support Team Projects	TeamWeb	Customize	Landscape
		Source	GardenCo
Chapter 10: Publishing Your Web Site	PublishWeb		GardenCo
Chapter 11: Managing Your Web Site	ManageSite		GardenCo

Uninstalling the Practice Files

After you finish working through this book, you should uninstall the practice files to free up hard disk space.

1 On the Windows taskbar, click the **Start** button, and then click **Control Panel**.

2 In Control Panel, click **Add or Remove Programs**.

3 In the list of installed programs, click **Microsoft Office FrontPage 2003 Step by Step Files,** and then click the **Remove** or **Change/Remove** button.

4 In the **Uninstall** dialog box, click **OK**.

5 After the files are uninstalled, click **Finish,** and then close the Add or Remove Programs window and Control Panel.

Important If you need additional help installing or uninstalling the practice files, please see "Getting Help" earlier in this book. Microsoft Product Support Services does not provide support for this book or its CD-ROM.

Conventions and Features

You can save time when you use this book by understanding how the *Step by Step* series shows special instructions, keys to press, buttons to click, and so on.

Convention	Meaning
New In Office 2003	This icon indicates a new or greatly improved feature in Microsoft Office FrontPage 2003.
(CD icon)	This icon indicates a reference to the book's companion CD.
BE SURE TO	These words are found at the beginning of paragraphs preceding or following step-by-step exercises. They point out items you should check or actions you should carry out either before beginning an exercise or after completing an exercise.
USE OPEN	These words are found at the beginning of paragraphs preceding step-by-step exercises. They draw your attention to practice files that you'll need to use in the exercise.
CLOSE	This word is found at the beginning of paragraphs following step-by-step exercises. They give instructions for closing open files or programs before moving on to another topic.
1 2	Numbered steps guide you through hands-on exercises in each topic.
●	A round bullet indicates an exercise that has only one step.
Troubleshooting	These paragraphs show you how to fix a common problem that might prevent you from continuing with the exercise.
Tip	These paragraphs provide a helpful hint or shortcut that makes working through a task easier.
Important	These paragraphs point out information that you need to know to complete a procedure.
☒ Close	The first time you are told to click a button in an exercise, a picture of the button appears in the left margin. If the name of the button does not appear on the button itself, the name appears under the picture.

Convention	Meaning
Ctrl + Home	A plus sign (+) between two key names means that you must hold down the first key while you press the second key. For example, "press Ctrl + Home" means "hold down the Ctrl key while you press the Home key."
Black bold characters	In steps, the names of program elements, such as buttons, commands, and dialog boxes, are shown in black bold characters.
Blue bold characters	Anything you are supposed to type appears in blue bold characters.
Blue italic characters	Terms that are explained in the glossary at the end of the book are shown in blue italic characters.

About the Authors

Online Training Solutions, Inc. (OTSI)

OTSI is a traditional and electronic publishing company specializing in the creation, production, and delivery of computer software training. OTSI publishes the Quick Course® series of computer and business training products. The principals of OTSI are:

Joyce Cox has over 20 years' experience in writing about and editing technical subjects for non-technical audiences. For 12 of those years she was the principal author for Online Press. She was also the first managing editor of Microsoft Press, an editor for Sybex, and an editor for the University of California.

Steve Lambert started playing with computers in the mid-seventies. As computers evolved from wire-wrap and solder to consumer products, he evolved from hardware geek to programmer and writer. He has written over 14 books and a wide variety of technical documentation and has produced training tools and help systems.

Gale Nelson honed her communication skills as a technical writer for a SQL Server training company. Her attention to detail soon led her into software testing and quality assurance management. She now divides her work time between writing and data conversion projects.

Joan Preppernau has been contributing to the creation of excellent technical training materials for computer professionals for as long as she cares to remember. Joan's wide-ranging experiences in various facets of the industry have contributed to her passion for producing interesting, useful, and understandable training materials.

The OTSI publishing team includes the following outstanding professionals:

Susie Bayers
Jan Bednarczuk
Keith Bednarczuk
RJ Cadranell
Liz Clark
Nancy Depper
Leslie Eliel
Joseph Ford
Jon Kenoyer
Marlene Lambert
Aaron L'Heureux
Lisa Van Every
Michelle Ziegwied

For more information about Online Training Solutions, Inc., visit *www.otsi.com*.

Quick Reference

36 **To insert text into a Web site**

1 Open the Web site, and open the page in which you want to add text in the Page view editing window.

2 Position the insertion point where you want the text to appear.

3 Type the text.

40 **To insert existing text into a Web page**

1 Open the page into which you want to insert text in the Page view editing window.

2 Position the insertion point where you want the text to appear.

3 On the **Insert** menu, click **File**.

4 Browse to the folder that contains the text you want to insert.

5 Click the file that contains the text in the list of available files, and then click **Open** to insert the full text of the document in your Web page.

45 **To format text**

● Select the text you want to format.

● To increase font size, on the Formatting toolbar, click the **Increase Font Size** button.

● To add italics, click the **Italic** button.

● To change the font, click the down arrow to the right of the **Font** box, and click the font you want in the drop-down list.

● To change the font color, on the Formatting toolbar, click the down arrow to the right of the **Font Color** button, and click a new font color.

● To add a border, on the Formatting toolbar, click the down arrow to the right of the **Borders** button, and click the option you want to apply.

● To format a paragraph, on the **Format** menu, click **Paragraph**. In the **Paragraph** dialog box, set the alignment, indentation, spacing, and any other settings you want, and then click **OK**.

50 **To insert a hyperlink**

1 Position the insertion point where you want to insert the hyperlink.

2 Type and select the text you want to hyperlink.

3 On the **Insert** menu, click **Hyperlink**.

4 In the **Insert Hyperlink** dialog box, click the **Browse for File** button, browse to the folder that contains the file you want to link to, click the file, and click **OK** twice.

52 **To preview a Web site**

1 Open the page in Design view.

2 At the bottom of the Page view editing window, click the **Show Preview View** button to switch to the Preview pane.

3 On the Standard toolbar, click the **Preview in Browser** button to see how the site looks in your default Web browser.

4 Click each of the navigation links to view the different pages of the site.

56 **To delete a Web site**

1 In the **Folder List**, right-click the top-level folder of the site you want to delete, and click **Delete** on the shortcut menu.

2 In the **Confirm Delete** dialog box, select the **Delete this Web site entirely** option, and then click **OK** to delete the Web site.

Chapter 3 **Presenting Information in Lists and Tables**

Page 60 **To add a new bulleted or numbered list item to an existing list**

● Position the insertion point at the end of a list item and press ⌷Enter⌷.

64 **To create a table**

● Position the insertion point where you want to insert the table, and on the Standard toolbar, click the **Insert Table** button.

● On the **Table** menu, point to **Insert**, and then click **Table**.

● On the **Table** menu, click **Draw Table**.

71 **To add information to a table**

● Position the insertion point in a cell, and then type the information.

74 **To edit a table**

● To delete a row or column, click in the row or column, point to **Select** on the **Table** menu, and click **Column** or **Row**. Then on the Tables toolbar, click the **Delete Cells** button.

● To adjust the size of the columns in a table, point to the right border of the column you want to adjust, and drag or double-click the border.

● To size the cells of a table to fit their contents, click anywhere in the table, and on the Tables toolbar, click the **AutoFit to Contents** button.

● To edit the structure of a table through the **Table Properties** dialog box, right-click anywhere in the table, click **Table Properties** on the shortcut menu, enter your table specifications, and then click **OK**.

xxiii

94 To size a picture

1 Double-click the picture to display the **Picture Properties** dialog box.

2 On the **Appearance** tab, select the **Specify size** check box, and set the **Width** to the desired number of pixels. (To prevent distortion, ensure that the **Keep aspect ratio** check box is selected.)

94 To crop a picture

1 Click the picture to select it, and on the Pictures toolbar, click the **Crop** button.

2 Drag the handles of the dashed-line crop box to redefine the size as you like.

3 Click the **Crop** button again or press `Enter` to crop the picture to the specified shape and size.

94 To convert a selected color picture to black and white

1 On the Pictures toolbar, click the **Color** button.

2 In the **Color** drop-down list, click **Grayscale**.

94 To add a bevel frame to a selected picture

● On the Pictures toolbar, click the **Bevel** button.

97 To create and test a thumbnail of a picture

1 Click the picture to select it and open the Pictures toolbar.

2 On the Pictures toolbar, click the **Auto Thumbnail** button.

3 On the Standard toolbar, click **Preview in Browser**. Save the page and embedded graphics if prompted to do so.

4 When your Web page opens in your browser, click the thumbnail to display the full-size graphic, and then click the browser's **Back** button to return to the thumbnail.

101 To add and modify a horizontal line

1 On the **Insert** menu, click **Horizontal Line**.

2 Right-click the line, and then click **Horizontal Line Properties** on the shortcut menu.

3 In the **Horizontal Line Properties** dialog box, set the width, height, and color to the desired settings, and click **OK**.

101 To insert a pre-defined shape

1 On the **Insert** menu, point to **Picture**, and then click **New Drawing**.

2 On the Drawing toolbar, click **AutoShapes** to see the menus of available shapes.

3 Click the shape category, and then click the shape you want to insert.

4 Repeat Step 3 and move the shapes as needed until you have completed your drawing.

101 **To rotate a shape**

● Click the shape, and drag its rotate handle (the green dot).

101 **To move a shape out from behind another shape**

● Right-click the shape, on the shortcut menu, point to **Order**, and then click **Bring to Front**.

101 **To select multiple shapes**

● Click one shape, and then hold down the [Shift] key while clicking the other shapes in turn to select them.

101 **To deselect one shape among many in a selected group**

● Hold down the [Shift] key, and click the shape you want to deselect.

101 **To group multiple shapes**

● Right-click the selected elements, and on the shortcut menu, point to **Grouping**, and then click **Group**.

101 **To ungroup elements in a drawing**

● Right-click the drawing, and on the shortcut menu, point to **Grouping**, and then click **Ungroup**.

101 **To create multiple copies of a shape**

1 Select a shape, and press [Ctrl]+[C] to copy it.

2 Press [Ctrl]+[V] to paste it, and while holding down the [Ctrl] key, repeat pressing the [V] key as many times as you want to paste the image into your drawing.

101 **To format an AutoShape**

1 Right-click the shape, and click **Format AutoShape**.

2 In the **Format AutoShape** dialog box, click the appropriate tab, and choose from among the available setting options.

3 Click **OK** to close the dialog box and apply your settings.

108 **To create a photo gallery in your open Web site**

1 On the **Insert** menu, click **Web Component**, and then select **Photo Gallery**.

2 In the **Choose a Photo Gallery Option** box, select the layout option you want, and click **Finish**.

3 In the **Photo Gallery Properties** dialog box, click **Add**, and then click **Pictures from Files**.

4 Browse to the folder that contains your picture files.

5 Select all the files at once by clicking the first file, holding down the [Shift] key, and clicking the last file. Then click **Open** to import them into the photo gallery.

6 Click **OK** to close the **Photo Gallery Properties** dialog box and generate the photo gallery.

111 **To insert text using WordArt**

1 On the **Insert** menu, point to **Picture**, and then click **WordArt**.

2 Select the style you want in the **WordArt Gallery** dialog box.

3 Click **OK**, and in the **Edit WordArt Text** dialog box, type your text in the **Text** box.

4 Set the font, font size, and any other formatting you want, and then click **OK**.

Chapter 5 **Creating a Web Site from Scratch**

Page 118 **To create a new Web site**

1 If the **New** task pane is not displayed, on the **File** menu, click **New**.

2 In the **New Web site** area of the **New** task pane, click **More Web site templates**.

3 Click the **Empty Web Site** icon.

4 Specify the location and name of your new Web site, preceding the location with C:\ or another drive letter for disk-based sites or with http:// for server-based sites, and then click **OK**.

121 **To create a new Web page**

1 On the Standard toolbar, click the **Create a new normal page** button.

2 Type the name you want to give your home page.

3 On the **File** menu, click **Save As** to open the **Save As** dialog box.

4 In the **Save in** drop-down list, browse to the folder where you want to save your file, and click **Save**.

123 **To change the name of your home page**

1 In the folder where you store your Web site, double-click the file name in **Folder List** to open it in the Page view editing window.

2 On the **File** menu, click **Save As**.

3 In the **Save As** dialog box, click the **Change title** button.

4 Change the page title, and click **OK**.

5 Click **Save** to close the **Save As** dialog box and save your change.

6 Click **Yes** when prompted to overwrite the existing file.

126 **To create a color background for a Web page**

1 On the **Format** menu, click **Background**.

2 In the **Colors** area, click the down arrow to the right of the **Background** box to expand the color selection area.

3 Click **More Colors**.

4 Select the color you want, click **OK** to close the **More Colors** dialog box, and then click **OK** to close the **Page Properties** dialog box and apply the selected background color to the Web page.

126 **To create a picture background for a Web page**

1 On the **Format** menu, click **Background**.

2 On the **Formatting** tab of the **Page Properties** dialog box, select the **Background picture** check box.

3 Click the **Browse** button, browse to the folder that contains your picture file, click the image you want to use, and click **Open**.

4 Select the options you want to apply to the image, and then click **OK**.

130 **To add a border**

1 On the **Format** menu, click **Borders and Shading**.

2 In the **Borders and Shading** dialog box, click the **Borders** tab and choose among your setting options.

3 Click **OK** to apply your settings.

133 **To create shared borders**

1 On the **Format** menu, click **Shared Borders**.

2 In the **Shared Borders** dialog box, select from the **All pages** and **Current page** options, and select any or all of the **Top**, **Left**, **Right**, and **Bottom** check boxes.

3 Click the **Border Properties** button to open the **Border Properties** dialog box, and set the properties the way you want.

4 Click **OK** twice to close the dialog boxes and apply the new border settings.

133 **To insert a page banner**

1 On the **Insert** menu, click **Page Banner**.

2 In the **Page Banner Properties** dialog box, select either the **Picture** or **Text** options, and click **OK**.

3   Make a copy of the page template for each page of your Web site. Rename each copy and change its page title.

4   Add the pages to the Web site's navigation structure.

5   Add elements to the individual pages as needed, and save the Web page.

164   **To create a frames page**

1   Open the **New** task pane.

2   In the **New page** area, click **More page templates** to open the **Page Templates** dialog box.

3   Click the **Frames Pages** tab.

4   Click the template you want, and then click **OK**.

168   **To convert existing static pages to a frame-based template**

1   Open the frame-based template in the Page view editing window.

2   To link an existing file to a frame, click **Set Initial Page**, browse to the file, and then click **Open**.

3   To create a new page for a frame, click **New Page**, create the file content, and save and name the file.

Chapter 7   **Enhancing the Capabilities of Your Web Site**

Page 180   **To create a new folder within the Web site structure**

1   At the top of the **Folder List**, click the **New Folder** button.

2   When the new folder appears at the bottom of the **Folder List**, type a name for the folder, and then press Enter.

180   **To sort the files by type**

●   In the **Folders** pane, click the **Type** heading.

180   **To sort the folders and files alphabetically**

●   In the **Folders** pane, click the **Name** heading.

180   **To move files into folders**

●   Select the files you want to move, and drag them to the folder.

183   **To make Web pages into a subweb**

●   Right-click the folder that contains the Web pages, on the shortcut menu, click **Convert to Web**, and in the warning that appears, click **Yes**.

186 **To create a link bar**

1 Open the Web page in Design view.

2 On the **Insert** menu, click **Navigation**.

3 In the **Component type** box, click **Link Bars**, pick a bar type from the **Choose a bar type** box, and then click **Next**.

4 Click the bar style you want, and click **Next**.

5 Specify the link bar's orientation, and then click **Finish**.

6 Enter a name for the new link bar, and then click **OK**.

7 Edit the Link Bar properties to specify the pages to which the bar will link.

186 **To create an image map**

1 Select the image to which you want to add links.

2 On the Pictures toolbar, click the hotspot shape you want.

3 Draw the hotspot.

4 In the **Insert Hyperlink** dialog box, browse to the location you want to link to, and then click **OK**.

193 **To insert a hyperlink to another Web site**

1 Select the words or object that you want to use as the link, and then click the **Insert Hyperlink** button.

2 In the **Insert Hyperlink** dialog box, enter the URL into the **Address** box.

3 If you want to specify a target frame, click **Target Frame** to open the **Target Frame** dialog box.

4 In the **Common targets** box, click **New Window**, or choose a different target.

5 Click **OK** to close the **Target Frame** dialog box, and then click **OK** to close the **Insert Hyperlink** dialog box and insert the hyperlink.

199 **To insert a Web component**

1 On the Standard toolbar, click the **Web Component** button to display the **Insert Web Component** dialog box.

2 In the **Component type** list, click the type of component you want to add, click the specific style or effect, and then click **Finish**.

3 Specify the properties for the component you chose, and click **OK**.

5 Navigate to the file you want to insert, select it, and then click **OK**.

6 Set the **Starting** date and time and the **Ending** date and time, and click **OK** to insert the Web component.

218 **To create a feedback form**

1 Open the **New** task pane.

2 In the **New page** area, click **More page templates** to open the **Page Templates** dialog box.

3 On the **General** tab, click **Feedback Form**, and then click **OK**.

4 On the Standard toolbar, click the **Save** button to display the **Save As** dialog box.

5 In the **File name** box, type a name for the file.

6 Click the **Change title** button. In the **Set Page Title** dialog box, type a title for the page.

7 Click **OK** to close the **Set Page Title** dialog box, and then click **Save** to close the **Save As** dialog box and save your file.

8 Switch to Navigation view.

9 Drag the feedback file from the **Folder List** to the navigation structure at the same level as the home page.

218 **To create a feedback confirmation page**

1 Open the **New** task pane.

2 In the **New page** area, click **More page templates** to open the **Page Templates** dialog box.

3 On the **General** tab, click **Confirmation Form**, and then click **OK**.

4 Save the page, typing a name and page title for it.

5 Switch to Navigation view, and drag the confirmation page to the navigation structure at the same level as the home page.

223 **To create a Frequently Asked Questions page**

1 Open the **New** task pane.

2 In the **New** page area, click **More page templates** to open the **Page Templates** dialog box.

3 Click **Frequently Asked Questions**, and then click **OK** to generate the new page.

4 On the **File** menu, click **Save As**.

5 In the **Save As** dialog box, in the **File** name box, type a name for the FAQ page.

6 Click **Change title**, type a page title, and click **OK** to close the dialog box.

7   Click **Save** to apply your changes.

8   Switch to Navigation view.

9   Drag the FAQ file from the **Folder List** to the navigation structure.

223   **To create a Search page using a page template**

1   Open the **New** task pane, and in the **New** page area, click **More page templates** to open the **Page Templates** dialog box.

2   On the **General** tab, click **Search Page**, and then click **OK**.

3   On the **File** menu, click **Save As** to open the **Save As** dialog box.

4   Name and save the file.

Chapter 9   **Creating a Web Site to Support Team Projects**

Page 234   **To create a project-management Web site**

1   Open the **New** task pane.

2   In the **New Web site** area, click **More Web site templates** to open the **Web Site Templates** dialog box.

3   On the **General** tab, click the **Project Web Site** icon.

4   In the **Options** area, click the **Browse** button, and navigate to the folder where you will store the new Web site.

5   On the toolbar, click the **Create New Folder** button.

6   In the **New Folder** dialog box, type a name for the new folder, and then click **OK**.

7   In the **New Web Site Location** dialog box, click **Open**.

8   In the **Web Site Templates** dialog box, click **OK**.

239   **To create a discussion Web site**

1   Open the **New** task pane.

2   In the **New Web site** area, click **More Web site templates** to open the **Web Site Templates** dialog box.

3   On the **General** tab, click the **Discussion Web Site Wizard** icon.

4   In the **Options** area, click the **Browse** button, and browse to the folder where you will store the new Web site.

5   On the toolbar, click the **Create New Folder** button.

6   In the **New Folder** dialog box, type a name for the new folder, and then click **OK**.

7   In the **New Web Site Location** dialog box, click **Open**.

8   In the **Web Site Templates** dialog box, click **OK**.

248   To create a SharePoint team Web site

1   On the Standard toolbar, click the down arrow to the right of the **Create a new normal page** button to expand the list of elements that can be created.

2   In the drop-down list, click **Web Site** to open the **Web Site Templates** dialog box.

3   Click the **General** tab.

4   Click the **SharePoint Team Site** icon.

5   In the **Specify the location of the new web** box, type http://<server>/<sitename>, where *<server>* is the name of your Web server and *<sitename>* is the name you want for your Web site. Then click **OK**.

251   To add a document library to a SharePoint team Web site

1   At the top of the page, click **Create**.

2   To add a new document library to the site, click **Document Library**.

3   In the **Name** box, type a name for the document library

4   In the **Description** box, type a description.

5   Select the other options you want, and then click **Create** to create the new document library.

251   To add a link to a SharePoint team Web site

1   On the Links page, click **New Item**.

2   On the Links: New Item page, type the URL in the **URL** box.

3   In the **Type the description** box, type a description, and then click **Save and Close** to save the Web site link to your **Links** list.

251   To apply a theme to a SharePoint team Web site

1   Display the Site Settings page.

2   In the **Customization** area, click **Apply theme to site**.

3   On the **Apply Theme to Web site** page, click the theme you want to apply, and at the bottom of the page, click **Apply**.

256   To turn on source control

1   On the **Tools** menu, click **Site Settings** to open the **Site Settings** dialog box.

2   On the **General** tab, select the **Use document check-in and check-out** check box, and then click **OK**.

3   If a message box appears, warning you that there will be a delay while FrontPage recalculates the Web site, click **Yes** to proceed.

283 **To generate reports**

1 On the **File** menu, click **Open Site**.

2 In the **Site name** box, type the address of your site, and then click **Open**.

3 On the **View** menu, point to **Reports**, point to the specific report that you want, and then click it.

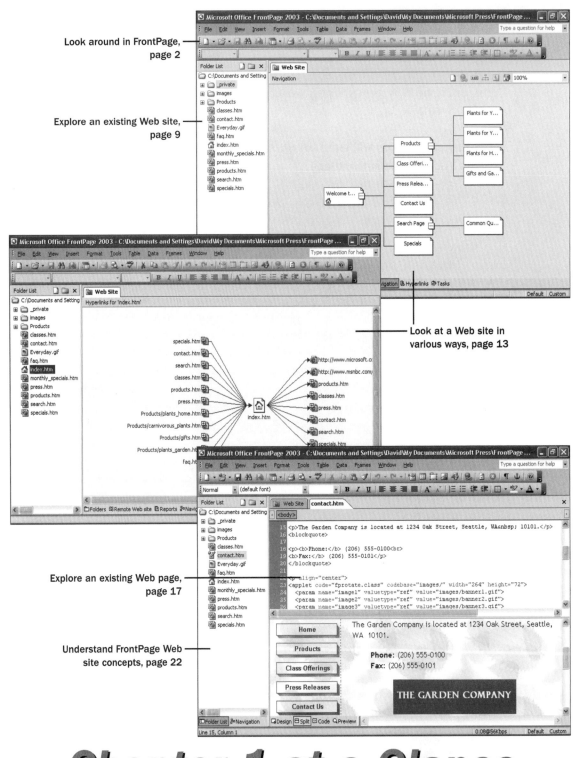

Look around in FrontPage, page 2

Explore an existing Web site, page 9

Look at a Web site in various ways, page 13

Explore an existing Web page, page 17

Understand FrontPage Web site concepts, page 22

Chapter 1 at a Glance

1 Understanding How FrontPage Works

In this chapter you will learn to:

✔ Look around in FrontPage.

✔ Explore an existing Web site.

✔ Look at a Web site in various ways.

✔ Explore an existing Web page.

✔ Understand FrontPage Web site concepts.

Microsoft Office FrontPage 2003 is a comprehensive application that you can use to develop Web sites. This sophisticated program includes everything you need to create Web sites ranging from a simple Web-based résumé to a complex Web-based retail store.

In spite of its sophistication, FrontPage is easy to use. As a member of *The Microsoft Office System 2003* suite of applications, it works pretty much the same way the other Office applications do. If you've avoided trying to create Web sites because you didn't want to learn how to program in *Hypertext Markup Language (HTML)*, FrontPage might well be the answer you've been waiting for. With FrontPage, you can easily create good-looking, interesting Web sites that incorporate complex elements, without typing a single line of programming code. But if you have some HTML programming experience or want to feel more in control, FrontPage gives you easy access to the code that it creates behind the scenes. You can view and edit the underlying HTML code at any time; but the great thing is that you don't have to. No programming experience is necessary to become a successful FrontPage developer.

This chapter introduces FrontPage and explains the concept of a FrontPage-based Web site. You will learn how to open an existing Web site, how to navigate between Web pages, and how to view the pages in different ways. You will then look at various ways of working in FrontPage and learn how to locate and control the FrontPage features you are likely to want to use in your own Web sites. In addition, you will learn how to view the underlying HTML code that makes all Web sites work. You will also get an overview of the different types of Web sites you can create with FrontPage and of the decision-making tools and resources that are necessary to create, manage, and maintain a personal or commercial Web site.

The exercises in this chapter and throughout the book are built around a Web site created for a fictitious garden and plant store called The Garden Company. The sample Web site, which is named *GardenCo*, contains realistic examples of content and structure that serve to demonstrate the concepts covered in each chapter.

See Also   Do you need only a quick refresher on the topics in this chapter? See the Quick Reference entries on page xxi.

Important   Before you can use the practice files in this chapter, you need to install them from the book's companion CD to their default location. See "Using the Book's CD-ROM" on page xiii for more information.

Looking Around in FrontPage

For those of you who don't have much experience with the other applications in the Office 2003 suite, here is a summary of some of the basic techniques you will use to work with FrontPage.

FrontPage 2003 commands are available from 11 *menus*. Office 2003 applications feature the same expanding, dynamic menus that were first made available in Office 2000. The menu commands you use most often move to the top of each menu, making them easier to access. The menu commands you don't use are tucked out of sight, but can be easily accessed by clicking the double chevron at the bottom of the menu. Menu commands that are followed by an arrowhead have submenus. Menu commands that are followed by an ellipsis (...) open dialog boxes or task panes where you provide the information necessary to carry out the command.

Most of the menu commands are also represented graphically on 15 *toolbars*, all of which are customizable. The graphic on the toolbar buttons corresponds to the graphic next to the same command on the menu. Each of the buttons has a *ScreenTip* to tell you the name of the command.

Menu and toolbar options are unavailable when the option can't be applied either to the environment you're working in or to the specific object that is selected. Available menu commands are displayed in black; unavailable commands are *dimmed*, or displayed in a gray font.

In this exercise, you will learn to start and exit FrontPage. You will also look at the commands that are available on the FrontPage 2003 menus and toolbars, experiment with different ways of displaying the toolbars, and close a file.

BE SURE TO start your computer, but don't start FrontPage before beginning this exercise.

1 At the left end of the taskbar at the bottom of your screen, click the **Start** button. On the **Start** menu, point to **All Programs**, point to **Microsoft Office**, and then click **Microsoft Office FrontPage 2003**.

Tip Depending on your system resources, you might see a message box notifying you of additional system requirements for using certain Office 2003 features, such as Speech Recognition. If you see this message box, click OK to continue.

When FrontPage opens for the first time, you see a new file called *new_page_1.htm* in the Page view editing window.

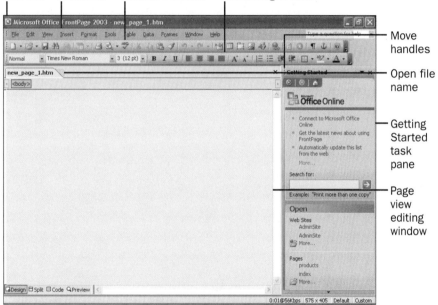

Title bar Menu bar Standard toolbar Formatting toolbar

Move handles

Open file name

Getting Started task pane

Page view editing window

The Getting Started task pane is open. This task pane is displayed when FrontPage starts with no Web site open.

Tip If you don't want the task pane to be shown by default, click the Tools menu and then click Options. On the General tab of the Options dialog box, clear the Startup Task Pane check box, and then click OK.

2 Click the **File** menu to open it, and then click the double chevron at the bottom of the menu to expand the complete menu.

3 Study the commands available on the menu, and think about how you might use each one.

The Close Site, Publish Site, and Export commands are dimmed because they are unavailable at this time—in this case, because they apply to Web sites rather than Web pages, and no Web site is open at the moment. If you haven't previously used FrontPage, the Recent Files command is also dimmed.

Ellipses (...) follow the New, Open, Open Site, Save As, File Search, Publish Site, Import, Export, Page Setup, Print, Send, and Properties commands to indicate that each has an accompanying task pane or dialog box.

4 Click the **Properties** command to open the **Page Properties** dialog box for the current file.

Dialog box tabs

5 Click each of the dialog box tabs to look at the available options. Then click **Cancel** to close the dialog box without effecting any changes.

6 Click the **File** menu to open it again.

Arrowheads follow the Preview in Browser, Recent Files, and Recent Sites commands to indicate that each has a submenu. Point to or click the Preview in Browser command to expand its submenu.

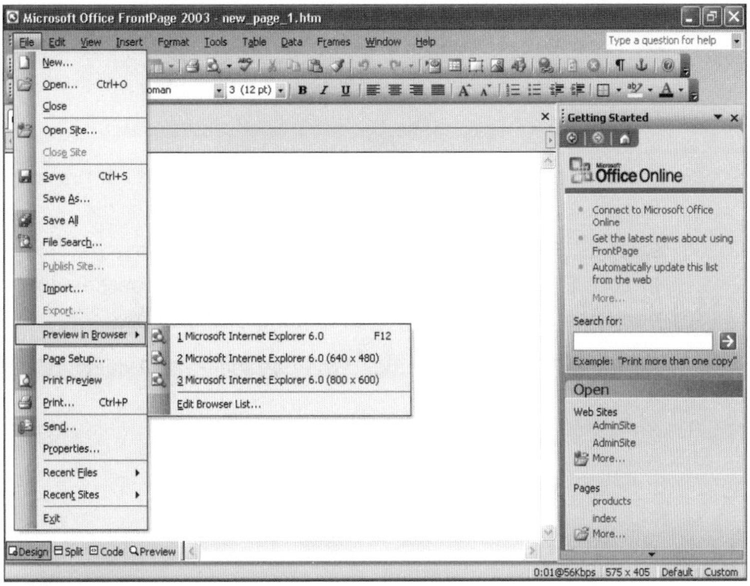

7 Repeat steps 2 through 6 for each of the remaining menus: **Edit**, **View**, **Insert**, **Format**, **Tools**, **Table**, **Data**, **Frames**, **Window**, and **Help**. Study the available and unavailable options, look at the dialog box options, and expand the submenus.

See Also For more information about getting help with Microsoft FrontPage, refer to the "Getting Help" section at the beginning of this book.

---

8 Right-click anywhere in the menu and toolbar area at the top of the window to open the toolbar shortcut menu.

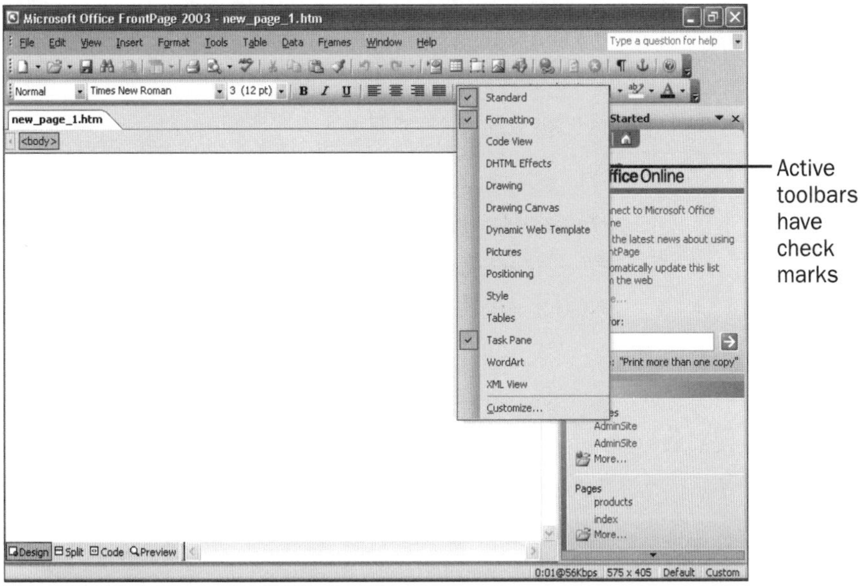

Active toolbars have check marks

Check marks indicate that the Standard and Formatting toolbars and a task pane are currently displayed. FrontPage automatically displays these two toolbars because they include buttons for the most commonly used page and file commands.

9 Press the [Esc] key to close the toolbar shortcut menu.

10 Point to each of the buttons on the Standard and Formatting toolbars to read their command names.

Each available button is highlighted as you point to it.

11 Drag the **Formatting** toolbar by its move handle to the center of the screen.

12 Drag the **Formatting** toolbar by its title bar to the left edge of the screen until it changes from horizontal to vertical orientation.

Moving a toolbar to one edge of the window is called *docking* the toolbar. You can dock the FrontPage toolbars at the top, left, bottom, or right edge of the window. The toolbar's orientation changes as it is moved. Toolbars docked on the left or right are vertically oriented; toolbars docked on the top or bottom and undocked toolbars are horizontally oriented.

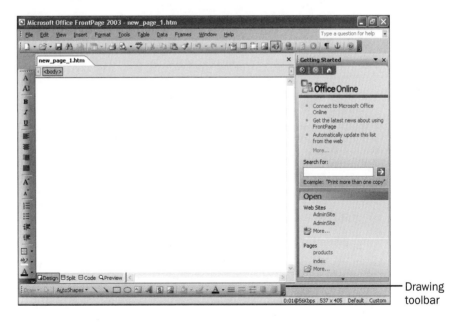

13 Right-click the Formatting toolbar to open the toolbar shortcut menu. On the toolbar shortcut menu, click **Drawing**.

The Drawing toolbar opens in its default location at the bottom of the screen.

Drawing toolbar

14 Click the down arrow at the right end of the Drawing toolbar to display the **Add or Remove Buttons** command. Point to **Add or Remove Buttons**, and then point to **Drawing** to open the list of the commands that are available from the Drawing toolbar.

Check marks indicate the currently displayed commands.

A similar list is available for each of the toolbars.

15 In the list, click the **AutoShapes**, **Line**, and **Arrow** buttons to remove them from the Drawing toolbar.

Notice that each button disappears from the toolbar as you click it.

16 Click **Reset Toolbar** to return the toolbar to its original state.

The list closes when you reset the toolbar.

Close

17 On the title bar, click the **Close** button to exit FrontPage.

18 Reopen FrontPage by clicking **Start**, pointing to **All Programs**, pointing to **Microsoft Office**, and then clicking **Microsoft Office FrontPage 2003**.

When FrontPage reopens, notice that the changes you made are still in effect; the Formatting toolbar is still docked at the left side of the window, and the Drawing toolbar is still open at the bottom.

19 Drag the Formatting toolbar by its move handle back to its original location below the Standard toolbar at the top of the window.

20 Right-click the Standard toolbar, and on the toolbar shortcut menu, click **Drawing** to close the Drawing toolbar.

21 On the **File** menu, click **Close** to close the *new_page_1.htm* file.

Exploring an Existing Web Site

When you work with other Office 2003 applications, you create self-contained documents that can be individually opened from within the application or from Microsoft Windows Explorer. When you work with FrontPage, you create a group of interconnected files that collectively make up a FrontPage-based Web site. As a result, Web sites must be opened from within FrontPage; clicking a single file name in Windows Explorer might open that file, but it won't open the Web site that the file belongs to.

After you open a Web site in FrontPage, you can look at the structure of the site in two views:

- In *Folders view*, you can see and modify the *file structure* of a Web site. You can organize the files and folders that make up your Web site by using techniques similar to those you use to organize files and folders in Windows Explorer. You can add new folders, delete or move existing folders, and view the contents of folders.

- In *Navigation view*, you can see or modify the *navigational structure* and hierarchical arrangement of the various pages on your Web site. In this view, you can click a page and drag it to another location in the Web site.

See Also For information about FrontPage's other views, see "Looking at a Web Site in Various Ways" in this chapter.

In this exercise, you will open a sample FrontPage-based Web site and look at the file structure and navigational structure of the site.

USE the *GardenCo* Web site in the practice file folder for this topic. This practice file is located in the *My Documents\Microsoft Press\FrontPage 2003 SBS\Understanding* folder and can also be accessed by clicking *Start/All Programs/Microsoft Press/FrontPage 2003 Step By Step*.
BE SURE TO start FrontPage before beginning this exercise.

1 On the **File** menu, click **Open Site** (do not click **Open**).

2 In the **Open Site** dialog box, browse to the *My Documents\Microsoft Press \FrontPage 2003 SBS\Understanding* folder.

Web site icon

A FrontPage-based Web site called *GardenCo* is located in this folder, indicated by the Web site icon preceding the name.

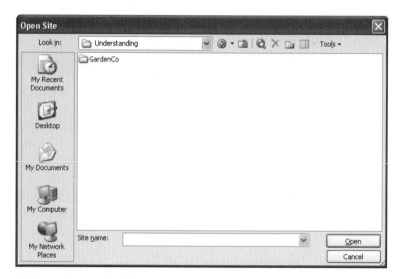

3   Click the **GardenCo** folder to select the Web site, and then click **Open**.

The open task pane closes and the Folder List opens, displaying in Folders view the accessible folders and files that make up the GardenCo Web site. You can double-click any file to open that file in FrontPage.

Important A FrontPage-based Web site includes hidden folders and files generated by FrontPage for behind-the-scenes operations. Deleting or changing these files and folders might "break" the site by damaging the navigation structure, rendering links invalid, or worse; so FrontPage designates them as hidden. Provided your computer is not set to show hidden files and folders (this setting is on the View tab of the Microsoft Windows Folder Options dialog box), you will never see these files, and there will be no danger that you might accidentally delete or alter them.

4 In the **Folder List**, click the plus sign preceding each of the folders to view the folder contents.

Different icons designate the various types of files that make up this site. For example, the Web page icon precedes the *file name* of each page of the FrontPage-based Web site, and the home page icon indicates the *home page* of the site.

Web page icon   home page icon

5 Click the **Close** button to close the **Folder List**.

Close [Window]

6 On the Standard toolbar, click the down arrow to the right of the **Toggle Pane** button, and then click **Folder List** in the drop-down list to redisplay the **Folder List**.

Toggle Pane

7 At the bottom of the **Folders view window**, click the **Navigation** button to switch to Navigation view.

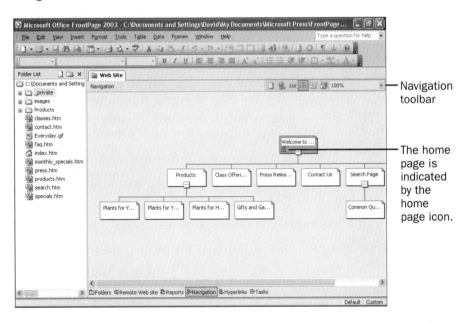

Navigation toolbar

The home page is indicated by the home page icon.

This view of the navigational structure is essentially a hierarchical map of how pages are connected within the site and what routes you can take to get from one page to another. As with the Folder List, you can open each of these files by double-clicking the page icon or title in the Navigation Pane.

8   Move the mouse pointer over each of the buttons on the Navigation toolbar to see the available commands.

Portrait/
Landscape

9   Click the **Portrait/Landscape** button to change the orientation of the Navigation view display.

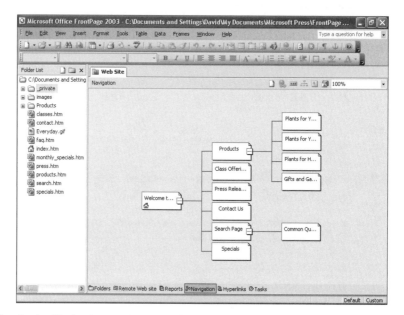

10   On the Navigation toolbar, click the down arrow to the right of the **Zoom** box, and then click **25%** in the drop-down list.

The drawing size changes.

11   In the **Zoom** drop-down list, click **Size To Fit** to optimize the navigation display within the current window.

12   Click the **Portrait/Landscape** button to return to the default navigational view.

13   Click the **Products** page (not the minus sign on its bottom edge) to select it.

View
Subtree Only

14   On the Navigation toolbar, click the **View Subtree Only** button.

If you are working with a particularly large Web site you can use this technique to single out one section of the navigation structure.

15   Click the **View Subtree Only** button again to see the entire *site map*.

16   On the **File** menu, click **Close Site** to close the Web site.

Looking at a Web Site in Various Ways

At the bottom of the working area, FrontPage 2003 provides six buttons for switching among different *views* of a Web site:

- *Folders view* displays the visible files and folders that are part of the open Web site. For each file, this view shows the file name, page title, file size, file type, the date the file was last modified and by whom, and any comments that have been added to the file information.

New in Office 2003 Remote Web Site view

- *Remote Web Site view* displays information about the published version of your Web site, so you can see the local and remote file structures simultaneously, similar to the view displayed by traditional *File Transfer Protocol (FTP)* programs. You can manipulate local and remote files and folders from this view.

- *Reports view* displays any of the 31 available basic reports about the open Web site. Reports view defaults to the last opened report. If no report has been open during the current FrontPage session, the default is a Site Summary report that collates the results of the other reports. To view one of the reports that make up the Site Summary, click the hyperlinked report name. The various reports can be chosen from the View menu or from the Reporting toolbar.

- *Navigation view* graphically displays a hierarchical view of all the files that have been added to the navigation structure of the open Web site. To add an existing file to the navigation structure, you simply drag the file into the Navigation view window, and drop it in the appropriate location. You can also create new files directly within Navigation view. To fit the site content into the window, you can switch between Portrait mode (vertical layout) and Landscape mode (horizontal layout) or zoom in or out using the buttons on the Navigation toolbar.

- *Hyperlinks view* displays the hyperlinks to and from any selected page in the open Web site. Internal hyperlinks are shown as well as external hyperlinks and e-mail hyperlinks. You select a file in the Folder List to see the hyperlinks to and from that file, and then select the plus sign next to any file name to further expand the view.

- *Tasks view* displays a list of *tasks* to be completed in the open Web site. FrontPage creates these tasks when you use a wizard to create a Web site, or you can create your own tasks. For each task, you see the status, name, and description. You can also see to whom the task is assigned; whether the task has been categorized as High, Medium, or Low priority; and when the task was last modified. Tasks are a useful way of tracking the readiness of a site.

You can switch between views by clicking the desired view on the View menu or by clicking the button for the view you want at the bottom of the working area.

Tip The View menu also provides a Page View command. You will do most of your development work in Page view.

In this exercise, you will look at Web pages in each of the FrontPage views to get an idea of what information is available to you in each view.

USE the *GardenCo* Web site in the practice file folder for this topic. This practice file is located in the *My Documents\Microsoft Press\FrontPage 2003 SBS\Understanding* folder and can also be accessed by clicking *Start/All Programs/Microsoft Press/FrontPage 2003 Step By Step*.
BE SURE TO start FrontPage before beginning this exercise.
OPEN the *GardenCo* Web site in Folders view.

🌐 Remote Web site
Remote Web
Site View

1 At the bottom of the window, click the **Remote Web site View** button.

Because this Web site has not yet been published, the view is blank.

Remote Web Site Properties...

2 Click the **Remote Web Site Properties** button.

3 In the **Remote Web Site Properties** dialog box, click each tab to see the publishing options you can set.

New in Office 2003
Optimize HTML

You can specify the location and server information of your published Web site. On the Optimize HTML tab, you can set options that decrease the size of your published file by removing elements such as authoring-specific comments, white space, and unnecessary tags and tag attributes from the published version.

4 When you finish looking at the options, click **Cancel**.

📄 Reports
Reports View

5 At the bottom of the working area, click the **Reports View** button.

FrontPage opens the Reports toolbar and displays the Site Summary report for the open Web site.

To see the individual reports that are collated into the Site Summary report, you can click the hyperlinked report names in the Site Summary; or you can click the Reports down arrow at the left end of the Reports toolbar and then click the desired report in the drop-down list.

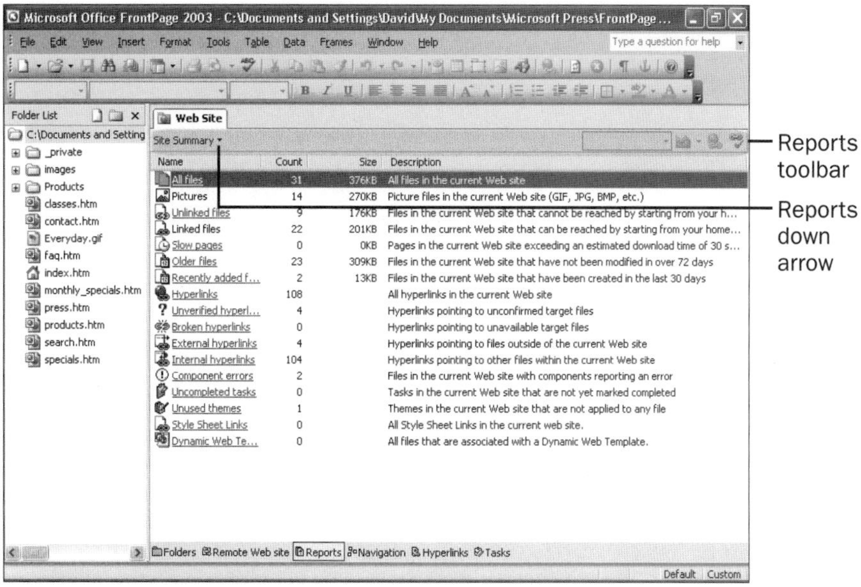

Reports toolbar

Reports down arrow

6 Move the mouse pointer over each of the buttons on the Reports toolbar to see the available commands.

7 In the Site Summary report, click the **Internal hyperlinks** link.

8 If a message box appears asking whether you want FrontPage to verify the hyperlinks, select the **Don't ask me this again** check box, and then click **Yes**.

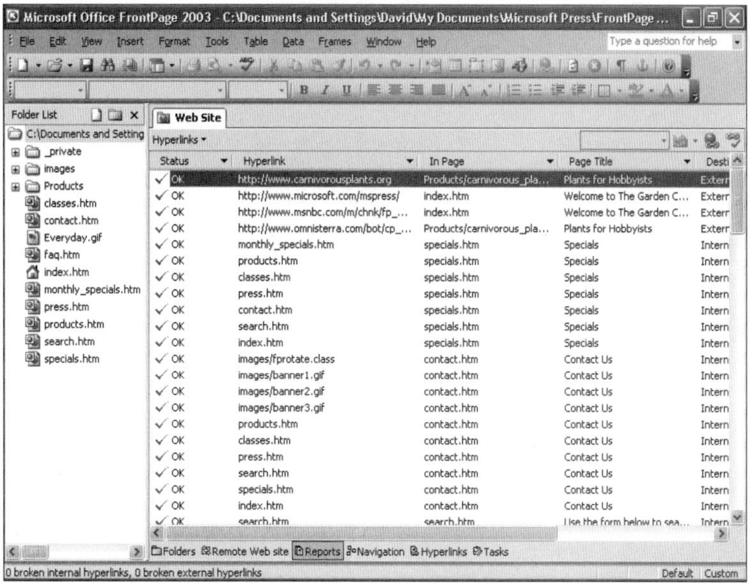

FrontPage tests each internal hyperlink and indicates whether it is good or bad by placing a green check mark or red X in front of the link.

9   At the far left end of the Reports toolbar, click the down arrow to the right of the **Report** box (which currently says **Hyperlinks**), and then click **Site Summary** in the drop-down list to return to the default report.

10   At the bottom of the working area, click the **Hyperlinks View** button.

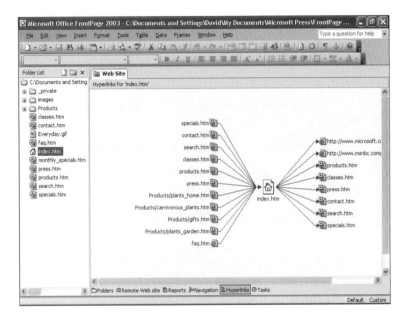

Because no specific page is selected, the screen reads *Select a page from the Folder List to view hyperlinks to and from that page.*

11   In the **Folder List**, click **index.htm**, the home page.

All the hyperlinks to and from the home page are displayed.

12   In the hyperlinks display, right-click **contact.htm**, and click **Move to Center** on the shortcut menu to move that file to the center point of the hyperlink structure.

Notice that different icons represent different types of links.

13   Click the plus sign next to any file icon to see the other hyperlinks from that file's page, and then click the minus sign to collapse the hyperlink view.

14   At the bottom of the working area, click the **Tasks View** button.

Tasks view shows you a reminder list of the things that need to be done in the open Web site. Tasks are automatically created when you use a FrontPage wizard to create a Web site. Tasks can also be created manually by anyone working on the Web site.

15 Double-click the task titled **Investigate FrontPage views** to open it.

16 In the **Assigned to** box, double-click or drag to select the current entry. Assign the task to yourself by typing your name, user name, or initials.

17 Read the description and study the task details, and then click **OK** to close the task.

18 Right-click the **Investigate FrontPage views** task, and click **Mark Complete** on the shortcut menu.

The task's Status setting changes from *Not Started* to *Completed*.

Important You can display previously completed tasks by right-clicking the background of the Tasks list, and then clicking Show History on the shortcut menu.

19 Double-click the task titled **Finish the book** to open it.

20 Read the description and study the task details, and then click **OK** to close the task.

CLOSE the *GardenCo* Web site.

Exploring an Existing Web Page

A Web site consists of one or more individual *Web pages*. When you develop a Web site, you work with the individual pages and the overall site structure. When you want to edit a Web page that is part of a FrontPage-based Web site, you first open the site in FrontPage, and then open the individual page. This avoids the possibility that you might make changes to a page and then disconnect it from the rest of the site. It also ensures that changes made on an individual page are reflected across the entire site, as appropriate.

Important   If FrontPage is your default HTML editor, you can open individual Web pages from outside FrontPage by double-clicking the page file in Windows Explorer. However, if FrontPage is not your default editor, accessing and changing files individually from outside FrontPage could result in damage to the Web site. To set FrontPage as your default HTML editor while starting FrontPage, click Yes when prompted to do so.

New in
Office 2003
Web Site tab

Page creation and editing tasks are done in *Page view*, which displays the open page or pages in the Page view editing window. At the top of the editing window is a tab for the current Web site and tabs for any open pages. You can open an existing page by double-clicking it on the Web Site tab. The tab at the top of each page shows the page's file name. If multiple pages are open, you can switch to another page by clicking its tab or by clicking its file name on the Window menu.

Tip   To see information about an entire site and access the Folders view, Remote Web Site view, Reports view, Navigation view, and Hyperlinks view options, click the Web Site tab at the top of the Page view editing window.

Page view provides four different ways to view your Web page:

New in
Office 2003
Web page
views

- The *Design pane* displays the Web page as it will appear in a Web browser, except that additional design guides, such as shared border indicators and table and cell outlines, are also visible. You work primarily in this pane when creating Web pages.

- The *Code pane* displays the HTML code behind the Web page. Elements are color-coded to make it easier for you to discern text and content from the surrounding code. Each line of code is numbered. Error messages often refer to line numbers within the HTML code so you can quickly locate problems.

New in
Office 2003
Split view

- The *Split pane* simultaneously displays the design view and HTML code. Selecting a page element in the design view simultaneously selects the element in the code so you don't have to scroll through the code to find what you're looking for.

- The *Preview pane* displays the Web page as it will actually appear in a Web browser. Hyperlinks and most page elements are active in the Preview pane.

Most FrontPage users will do almost all page design work in the Design pane, which offers the simplest interface.

In this exercise, you will open an individual Web page in Page view and look at the page in the different Page view panes.

USE the *GardenCo* Web site in the practice file folder for this topic. This practice file is located in the *My Documents\Microsoft Press\FrontPage 2003 SBS\Understanding* folder and can also be accessed by clicking *Start/All Programs/Microsoft Press/FrontPage 2003 Step By Step.*
BE SURE TO start FrontPage before beginning this exercise.

Open

1 On the Standard toolbar, click the down arrow to the right of the **Open** button, and then click **Open Site** in the drop-down list.

2 In the **Open Site** dialog box, browse to the *My Documents\Microsoft Press \FrontPage 2003 SBS\Understanding* folder, click **GardenCo**, and then click **Open**.

The Web site opens in FrontPage with the Folder List displayed.

Tip If the Folder List is not displayed, click Folder List on the View menu to display it.

3 In the **Folder List**, right-click the **contact.htm** file, and then click **Open** on the shortcut menu.

open Web page icon

The file icon changes to an open Web page icon, and the file opens in the *Page view editing window*. Folder List and Navigation buttons appear at the bottom of the Folder List; you can click these to switch between the Folder List and the Navigation Pane.

Web site tab   Web page tab

Page view options

At the top of the editing window, tabs appear for the current Web site and the open page. You can use the four buttons at the bottom to switch between different views of the open Web page.

4 Use the scroll bars to look at the entire page.

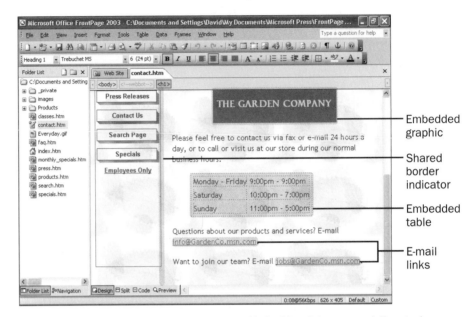

This page has *shared borders* at the top and left side of the page, delineated by dotted lines.

Shared borders appear on every page of the Web site and contain the same information, giving the site a consistent look. The top shared border of this site contains a corporate logo and the page title, or *page banner*. The left shared border contains a *link bar* displaying graphic *hyperlinks* that you can click to jump to other pages in the site.

The content area in the center of the page contains text, a graphic, a table, and two *e-mail links*.

5 At the bottom of the Page view editing window, click the **Show Code View** button to switch to the Code pane.

Code
Show
Code View

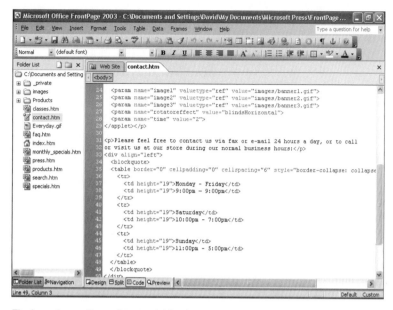

6 Find each section of text within the page code, and study the surrounding HTML code. Try to identify the code that creates each page element.

7 Click the **Show Split View** button to switch to the Split pane.

🗗 Split

Show Split
View

*New in
Office 2003*

Split view

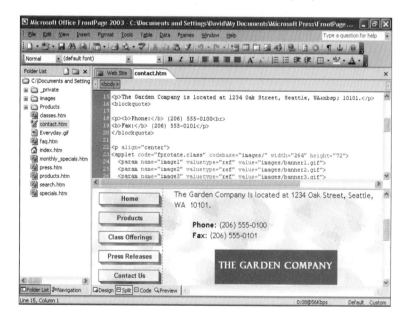

Q Preview

Show
Preview View

8   Click the **Show Preview View** button to switch to the Preview pane.

9   Click the hyperlinked buttons on the link bar to switch to other pages.

✕

Close [Window]

10   When you're done looking at the page, click the **Close** button in the upper right corner of the Page view editing window to close the file.

CLOSE the *GardenCo* Web site. If you are not continuing on to the next chapter, quit FrontPage.

Understanding FrontPage Web Site Concepts

This section discusses the types of sites that can be developed with FrontPage and the system requirements that are necessary to take full advantage of the FrontPage 2003 development environment.

There are two kinds of Web sites: *disk-based Web sites* and *server-based Web sites*. A disk-based Web site can be run on any kind of computer, or even from a floppy disk or CD-ROM. Disk-based Web sites support only basic HTML functionality. Many of the more interesting *Web components* that FrontPage supplies won't work on a disk-based site.

Server-based Web sites run on a Web server—a computer that is specifically configured to *host* Web sites. On a small scale, a Web server might be a local computer such as your own, or it might be an intranet server within your company. On a larger scale, Web servers that host corporate Internet sites are usually located at professional *server farms* run by an *Internet service provider (ISP)* or *Web hosting company*.

Most Web sites are initially developed as disk-based sites; that is, you develop them on your local computer. You then *publish* them to a Web server, either within your organization or at your hosted Web location.

- Some FrontPage *Web components*—ready-made elements that provide capabilities such as link bars and tables of contents—work only when they are placed on a page that is part of a FrontPage-based Web site.

- Some components require that the Web page or site be located on a Web server running Microsoft Windows SharePoint Services.

- Other common Web components work only in a server-based Web site located on a Web server running FrontPage Server Extensions.

- Some components pull their content directly from other Web sites, so they require an Internet connection to be visible.

- Server administration features are available only for server-based Web sites stored on Web servers running Windows SharePoint Services or FrontPage Server Extensions.

■ To display database information, your site must be hosted on a Web server that supports Active Server Pages (ASP) and ActiveX Data Objects (ADO).

FrontPage-based Web sites can run on any kind of Web server, but the full functionality of your Web site might not be available unless your site is hosted on a server with FrontPage Server Extensions installed. If you maintain your own Web server, installing the server extensions is a simple exercise; they are available on The Microsoft Office System 2003 installation CD-ROM. If you are looking for a company to host your Web site, or if you already have an ISP but you have never asked it to host a FrontPage–based Web site before, be sure to ask whether its servers have FrontPage Server Extensions installed.

Key Points

■ FrontPage is an easy-to-use program that provides all the tools you need to develop a simple or complex Web site.

■ FrontPage uses a menu and toolbar command structure like that of the other Microsoft Office System applications.

■ FrontPage Web sites consist of numerous files, some hidden, and should be opened for editing from within FrontPage rather than from Windows Explorer.

■ You can see and work with your Web site from several different viewpoints: Folders view, Remote Web Site view, Reports view, Navigation view, Hyperlinks view, and Tasks view.

■ A Web site consists of individual Web pages. The structure of each page is determined by the underlying HTML code. You can see and work with the HTML code in the Page view Code pane or Split pane, but you do most of your work in the Design pane. FrontPage makes it unnecessary for you to know how to create HTML code.

■ Web sites are initially developed on your local computer and then published to the Internet. Many features are not available for use until the Web site is published to a server running FrontPage Server Extensions.

Our Mission

Comment: Write one or two short sentences that describe your company's philosophy and ambitions. Something like, 'To become the leading provider of ...'. At The Garden Company, we take pride in offering only the highest-quality plants and garden-related products to our customers.

Contact Information

Comment: Tell readers how people can connect to your international versions of te customary to provide e-mail sales and customer support e-mail 24 hours a day, or to normal business hours: Mor Saturday and Sunday 10:00

Insert and edit text, page 36

Insert hyperlinks, page 50

Format text, page 45

See your Web site as visitors will, page 52

Class Offerings

The Garden Company offers a variety of classes on plant selection for your geographical area, general and seasonal plant care, and garden-related craft activities.

n Planning for Spring Splendor
's never too early to get started on a eautiful Spring garden! This class is taught y David Ortiz, a Pacific Northwest native and cal gardening expert. This is a very

Reuse existing text, page 40

Create a new Web site by using a template or wizard, page 26

Delete a Web site, page 56

Home

Welcome to **The Garden Company** Web site. We are a quality retail gardening business located in the Pacific Northwest. Our products and services are featured on this Web site. *Whether you visit us on the Web or in our store, please feel free to browse, and let us know if you require assistance or have any questions!*

Our Mission

At The Garden Company, we take pride in offering only the highest-quality plants and garden-related products to our customers.

We also offer a variety of classes on plant selection for rainy regions

Confirm Delete

Deleting this Web site is a permanent action. Are you sure you want to delete "C:\...\My Web Sites\OnePage" ?

● Remove FrontPage information from this Web site only, preserving all other files and folders.

○ Delete this Web site entirely.

OK   Cancel

Chapter 2 at a Glance

2 Creating a Web Site to Promote Yourself or Your Company

In this chapter you will learn to:

✔ Create a new Web site by using a template or wizard.

✔ Insert and edit text.

✔ Reuse existing text.

✔ Format text.

✔ Insert hyperlinks.

✔ See your Web site as visitors will.

✔ Delete a Web site.

All Microsoft Office System 2003 applications provide tools for jump-starting the creation of common types of files. Microsoft Office FrontPage 2003 includes templates and wizards you can use to set up the structure for basic types of Web pages and even entire Web sites. When you use one of these tools, FrontPage does most of the structural work for you, leaving you free to concentrate on the site's content.

You can use the FrontPage templates and wizards to create everything from a very basic Web page to a complex, multi-page, interactive site. These are great tools to use if you are new to Web design and want to explore the possibilities, or if you are looking for a quick way to get started on the creation of a real Web site.

In this chapter, you will walk through the steps for creating a couple of Web sites, including a corporate site that we will work with throughout most of the book. You will learn how to enter and format text, how to preview a Web site, and how to delete a site you no longer need.

See Also Do you need only a quick refresher on the topics in this chapter? See the Quick Reference entries on pages xxi–xxiii.

Important Before you can use the practice files in this chapter, you need to install them from the book's companion CD to their default location. See "Using the Book's CD-ROM" on page xiii for more information.

Creating a New Web Site by Using a Template

The easiest way to create a new Web site is by using one of FrontPage's *templates*. Templates create the layout for a specific type of Web page or Web site, designating with placeholders the type of content you should put in each location. All you have to do is replace the placeholders with your own content, and you have a finished page or site to show off.

To create a Web site using a template, you simply select the template and specify the location where the site should be created. FrontPage then creates the new Web site and applies the template's structure to it, leaving it up to you to fill in the content and customize the look of the site to suit your needs.

In this exercise, you will create two different types of Web sites by using templates: a simple one-page site and a personal Web site.

BE SURE TO start FrontPage before beginning this exercise.

1   If the **New** task pane is not open, on the **File** menu, click **New**.

New task pane

2 In the **New Web site** area of the **New** task pane, click **More Web site templates**.

3 In the **Web Site Templates** dialog box, make sure the **One Page Web Site** icon is selected.

Tip   You need to specify the location and name of the new Web site. FrontPage provides a special folder in which you can store your Web sites, called My Web Sites. This folder is located in your My Documents folder.

4 In the **Options** area, click the **Browse** button.

The New Web Site Location dialog box opens.

5 In the **New Web Site Location** dialog box, click the **My Documents** icon on the Places bar.

6 In the file list, double-click **My Web Sites**.

7 On the dialog box toolbar, click the **Create New Folder** button.

The New Folder dialog box opens.

Create
New Folder

8 In the **New Folder** dialog box, type **OnePage** in the **Name** text box, and then click **OK**.

9 In the **New Web Site Location** dialog box, click the **Open** button.

10 In the **Web Site Templates** dialog box, click **OK**.

In about three seconds, FrontPage displays the structure of your newly created one-page Web site.

Tip FrontPage opens your new Web site in the view that was last active. If your screen doesn't look like our graphic, check the Views bar and make any adjustments necessary to make your view the same as ours.

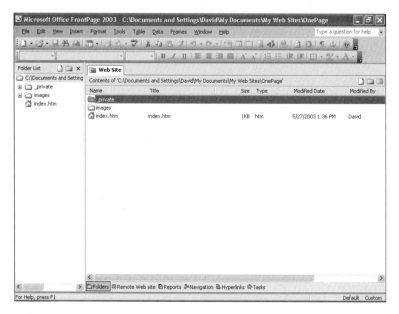

In FrontPage, it appears that your one-page Web site consists of a single file called *index.htm* and two empty folders called *_private* and *images*. However, if you look at the site's folder in Microsoft Windows Explorer, you will see that many files and folders (some of them hidden) support this single page.

Tip If your Folder Options are not set to "Show hidden files and folders," you won't see all of the files and folders that support this page.

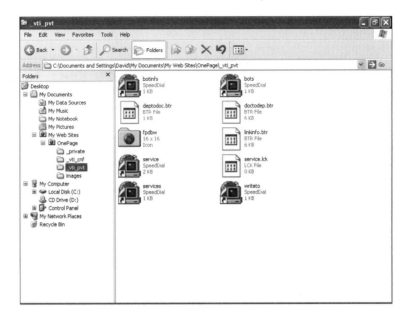

11 In the **Folder List**, double-click **index.htm** to open it in Page view.

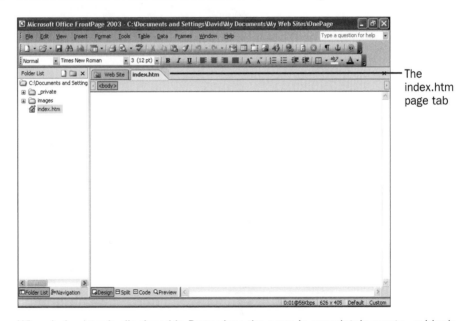

The index.htm page tab

When index.htm is displayed in Page view, the page is completely empty—a blank canvas upon which you can create a veritable work of art. By the time you finish this book, you will know how to create a fairly sophisticated page from scratch, but until then, it is a good idea to lean on FrontPage to give you a starting framework. Now you will test another template by creating a personal site to showcase your new skills.

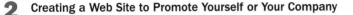

Create a new
normal page

12   Click the down arrow to the right of the **Create a new normal page** button, and then click **Web Site**.

The Web Site Templates dialog box appears.

13   In the **Web Site Templates** dialog box, click (don't double-click) the **Personal Web Site** icon.

Tip   FrontPage suggests a location for your new Web site based on the location of the last Web site you created.

14   In the **Options** area, click the **Browse** button, and then navigate to the *My Web Sites* folder. Create a new folder named Personal, and click **Open**. In the **Web Site Templates** dialog box, click **OK**.

A second FrontPage window opens, displaying your newly created personal Web site. You now have two instances of FrontPage running on your computer at the same time.

15 In the **Folder List**, double-click the **index.htm** file to open the home page of the Web site in Page view.

The home page provides placeholders for information about you and your interests, and links to your favorite Web sites. You can display photos of yourself, your family, your friends, your dog, and your vacations (real or imagined) in the photo gallery, and Web visitors can contact you by using the feedback page.

Placeholders currently represent all the information in this Web site. By replacing the placeholders with your own information, you can have an attractive site ready to publish in no time at all.

16 On the **File** menu, click **Close Site** to close the personal Web site.

Close

17 Click the FrontPage window's **Close** button to close the second instance of FrontPage and return to the first instance.

18 On the **File** menu, click **Close Site** to close the one-page Web site.

The New Task Pane

The New task pane contains convenient links to the Web sites and individual pages that you have created or worked with in FrontPage. It also contains links to templates and wizards you can use to create new Web pages or sites. If this task pane is not already open, you can open it using one of the following methods:

1 On the **File** menu, click **New**.

2 On the **View** menu, click **Task Pane**. If a different task pane is displayed, click the down arrow at the right end of the task pane's title bar, and click **New** in the drop-down list.

3 Right-click the toolbar, and click **Task Pane** on the toolbar shortcut menu. If a different task pane is displayed, click **New** in the task pane title bar's drop-down list.

4 Press Ctrl + F1 .

To open the task pane every time you start FrontPage:

● On the **Tools** menu, click **Options,** and then on the **General** tab, select the **Startup Task Pane** check box.

Creating a New Web Site by Using a Wizard

In addition to using templates to create Web sites, you can create sites that are a little more complex by using one of FrontPage's *wizards*. Wizards are similar to templates, but even better. A wizard not only creates the layout of a page or site for you, it also leads you through the process of personalizing the content and the appearance of the final product.

For example, suppose that Karen Berg, the owner of a small, fictitious plant and garden store called The Garden Company, wants to communicate with her existing customers and expand her customer base by having a corporate presence on the Internet. If maintaining a Web site meets these modest goals, she might later choose to expand the site's capabilities to permit online retailing beyond the store's Seattle, Washington, location. However, to begin with, she wants to use FrontPage to create a good-looking Web site. This is a job for one of FrontPage's wizards.

In this exercise, you will use the Corporate Presence Web Wizard to create the basic corporate Web site.

Online Retailing

On the surface, expanding your business by selling goods or services over the Internet seems like a good idea. However, this decision should not be made without a good deal of analysis and planning. First, what you have to offer has to be so compelling that people will want to buy it, and second, you have to offer it under terms and conditions that will make people want to buy it from you, rather than from someone else. Unless you have an exclusive right to sell your particular product, you are going to be competing on many fronts, including price, cost and speed of delivery, and customer service. You must also consider how you will provide a secure environment for the handling of other people's money. All these topics are beyond the scope of this book, but if you are interested in learning more about online retailing, you might want to check out *Small Business Solutions for E-Commerce* by Brenda Kienan (Microsoft Press, 2000).

BE SURE TO start FrontPage before beginning this exercise.

Create a new normal page

1 Click the down arrow to the right of the **Create a new normal page** button, and then click **Web Site**.

The Web Site Templates dialog box appears.

2 In the **Web Site Templates** dialog box, click (don't double-click) the **Corporate Presence Wizard** icon.

3 In the **Options** area, click the **Browse** button, and browse to the *My Web Sites* folder.

Create New Folder

4 On the dialog box toolbar, click the **Create New Folder** button. Name the new folder CorpSite, and click **OK**.

5 Back in the **New Web Site Location** dialog box, click **Open** and then click **OK**.

The first of a series of Corporate Presence Web Wizard dialog boxes, called *pages*, appears. The wizard uses these pages to prompt you to make choices and enter basic corporate information.

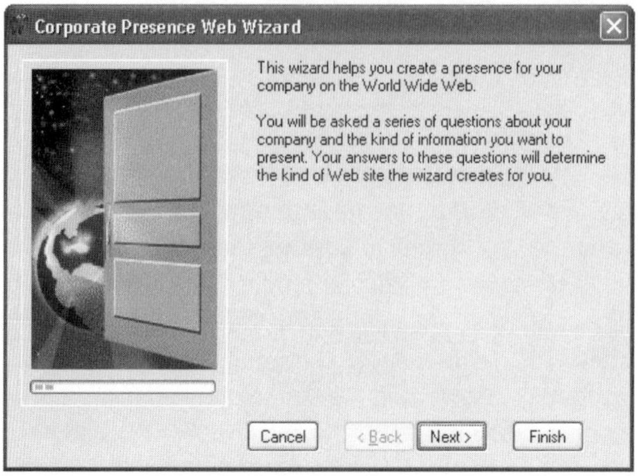

6   Read the information on the first page, and then click **Next** to move to the second page.

7   Continue reading the information and clicking **Next** to accept all the default selections in each of the **Corporate Presence Web Wizard** pages, until you come to the one that requests the name and address of the company.

8   Enter the information shown here (or your own personalized information), and then click **Next**:

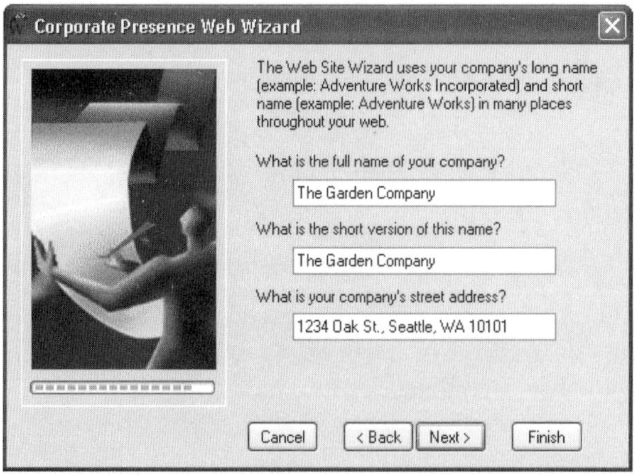

9   Enter the corporate contact information shown here (or your personalized information):

10 Click **Next**, and then click **Finish**.

FrontPage creates your site using the information you provided and then displays a list of the tasks that need to be completed to finish the site.

11 In the **Folder List**, double-click **index.htm** to open the home page in Page view.

12 Scroll to the bottom of the page, and notice the contact information you provided in the wizard.

CLOSE the *GardenCo* Web site.

E-Mail Aliases

When creating a Web site for a company or organization, it's wise to use generic e-mail addresses (called *aliases*) in your Web site contact information rather than specific people's e-mail addresses, so the address can stay the same no matter who is actually assigned to respond to the inquiry. For example, if The Garden Company listed its information contact address as that of Karen Berg and then Karen was away for an extended period of time, messages might build up in her mailbox with no one to answer them. Similarly, if all Web site inquiries were directed to David Ortiz and then David left the company, valuable customer contacts could go unnoticed. Using an e-mail alias that automatically forwards received e-mail messages to one or more individuals ensures that customers' questions are always received by the appropriate person.

Inserting and Editing Text

You can enter new text in a Web page by typing it directly in each page. When you use a FrontPage wizard to create a new Web site, the wizard uses *comments* as place-holders for the text that you need to personalize. The comments inserted by the wizard suggest the type of information you should enter in each area.

In this exercise, you will replace each of the three main blocks of placeholder text on the home page of a Web site created by the Corporate Presence Web Wizard. Then you will add additional text and mark this task as complete.

USE the *GardenCo* Web site in the practice file folder for this topic. This practice file is located in the *My Documents\Microsoft Press\FrontPage 2003 SBS\CreateWeb\InsertText* folder and can also be accessed by clicking *Start/All Programs/Microsoft Press/FrontPage 2003 Step By Step*.

Open

1   On the Standard toolbar, click the down arrow to the right of the **Open** button, and then click **Open Site** in the drop-down list.

2   In the **Open Site** dialog box, browse to the *GardenCo* Web site that is located in the practice file folder, and click **Open** to open the Web site in FrontPage.

3   In the **Folder List**, double-click **index.htm** to open the home page in the Page view editing window.

×
Close

4 In the bar at the top of the **Folder List** pane, click the **Close** button to enlarge your work area by closing the Folder List.

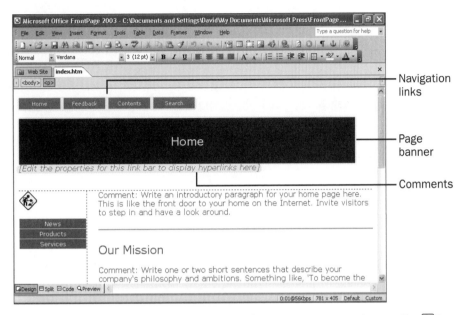

Navigation links

Page banner

Comments

5 In the body of the home page, click the introductory comment, and press the ⌷End⌷ key to position the insertion point at the end of the paragraph.

Tip You can delete the comments before typing new text, but you don't have to. The comments will not be visible to your Web visitors.

6 Type the following text:
Welcome to The Garden Company. We are a quality retail gardening business located in the Pacific Northwest. Our products and services are featured on this Web site. Whether you visit us on the Web or in our store, please feel free to browse, and let us know if you require assistance or have any questions!

7 Position the insertion point at the end of the comment under the *Our Mission* heading, and then enter the following text:
At The Garden Company, we take pride in offering only the highest-quality plants and garden-related products to our customers.

8 After the comment under the *Contact Information* heading, enter the following text: **Please feel free to contact us via fax or e-mail 24 hours a day, or to call or visit us at our store during our normal business hours: Monday - Friday 9:00 a.m. - 9:00 p.m., Saturday and Sunday 10:00 a.m. - 5:00 p.m.**

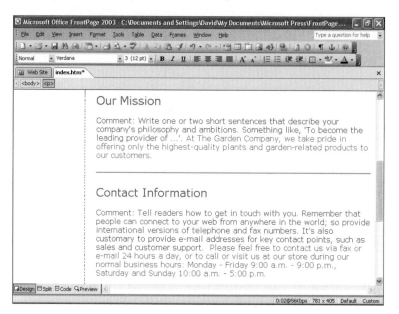

You can change the text that you've entered or add more text at any time.

9 Position the insertion point at the end of the paragraph under the *Our Mission* heading.

10 Press ⌈Enter⌋ to create a new paragraph, and then type the following text: **We also offer a variety of classes on plant selection for rainy regions, general and seasonal plant care, and garden-related craft activities.**

11 At the bottom of the Page view editing window, click the **Show Preview View** button.

Show
Preview View

Now you can see the page as your Web visitors will see it.

12 On the Standard toolbar, click the **Save** button to save your Web page.

Save

CLOSE the *GardenCo* Web site.

Making Comments in Web Pages

You can use comments to make notes to yourself or to communicate with other people working on a Web site. Comments don't show up in the published version of a Web page. You can insert, edit, and delete comments when you're working with a page in Design, Split, or Code view.

To insert a comment:

1 On the **Insert** menu, click **Comment**.

2 In the **Comment** text box, type your notes, and then click **OK**.

To edit a comment:

1 Double-click anywhere in the comment text block to open the **Comment** dialog box.

2 In the **Comment** text box, make your changes, and then click **OK**.

To delete a comment:

● Click the comment once to select it, and then press the Del key.

Reusing Existing Text

If you have already created material for another purpose, such as a press release or company brochure, you probably don't want to have to create it all over again in your Web site. And you don't have to.

FrontPage makes it simple to copy and paste text into a template-based Web site. You can insert chunks of text, graphics, spreadsheets, or drawings cut or copied from other Office applications. You can even insert entire files.

You can copy or cut multiple pieces of content from Microsoft Office System programs, and then paste the content into your Web pages. The Office Clipboard task pane stores text, tables, graphics, and other file elements in a convenient and accessible location and can archive up to 24 different elements across all The Microsoft Office System applications.

Each time you paste content from the Clipboard into FrontPage, the floating Paste Options button appears, which you use to apply the destination styles, keep the source formatting, or keep only the text for your pasted selection. You can ignore the Paste Options button if you want to keep the source formatting.

In this exercise, you will insert text from external files into the News and Services pages, and change the page banner. The text on the News page currently consists of a Web Changes heading and a discussion of site updates. Because you have decided that site updates won't be of interest to patrons of The Garden Company, you will change this page to one that contains press releases. You will also modify the three Services pages using text contained in a Microsoft Office Word document, and update the page titles to reflect their new content.

See Also For more information about page banners, refer to "Using Page Banners and Shared Borders" in Chapter 5.

USE the *GardenCo* Web site and the *PR2* and *Classes* documents in the practice file folder for this topic. These practice files are located in the *My Documents\Microsoft Press\FrontPage 2003 SBS\CreateWeb \InsertExist* folder and can also be accessed by clicking *Start/All Programs/Microsoft Press/FrontPage 2003 Step By Step.*
OPEN the *GardenCo* Web site.

1 If the **Folder List** is not visible, on the **View** menu, click **Folder List**.

2 In the **Folder List**, double-click the **news.htm** file to open it in the Page view editing window.

3 Triple-click the **Web Changes** heading to select it, and type Press Releases.

The text of the heading is replaced, but its formatting is retained.

4 Replace the default opening paragraph, above the comment, with the following text: **Keep up with the news! Recent press releases and links to archived press releases are available here.**

5 Click the comment below the paragraph you just typed to select it.

6 On the **Insert** menu, click **File**.

The Select File dialog box appears.

7 Browse to the practice file folder for this exercise.

8 In the **Files of type** drop-down list, click **Word 97-2003 (*.doc)**.

9 Click **PR2** in the list of available files, and then click **Open** to insert the full text of the document in your Web page.

The text of the document is converted to rich text format and then to HTML and inserted into the News page, just as if you had created it there originally. The original formatting is retained.

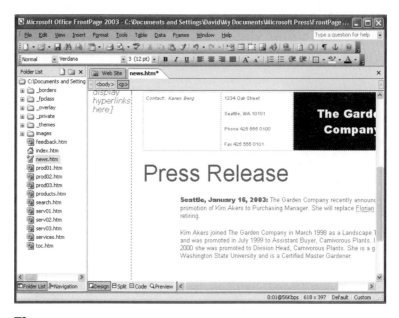

Tip Don't spend time making a document perfect before you import it. You can always make adjustments to the text of the document after it is imported into your Web page.

The contact information at the top of the imported text is contained in a table. The table cells are indicated by dotted lines.

10 Click anywhere in the table. On the **Table** menu, point to **Select**, and then click **Table**.

The table and its contents are selected.

11 Right-click the selection, and click **Delete Cells** on the shortcut menu to delete the table.

12 Triple-click the **Press Release** heading to select the entire paragraph, and press the ⌨ key to remove it from the Web page.

13 Click the **Save** button to save your Web page.

Save

Your Web page is saved.

14 Click the **Close** button in the top right corner of the work area to close the page file.

☒
Close

15 Open the *Services* page.

16 Right-click the **Services** page banner, and click **Page Banner Properties** on the shortcut menu.

The Page Banner Properties dialog box appears.

17 In the **Page banner text** box, select and delete the current text, and then type Class Offerings.

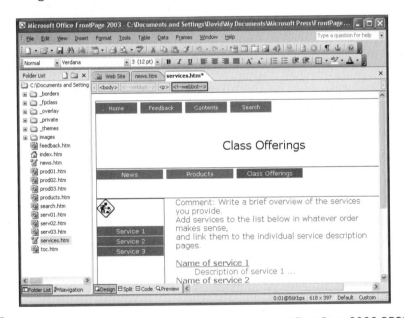

18 Click **OK** to close the dialog box and change the page title.

This change affects the page title shown both on the page banner and in Navigation view.

19 In Windows Explorer, browse to the *My Documents\FrontPage 2003 SBS\CreateWeb \InsertExist* folder, and double-click **Classes** to open it in Word.

20 Triple-click anywhere in the introductory paragraph to select it, and press [Ctrl]+[C] to copy the text to the Office Clipboard.

21 Return to FrontPage. On the services.htm page, click the comment text to select it, and then press [Ctrl]+[V] to paste the overview text of the *Class Offerings* document from the Office Clipboard.

The copied text replaces the comment.

22 Select and delete the extra (empty) paragraph inserted with the text.

23 In the **Folder List**, open **serv01.htm**, **serv02.htm**, and **serv03.htm** (the three individual service files) for editing.

24 In each file, repeat steps 16 through 18 to change the page title to these short versions of the class names described in the *Class Offerings* document:

■ Change *Service 1* to **Spring Splendor**.

■ Change *Service 2* to **Carnivorous Plants**.

■ Change *Service 3* to **Organic Byproducts**.

As you update each page banner, the navigational links under the page banners are updated simultaneously, as are the links on the services.htm page.

25 Return to the *services.htm* file, and note that the vertical navigation links along the left have also been updated to reflect the new page titles.

26 For each of the three *Name of service* links, double-click the link to select it, and type the full name of the corresponding course from the *Class Offerings* document, as follows:

■ Replace *Name of service 1* with **Autumn Planning for Spring Splendor**.

■ Replace *Name of service 2* with **Carnivorous Plants: Vicious or Delicious?**

■ Replace *Name of service 3* with **Organic Byproducts: Use Them or Lose Them!**

Because these are hyperlinks, it is preferable to retype the link than to copy and paste it, to ensure that the link remains active.

See Also For more information about hyperlinks, refer to "Inserting Hyperlinks," later in this chapter.

---

27 Copy and paste the first descriptive paragraph for each class from the *Class Offerings* document into *services.htm*, replacing the corresponding service description.

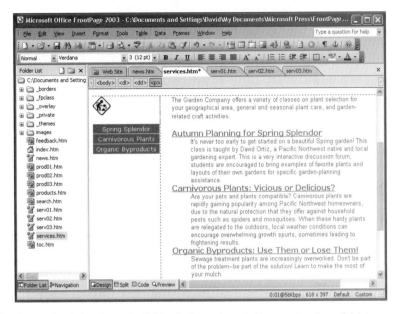

28   On each of the three individual class description pages (*serv01.htm*, *serv02.htm*, and *serv03.htm*), click anywhere in the body of the page, press `Ctrl`+`A` to select all the content, and then press the `Del` key.

29   In the *Class Offerings* document (the Word file), select and copy the descriptive text, learning objectives, and class schedule for each class, and then paste the information into the appropriate service page.

30   On the **File** menu, click **Save All** to save your changes to all the open files.

CLOSE the *GardenCo* Web site and the *Class Offerings* document, and quit Word.

Formatting Text

Web sites and Web pages created by FrontPage wizards are already formatted to look terrific without any additional effort from you. However, there are times when you will want to give a word or two a special look or make a paragraph stand out in some way. Most of the techniques you use in FrontPage to format text are the same as those you use in the other Microsoft Office System applications, so in this section, you will quickly review the types of formatting you are most likely to want to apply to your text, without much explanation.

In this exercise, you will format text and paragraphs using common Office formatting techniques.

USE the *GardenCo* Web site in the practice file folder for this topic. This practice file is located in the *My Documents\Microsoft Press\FrontPage 2003 SBS\CreateWeb\FormatText* folder and can also be accessed by clicking *Start/All Programs/Microsoft Press/FrontPage 2003 Step By Step*.
OPEN the *GardenCo* Web site.

1   Open **index.htm** (the home page) in the Page view editing window.

2   Select and delete the three comment blocks and the following spaces to make the page easier to read.

3   In the first paragraph, select the company name.

4   On the Formatting toolbar, click the **Increase Font Size** button.

Increase
Font Size

The font size shown in the Font Size box changes from *3 (12 pt)* to *4 (14 pt)* as the text size increases.

Tip   Font sizes are expressed in FrontPage in two ways: in points (as you are used to seeing in other applications, such as Microsoft Word and Microsoft Excel) and in sizes of 1 through 7. Eight options are available in the Font Size drop-down list: *Normal, 1 (8 pt), 2 (10 pt), 3 (12 pt), 4 (14 pt), 5 (18 pt), 6 (24 pt),* and *7 (36 pt)*.

Italic

5   Select the last sentence in the first paragraph (beginning with *Whether you visit us*), and click the **Italic** button to italicize the text.

6   Open **services.htm** (the Class Offerings page) in Page view.

Notice that the font used on this page is different from the default font on the home page.

7   Select the first paragraph.

Font

8   Click the down arrow to the right of the **Font** box, and click **Verdana** in the drop-down list.

Notice that the font size is still different from that on the home page.

9   With the first paragraph still selected, press Ctrl + Space to apply the default page formatting, which is 12-point Verdana. Repeat this step with each of the three class description paragraphs.

10   In the introductory paragraph, select the words **plant selection**.

Font Color

11 On the Formatting toolbar, click the down arrow to the right of the **Font Color** button, and change the font color to **Blue**. Repeat this procedure to change the words *plant care* to **Green** and *craft activities* to **Red**.

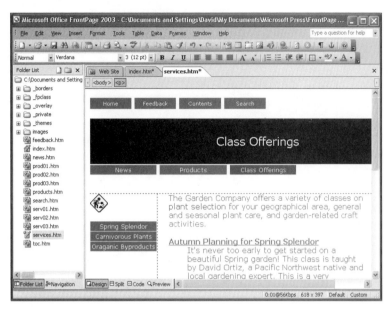

12 Open **serv01.htm** (the Spring Splendor page) in the Page view editing window.

Notice that the font on this page does not match the default site font on the home page.

13 Click [Ctrl]+[A] to select all the page content. In the **Font** drop-down list, click **(default font)**.

The font of each of the page elements changes to the default element font.

14 Select the paragraph that gives details about the class location and size.

Borders

15 On the Formatting toolbar, click the down arrow to the right of the **Borders** button to display the **Borders** palette.

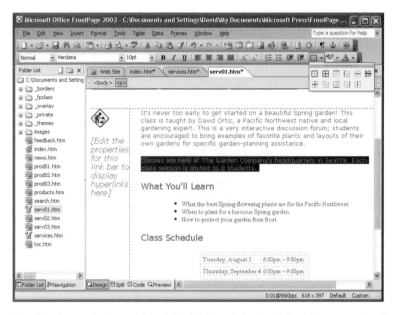

The Borders palette can be detached and docked elsewhere as a toolbar, or it can be detached and left as a floating toolbar.

Outside
Borders

16 Click the **Outside Borders** option to apply a border to the paragraph.

17 With the paragraph still selected, on the **Format** menu, click **Paragraph**.

The Paragraph dialog box appears.

18 In the **Paragraph** dialog box, do the following:

■ In the **Alignment** drop-down list, click **Center**.

■ In the **Indentation** section, set **Before text** and **After text** to 15.

■ In the **Spacing** section, set **Before** and **After** to 0.

Notice that your changes are reflected in the Preview area as you make them.

19 Click **OK** to apply the paragraph formatting.

20 Click an insertion point at the beginning of the second sentence in the bordered paragraph, and press Shift + Enter to insert a line break.

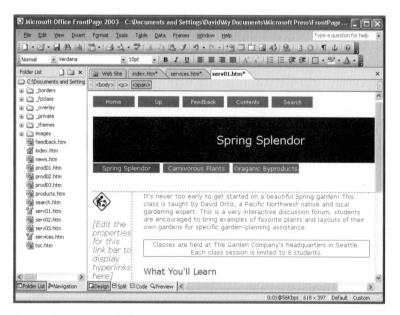

21 On the **File** menu, click **Save All** to save all the open files.

CLOSE the *GardenCo* Web site.

Cascading Style Sheets

Cascading style sheets (CSS) are documents that define formats and styles for page elements including headings, paragraphs, tables, lists, and so forth. The style sheet can be either an *embedded cascading style sheet* within a Web page, or as an *external cascading style sheet*. External style sheets can be referenced by multiple documents to provide a consistent look across pages and sites.

Web authors can also use cascading style sheets to stipulate how page elements are to be displayed by different browsers. Many Web sites utilize a *browser sniffer* that detects the Web browser and version used by each Web visitor and attaches the appropriate cascading style sheet to the site at that time.

To create an embedded cascading style sheet in FrontPage, click Style on the Format menu, and then define your own styles. The definitions are saved in the HTML code of the page.

To create an external cascading style sheet in FrontPage, select the CSS type from the options available on the Style Sheets tab of the Page Templates dialog box, click OK to create a CSS file, and then define your styles within the file.

To attach a style sheet in FrontPage, click Style Sheet Links on the Format menu, click Add, and browse to the CSS file on your computer or (if you have an Internet connection) anywhere on the Web.

The World Wide Web Consortium (W3C) originally developed cascading style sheets. For more information about current and future CSS specifications and how various browsers support CSS, visit their Web site at *www.w3c.org*.

Inserting Hyperlinks

When you use a wizard to generate a Web site, the wizard creates hyperlinks between the pages of the Web site. You can also add hyperlinks of your own. These hyperlinks might be to specific items of information on the same page or on a different page, to other Web sites, or to documents that are not part of any Web site.

In this exercise, you will create hyperlinks from the News page of the *GardenCo* Web site to important press releases that are stored in an external Word document.

USE the *GardenCo* Web site and the *PR1* document in the practice file folder for this topic. These practice files are located in the *My Documents\Microsoft Press\FrontPage 2003 SBS\CreateWeb\InsertHype* folder and can also be accessed by clicking *Start/All Programs/Microsoft Press/FrontPage 2003 Step By Step*. OPEN the *GardenCo* Web site.

1   Open **news.htm** in Page view.

2   Press Ctrl+End to move the insertion point to the end of the document.

3   Press Enter, type **Archived Press Releases**, and press Enter again.

4   On the **Insert** menu, click **Hyperlink**.

Browse for File

5   In the **Insert Hyperlink** dialog box, click the **Browse for File** button, browse to the *My Documents\FrontPage 2003 SBS\CreateWeb\InsertHype* folder, click **PR1**, click **OK** to select the file, and then click **OK** again.

A hyperlink to the press release is inserted at the insertion point.

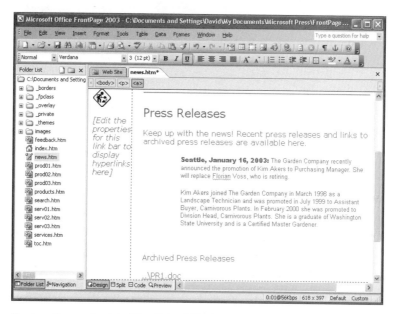

6   To view the contents of the linked file from within FrontPage, press the Ctrl key, and click the link.

A press release dated September 23, 2002 opens in Word.

7   Close the Word window to return to your Web site.

8   Save and close the *news.htm* file.

CLOSE the *GardenCo* Web site.

Making Your Site Accessible for Visitors

**New In
Office 2003**
Accessibility
checking

If you want your Web site to be comfortably viewed by the widest possible audience, you'll want to avoid including elements in your site that might affect its accessibility. For example, you will want to make navigation methods consistent throughout the site, and you'll want to group blocks of information so that they are more manageable. You can make your site accessible to viewers who have vision problems by using contrasting foreground and background colors and avoiding screen flicker. Paying attention to these and other issues while constructing your Web site will ensure that you do not inadvertently limit your audience.

FrontPage 2003 includes a new accessibility-checking feature that you can use to quickly check one or more pages of your Web site for potential accessibility problems. You can check your site against the World Wide Web Consortium's Web Content Accessibility Guidelines and the U.S. government Section 508 guidelines. The accessibility checker creates a list of errors, warnings, and suggestions for improving your Web site's accessibility.

To check the accessibility of a Web site:

1   Open the site that you want to check.

2   On the **Tools** menu, click **Accessibility**.

3   In the **Check where** area, select the **All pages** option.

4   Click the **Check** button.

5   When a message appears that FrontPage has finished searching the document, click **OK**.

6   When FrontPage displays a list of possible accessibility issues, click one of the problems to see a description in the **Problem Details** area, or double-click one of the problems to open the pertinent file to that location.

7   To create a printable problem report, click the **Generate HTML Report** button.

Seeing Your Web Site as Visitors Will

We've made a pretty good start at personalizing The Garden Company's Web site, and you are probably anxious to see the results of your work. There are two ways to view a Web site created with FrontPage before it is published: in FrontPage or in a browser.

Previewing your Web site in FrontPage is a good way to look at the basic layout and evaluate the overall presentation of the site, but it doesn't always represent the site as a visitor will experience it. Apart from the fact that you probably can't see as much of the page as you intend your visitors to see, none of the advanced controls that you might choose to add later will work in this view.

To see an accurate preview of your Web site before it is published, you will want to preview it in a *Web browser*. Viewing the Web site in a browser is a great opportunity to test its usability and functionality before exposing it to the scrutiny of the real world. Always be sure to take the time to test your site before publishing it.

In this exercise, you will look at the *GardenCo* Web site in the Preview pane, preview it in your default Web browser, and then see how it looks to Web visitors using other screen resolutions.

USE the *GardenCo* Web site in the practice file folder for this topic. This practice file is located in the *My Documents\Microsoft Press\FrontPage 2003 SBS\CreateWeb\Preview* folder and can also be accessed by clicking *Start/All Programs/Microsoft Press/FrontPage 2003 Step By Step*.
OPEN the *GardenCo* Web site.

1 Open the home page in Design view.

2 At the bottom of the Page view editing window, click the **Show Preview View** button to switch to the Preview pane.

Show
Preview View

The Web page is displayed in FrontPage.

At the top of the screen, a message tells you the page contains elements that might need to be saved or published to be previewed correctly.

Important   You can't preview a Web site in an Internet browser without first selecting a file.

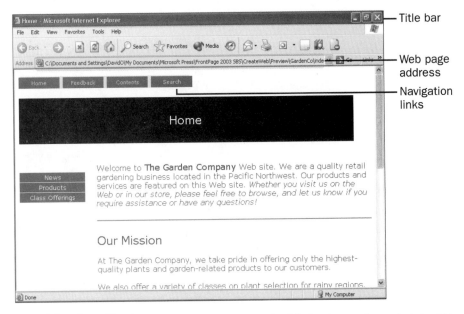

Preview in Browser

3   On the Standard toolbar, click the **Preview in Browser** button to see how the site looks in your default Web browser.

Troubleshooting   The Preview in Browser button's ScreenTip displays "Preview in (your default Web browser)".

Your default Web browser opens, displaying the *GardenCo* Web site home page.

Troubleshooting   The Web site previews in this book are shown in Internet Explorer 6.0 with the default settings. If you are using another Internet browser or have made changes to your Internet Explorer settings, your display might be different.

4   Click each of the navigation links to view the different pages of the site.

Troubleshooting   You cannot edit a file in FrontPage while you are previewing it in a browser. Attempting to do so causes an error called an *access violation*. Always close the browser, and then make any necessary changes to your site in FrontPage.

Close

5   When you're done, click the **Close** button to close the browser.

New in Office 2003

Browser and resolution reconciliation

6 Click the down arrow to the right of the **Preview in Browser** button.

A drop-down list displays your browser viewing options, which might include multiple Internet browsers and/or multiple screen resolutions.

7 To see how the sample Web site appears at a screen resolution other than your own setting, click one of the commands that is different from your default setting.

8 Preview the site. When you're done, click the **Close** button to close the browser.

CLOSE the *GardenCo* Web site.

Optimizing Your Screen Display Properties

The width and height of your computer monitor display in pixels is called the *screen resolution*. When personal computers first became popular, most computer monitors were capable of displaying a screen resolution of only 640 pixels wide by 480 pixels high (more commonly known as *640 x 480*). Now most computer monitors can display at 800 x 600 pixels and 1024 x 768 pixels. Some monitors can even display a screen resolution of 1280 x 1024 pixels, or larger. Newer monitors no longer offer a 640 x 480 screen resolution.

Most computer users have the choice of at least two different screen area sizes. Some people prefer to work at an 800 x 600 screen resolution because everything on the screen appears larger. Others prefer being able to fit more information on their screen with a 1024 x 768 display.

When designing a Web page that consists of more than free-flowing text, it is important to consider the likely screen resolution of your Web visitors and design for the lowest common denominator. It is currently common practice to design Web sites to look their best when the visitor's screen area is set to 800 x 600 pixels. (This means that visitors who view your site with a 640 x 480 area will have to scroll to display the entire page.)

To check and change your screen resolution on a Windows XP computer:

1 At the left end of the Windows taskbar, click **Start**, and then click **Control Panel**.

2 In the Control Panel window, click **Appearance and Themes**, and then click **Display** to open the **Display Properties** dialog box.

3 On the **Settings** tab, look at the **Screen resolution** slider. The current screen resolution appears beneath the slider.

4 Drag the slider to change the screen resolution, and click **Apply** to apply your changes.

5 If a dialog box appears prompting you to confirm the change, click **Yes**.

6 When the screen resolution is the way you want, click **OK**.

Deleting a Web Site

When you first start creating Web sites with FrontPage, you will probably want to experiment. As a result, you will more than likely end up with Web sites on your hard disk drive that you no longer need. What's more, if you make a mess when creating a real Web site and decide to start over, because you already have a Web site with your chosen name stored on your hard disk drive, FrontPage will not allow you to overwrite the existing site with a new one. You must create a whole new set of files by appending a number to the name you want to use.

To solve these problems, you might be tempted to simply delete existing sites in Windows Explorer, but if you do, you risk leaving behind extraneous hidden files. Instead you must delete the sites from FrontPage. In this exercise, you will delete the two Web sites you created with templates at the beginning of the chapter.

Important If you did not create the *OnePage* and *Personal* Web sites in the first exercise of this chapter, skip this exercise.

USE the *OnePage* and *Personal* Web sites you created in the first exercise of this chapter.
OPEN the *OnePage* Web site.

1 In the **Folder List**, right-click the top-level folder of the site, and click **Delete** on the shortcut menu to open the **Confirm Delete** dialog box.

2 Select the **Delete this Web site entirely** option, and then click **OK** to delete the Web site.

The Web site is deleted and the Folder List closes because the displayed content no longer exists.

Open

3 Click the down arrow to the right of the **Open** button, and click **Open Site** in the drop-down list.

4 Browse to and open the *Personal* Web site created at the beginning of this chapter.

5 Repeat steps 1 and 2 to delete the *Personal* Web site.

BE SURE TO quit FrontPage if you are not continuing on to the next chapter.

Key Points

- You can quickly and easily create FrontPage Web sites by using a template or wizard. Both tools create and populate the basic Web site by using comments to suggest the types of text you can use to personalize the site. A wizard walks you through the process of personalizing the site.

- You can format text and paragraphs in FrontPage by using the same familiar commands as you do in other Office applications.

- To test the full functionality of a Web site, you must preview it in a Web browser. FrontPage 2003 makes it easy to preview your site in multiple browsers and screen resolutions.

- You should delete Web sites from within FrontPage rather than from Windows Explorer to ensure that all the hidden files and folders are correctly deleted.

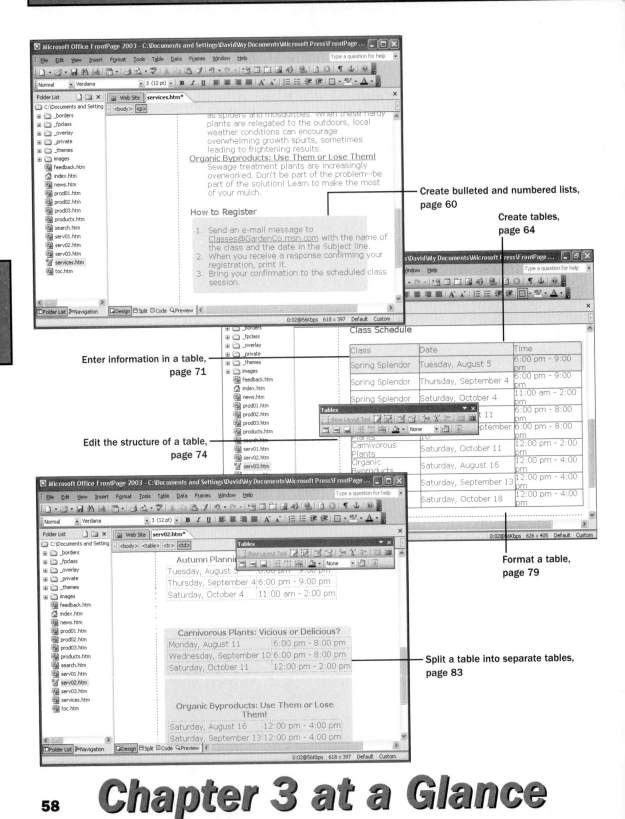

Create bulleted and numbered lists,
page 60

Create tables,
page 64

Enter information in a table,
page 71

Edit the structure of a table,
page 74

Format a table,
page 79

Split a table into separate tables,
page 83

Chapter 3 at a Glance

3 Presenting Information in Lists and Tables

In this chapter you will learn to:

✔ Create bulleted and numbered lists.

✔ Create tables.

✔ Enter information in a table.

✔ Edit the structure of a table.

✔ Format a table.

✔ Split a table into separate tables.

You are probably familiar with the kinds of *lists* and *tables* you can create in applications such as Microsoft Office Word 2003 and Microsoft Office PowerPoint 2003. In Microsoft Office FrontPage 2003, you use similar techniques to create lists and most kinds of tables.

Lists and tables are traditionally used to present information in structured, easy-to-grasp formats. In addition, you can use tables to structure entire Web page layouts. Using tables to establish the look of an entire Web page minimizes browser display variations and gives you more control than if you depend on a non-structured presentation. For instance, you can use a table to create a Web page that is a specific height and width, and to lay out content in specific positions on the page.

In this chapter, you will learn how to create bulleted lists, numbered lists, and tables in a FrontPage Web page. First you will add lists to a few pages of The Garden Company's Web site. Then you will create tables by using three different methods:

■ By using the Insert Table button.

■ By using the Insert Table command.

■ By drawing lines to create the table's rows and columns.

By learning a variety of methods, you will be able to select the simplest method for creating your own tables in the future.

See Also Do you need only a quick refresher on the topics in this chapter? See the Quick Reference entries on pages xxiii–xxiv.

Important Before you can use the practice files in this chapter, you need to install them from the book's companion CD to their default location. See "Using the Book's CD-ROM" on page xiii for more information.

Creating Bulleted and Numbered Lists

You use lists to separate items of information that might otherwise be buried in a text paragraph. If the items don't have to appear in a particular order, they usually appear in *bulleted lists*; for example, a list of drought-tolerant plants would be presented in a bulleted list. If the items have to appear in a particular order, they usually appear in *numbered lists*; for example, instructions for repotting a particular houseplant would be presented in a numbered list.

To convert a series of regular paragraphs to a bulleted list, you select the paragraphs and on the Formatting toolbar, click the Bullets button. Similarly, to convert regular paragraphs to a numbered list, you select the paragraphs and on the Formatting toolbar, click the Numbering button. To convert bulleted or numbered items back to regular paragraphs, select the items, and click the corresponding button to toggle it off.

In this exercise, you will create a new bulleted list, add an item to an existing bulleted list, and create a numbered list.

USE the *GardenCo* Web site in the practice file folder for this topic. This practice file is located in the *My Documents\Microsoft Press\FrontPage 2003 SBS\ListsTables\CreateList* folder and can also be accessed by clicking *Start/All Programs/Microsoft Press/FrontPage 2003 Step By Step*.
BE SURE TO start FrontPage before beginning this exercise.
OPEN the *GardenCo* Web site.

Important The exercises in this chapter build on the results of the previous exercise. If you work through all the exercises sequentially, you can continue working with your own file rather than closing and opening the sample Web sites from the practice file folders. When using the practice files, be sure to use the files from the correct practice file folder for each exercise.

1 If the **Folder List** is not already open, on the **View** menu, click **Folder List**.

2 In the **Folder List**, double-click **serv01.htm** to open the Spring Splendor page in the Page view editing window.

3 Position the insertion point on the blank line under the *What You'll Learn* heading.

4 Type Which Spring-flowering plants are best for the Pacific Northwest.

5 Press Enter to start a new line, and then type When to plant for a luscious Spring garden.

6 Press Enter, and then type How to protect your garden from frost.

Bullets

7 Select the three lines you just typed, and on the Formatting toolbar, click the **Bullets** button.

The text is converted to a bulleted list.

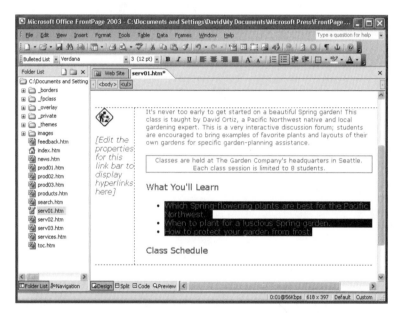

Close [Page]

8 Click the serv01.htm file's **Close** button to close the Spring Splendor page, saving your changes when prompted.

9 In the **Folder List**, double-click **serv03.htm** to open the Organic Byproducts page in the Page view editing window.

10 To add a new bulleted item to the **What You'll Learn** list, position the insertion point at the end of the second item, and press Enter.

A new, blank bulleted list line is created.

11 Type When and where to use your mulch for maximum effectiveness.

12 Close the Organic Byproducts page, saving your changes when prompted.

13 In the **Folder List**, double-click **services.htm** to open the Class Offerings page in the Page view editing window.

14 Press Ctrl+End to move the insertion point to the end of the page.

15 Press Enter to create a new line.

16 Type Send an e-mail message to Classes@GardenCo.msn.com with the name of the class and the date in the Subject line.

As you type, the e-mail address is automatically formatted as a hyperlink.

Numbering

17 On the Formatting toolbar, click the **Numbering** button to turn the paragraph into a numbered item.

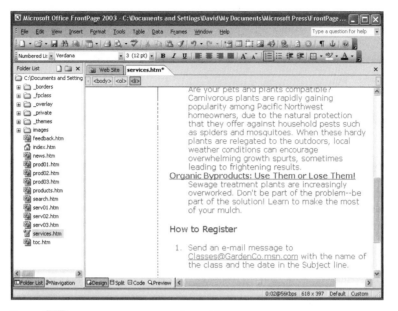

18 Press `Enter` to create a new numbered item.

19 Type When you receive a response confirming your registration, print it.

20 Press `Enter`, and then type Bring your confirmation to the scheduled class session.

21 Press `Enter` to create a new line, and then click the **Numbering** button to turn off numbering and convert the new numbered item to a regular paragraph.

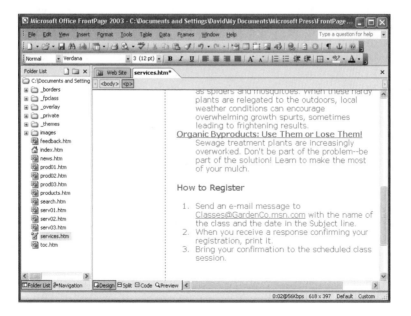

If you're interested, you might want to click the Code button to display the underlying source code for the numbered list in the Code pane. As you will see, FrontPage designates the entire list as an *ordered list* by enclosing it in <ol> and </ol> tags. Each list item is enclosed in <li> and </li> tags. A bulleted list has a similar structure, except that the entire list is designated as an *unordered list* by enclosing it in <ul> and </ul> tags.

22 Close the Class Offerings page, saving your changes when prompted.

CLOSE the *GardenCo* Web site.

Creating Tables

A *table* consists of vertical *columns* and horizontal *rows*. A table might have an overall *table title* that appears either as a separate paragraph above the body of the table or in the table's top row. It usually has a *header row*, which contains a title for each column, and it might have a *header column*, which contains a title for each row.

Tip Sometimes text or numbers would stand out better for your Web visitors if they were presented in columns and rows, but they don't need the structure of a table. In Word, you can use a tabular list—a set of pseudo columns and rows in which you use tabs to line everything up—instead of setting up a table structure. But FrontPage doesn't accommodate this type of list. When you want to put information in columns and rows, you need to create a real table.

In this exercise, you'll learn one way of creating a table as you set up the structure for a Class Schedules table. You will use this table to organize information about the gardening classes offered by The Garden Company.

USE the *GardenCo* Web site in the practice file folder for this topic. This practice file is located in the *My Documents\Microsoft Press\FrontPage 2003 SBS\ListsTables\CreateTable* folder and can also be accessed by clicking *Start/All Programs/Microsoft Press/FrontPage 2003 Step By Step*.
OPEN the *GardenCo* Web site.

1 In the **Folder List**, double-click the **serv01.htm** file to open the Spring Splendor page in the Page view editing window.

2 Press `Ctrl`+`End` to move the insertion point to the end of the page, and then press `Enter` to insert a blank line following the *Class Schedule* heading.

3 On the Standard toolbar, click the **Insert Table** button.

Insert Table

A grid drops down, on which you can indicate the size of your table.

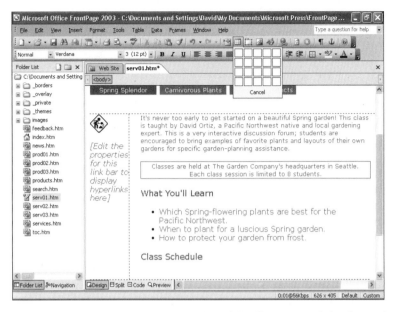

4 Point to the first *cell*—the intersection of the first row and the first column—and hold down the left mouse button. Drag the pointer until an area three cells wide by ten cells high is highlighted (the grid will expand as you drag the mouse to the edge), and then release the mouse button.

FrontPage inserts a table with the number of rows and columns you highlighted.

5 If necessary, scroll to the bottom of the page to see the entire table.

Close [Page]

6   Click the serv01.htm file's **Close** button to close the Spring Splendor page, saving your changes when prompted.

7   In the **Folder List**, double-click **serv02.htm** to open the Carnivorous Plants page in the Page view editing window.

8   Repeat step 2 to insert a blank line at the end of the page.

9   On the **Table** menu, point to **Insert**, and then click **Table**.

The Insert Table dialog box appears.

Tip   Unlike most corresponding menu commands and toolbar buttons in Microsoft Office 2003, the Insert Table menu command and the Insert Table button work differently. The command displays a dialog box, whereas the button displays a grid.

10   In the **Size** area, specify **9** rows and **4** columns for your table.

11   In the **Layout** area, set the **Cell padding** to **3**, and verify that the width is set to 100 percent.

Tip   *Cell padding* is space between the borders of the cells and the text inside them. This padding is similar to the margins of a page.

12   In the **Borders** area, set the **Size** to **0**.

13 Click **OK** to create the table.

14 If necessary, scroll to the bottom of the page to see the entire table.

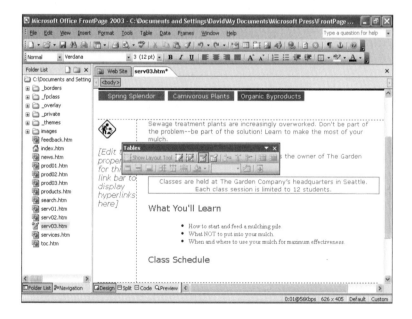

15 Close the Carnivorous Plants page, saving your changes when prompted.

16 In the **Folder List**, double-click **serv03.htm** to open the Organic Byproducts page in the Page view editing window.

17 Repeat step 2 to insert a blank line at the end of the page.

18 On the **Table** menu, click **Draw Table**.

The Tables toolbar opens, and the mouse pointer changes to a pencil.

19 Scroll down so you can see the bottom of the page.

20 Click under the *Class Schedule* heading, and then drag the pencil pointer down and to the right, to create a table of approximately the same size as those you previously created in this exercise.

When you release the mouse button, FrontPage creates a single-cell table.

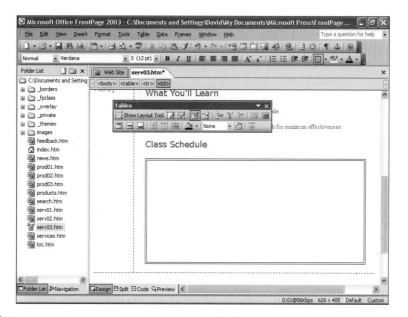

21 Using the pencil pointer, draw two vertical lines within the table to divide it into three columns.

22 Draw nine horizontal lines within the table to divide it into ten rows.

Tip This will be easiest if you first divide the table into two rows, and then divide each row into five rows.

[Screenshot of Microsoft Office FrontPage 2003 showing the Class Schedule table and Tables toolbar]

Tip Experiment with the locations of the lines separating columns and rows; you will find that the table expands to meet your needs.

23 When you're done drawing the rough table, press the ⎋ key to change the pointer back to its original shape.

24 Drag through the table's cells to select them all.

Distribute
Rows Evenly

25 On the **Tables** toolbar, click the **Distribute Rows Evenly** button to make all ten rows an equal height.

Distribute
Columns
Evenly

26 On the **Tables** toolbar, click the **Distribute Columns Evenly** button to make all three columns an equal width.

27 Close the Organic Byproducts page, saving your changes when prompted.

Close (Toolbar)

28 At the right end of the **Tables** toolbar's title bar, click the **Close** button to close the toolbar.

CLOSE the *GardenCo* Web site.

Tip   If you want to close a floating toolbar to reduce screen clutter, you can either click the Close button at the right end of the title bar of a floating toolbar, or right-click the toolbar, and click its name on the shortcut menu. To display a hidden toolbar, right-click any toolbar, and then click the name of the toolbar you want on the shortcut menu.

Converting Existing Text to a Table

If you have an existing block of text with items separated by commas, tabs, or paragraph marks, you can convert the text to a table.

To convert existing text:

1   Select the text you want to convert, and then on the **Table** menu, point to **Convert**, and click **Text to Table**.

The Convert Text To Table dialog box appears, in which you can tell FrontPage how the elements of the selected text are separated.

2   Make your selection, and click **OK**.

FrontPage converts the text to a table. You can use the Tables toolbar to make any necessary adjustments.

You can also convert a table to text by selecting the table, and on the Table menu, pointing to Convert and clicking Table to Text.

Entering Information in a Table

In the previous exercise, you created the structure for three tables on three separate pages of The Garden Company's Web site. Now you need to fill the tables with information to make them useful. You enter information in FrontPage tables the same way you enter it in Word tables.

In this exercise you will fill three existing tables with information. For The Garden Company's Web site, you'll place the same information in each table, but you would probably fill your own tables with different types of information.

USE the *GardenCo* Web site in the practice file folder for this topic. This practice file is located in the *My Documents\Microsoft Press\FrontPage 2003 SBS\ListsTables\TableText* folder and can also be accessed by clicking *Start/All Programs/Microsoft Press/FrontPage 2003 Step By Step*.
OPEN the *GardenCo* Web site.

1   In the **Folder List**, click the **serv01.htm** file to select it, and then hold down the Ctrl key, and click **serv02.htm** and **serv03.htm** so that all three files are selected.

2 Press [Enter] to open the three files in the Page view editing window.

3 On the Spring Splendor page, scroll down so you can see the entire table.

4 Position the insertion point in the first cell of the table, and then type Class.

Tip If the Tables toolbar opens when you position the insertion point inside a table, you can drag it out of the way by its title bar, or you can close it by clicking the Close button at the right end of its title bar.

As you type, the table column widths adjust automatically to reflect the relationship between the contents of each column.

5 Press the [Tab] key to move the insertion point to the second cell, and then type Date.

The table column widths adjust automatically as you type each word.

6 Press [Tab] to move the insertion point to the third cell, and then type Time to complete the table's header row.

7 Enter the following information in the three columns of the table, under the respective headings:

Class	Date	Time
Spring Splendor	Tuesday, August 5	6:00 pm – 9:00 pm
Spring Splendor	Thursday, September 4	6:00 pm – 9:00 pm
Spring Splendor	Saturday, October 4	11:00 am – 2:00 pm
Carnivorous Plants	Monday, August 11	6:00 pm – 8:00 pm
Carnivorous Plants	Wednesday, September 10	6:00 pm – 8:00 pm
Carnivorous Plants	Saturday, October 11	12:00 pm – 2:00 pm
Organic Byproducts	Saturday, August 16	12:00 pm – 4:00 pm
Organic Byproducts	Saturday, September 13	12:00 pm – 4:00 pm
Organic Byproducts	Saturday, October 18	12:00 pm – 4:00 pm

Tip   If you don't feel like typing, you can copy and paste this information from the *ClassList* document stored in the practice file folder for this topic.

8   At the top of the Page view editing window, click the **serv03.htm** page tab to switch to that file.

9   On the Organic Byproducts page, fill the hand-drawn table with the same header row and the same three columns of information.

Note that the column widths do not adjust as you enter information into this table because you specified when creating it that the columns should be distributed evenly.

10   At the top of the Page view editing window, click the **serv02.htm** page tab to switch to that file.

11   The table on the Carnivorous Plants page has only nine rows, so this table will not have a header. Fill in the first two columns with the class and date information, and then fill in the fourth column with the time information.

12 On the **File** menu, click **Save All** to save the open files.

CLOSE the *GardenCo* Web site.

Editing the Structure of a Table

Unless you are very skilled at creating tables, you will rarely create one that you don't have to later adjust in one way or another. Most likely, you will have to add or delete rows or columns and move information around until it is in the right place. Almost certainly, you will also have to adjust the size of rows and columns that are too big, too small, or unevenly spaced. Luckily, with FrontPage it is simple to fix all these structural problems.

Tip When columns are much wider than the information they contain, your Web visitors might have to scroll from side to side to see all of the information in a table. When columns are too narrow, the text within will wrap, and your Web visitors might have to scroll up and down. Whenever possible, avoid these problems by resizing one or more of the rows or columns in a table as needed.

In this exercise, you will change the structure of an existing table to re-arrange the information it contains. On the Carnivorous Plants page of the sample Web site, the class schedule is currently presented in nine rows and four columns, one of which is blank. You will move information between columns, delete the unused column, and add a header row to this table.

USE the *GardenCo* Web site in the practice file folder for this topic. This practice file is located in the *My Documents\Microsoft Press\FrontPage 2003 SBS\ListsTables\TableStruct* folder and can also be accessed by clicking *Start\All Programs\Microsoft Press\FrontPage 2003 Step By Step*. OPEN the *GardenCo* Web site.

1 In the **Folder List**, double-click **serv02.htm** to open the Carnivorous Plants page in the Page view editing window.

2 On the Carnivorous Plants page, click anywhere in the fourth column of the table.

The Tables toolbar opens.

Troubleshooting If the Tables toolbar does not open, right-click an open toolbar, and click Tables on the shortcut menu.

3 On the **Table** menu, point to **Select**, and then click **Column**.

4 Point to the upper-left corner of the selection, and drag the time information from the fourth column to the top cell of the third column.

Troubleshooting If you drag the selected cells to a cell other than the top cell of the column, the entire contents of the selection will be inserted in the cell to which you drag it.

5 Click anywhere in the top row of the table.

6 On the **Tables** toolbar, click the **Insert Rows** button.

Insert Rows

A new row is inserted at the top of the table.

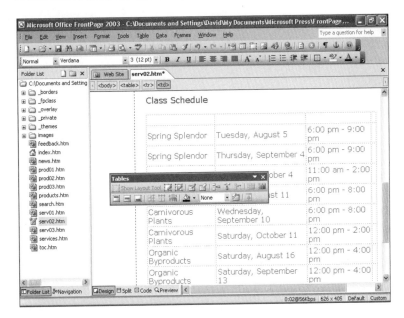

7 Click anywhere in the empty fourth column of the table.

8 On the **Table** menu, point to **Select**, and then click **Column**.

Delete Cells

9 On the **Tables** toolbar, click the **Delete Cells** button to delete the blank column from the right side of the table.

10 In the new header row, enter Class, Date, and Time as the column headings.

The table on the Carnivorous Plants page now looks like those on the Spring Splendor and Organic Byproducts pages.

Close [Page]

11 Click the serv02.htm file's **Close** button to close the Carnivorous Plants page, saving your changes when prompted.

12 In the **Folder List**, double-click **serv03.htm** to open the Organic Byproducts page in the Page view editing window.

13 Scroll down so you can see the entire table.

14 To adjust the size of the columns in the table on this page, start by pointing to the right border of the table's **Date** column.

The pointer changes to a double-headed arrow.

15 Double-click the border.

FrontPage resizes the column to exactly fit its contents.

AutoFit to Contents

16 Click anywhere in the table, and on the **Tables** toolbar, click the **AutoFit to Contents** button.

All the table columns adjust to the exact width of their contents.

17 Right-click anywhere in the table, and then click **Table Properties** on the shortcut menu to display the **Table Properties** dialog box.

18 In the **Table Properties** dialog box, do the following:

- In the **Alignment** drop-down list, click **Left**.

- Set **Cell padding** to **3**.

- Select the **Specify width** check box.

- In the **Specify width** box, type **100**, and then select the **In percent** option.

- In the **Borders** area, set **Size** to **0**.

Table Properties

Layout Tools
- ○ Enable layout tools
- ○ Disable layout tools
- ⊙ Automatically enable layout tools based on table content

Size

Rows: 10   Columns: 3

Layout

Alignment:	Left	☑ Specify width:
Float:	Default	100 ○ In pixels ⊙ In percent
Cell padding:	3	☑ Specify height:
Cell spacing:	0	278 ⊙ In pixels ○ In percent

Borders

Size:	0	Light border: ☐ Automatic
Color:	☐ Automatic	Dark border: ☐ Automatic
☑ Collapse table border		

Background

Color: ☐ Automatic
☐ Use background picture

Browse...   Properties...

Set

☐ Set as default for new tables

Style...   OK   Cancel   Apply

■ Click **OK** to close the dialog box and apply your changes.

Microsoft Office FrontPage 2003 - C:\Documents and Settings\David\My Documents\Microsoft Press\FrontPage ...

File Edit View Insert Format Tools Table Data Frames Window Help   Type a question for help

Normal   Verdana   3 (12 pt)   B I U

Folder List   Web Site serv03.htm*

C:\Documents and Setting   <body> <div> <table> <tr> <td>

- _borders
- _fpclass
- _overlay
- _private
- _themes
- images
- feedback.htm
- index.htm
- news.htm
- prod01.htm
- prod02.htm
- prod03.htm
- products.htm
- search.htm
- serv01.htm
- serv02.htm
- serv03.htm
- services.htm
- toc.htm

Class Schedule

Class	Date	Time
Spring Splendor	Tuesday, August 5	6:00 pm - 9:00 pm
Spring Splendor	Thursday, September 4	6:00 pm - 9:00 pm
	ber 4	11:00 am - 2:00 pm
	st 11	6:00 pm - 8:00 pm
Carnivorous Plants	Wednesday, September 10	6:00 pm - 8:00 pm
Carnivorous Plants	Saturday, October 11	12:00 pm - 2:00 pm
Organic Byproducts	Saturday, August 16	12:00 pm - 4:00 pm
Organic Byproducts	Saturday, September 13	12:00 pm - 4:00 pm
Organic		12:00 pm - 4:00

Tables
Show Layout Tool   None

Folder List Navigation   Design Split Code Preview

0:02@56Kbps 626 x 405 Default Custom

19 Move the mouse pointer to the top of the first column so that it changes to a down arrow. Hold down the left mouse button to select the column, and then drag to the right until all three columns are selected.

20 On the **Tables** toolbar, click the **Distribute Columns Evenly** button to make all the columns the same width.

Distribute
Columns
Evenly

21 Close the Organic Byproducts page, saving your changes when prompted.

CLOSE the *GardenCo* Web site.

Formatting a Table

In FrontPage, as in Word, you have several options for formatting tables. You can choose from a large variety of pre-formatted table styles or create your own look. You can even merge two or more cells into one cell so that a table entry spans several columns or rows.

FrontPage 2003 supports many of the standard Microsoft Office System table-formatting options, including the following:

- By using Fill Right and Fill Down, you can quickly copy content from one table cell to several others.

- By using AutoFormat, you can quickly create professional-looking tables by simply selecting a pre-formatted option from a list.

- By using the Borders button, you can format selected table and cell borders as easily as you can in Word and Excel, simply by clicking the type of border you want.

In this exercise, you'll format the tables in The Garden Company's Web site, first by doing things "the hard way"—and seeing just how easy that can be—and then by checking out a few of FrontPage's ready-made formats.

USE the *GardenCo* Web site in the practice file folder for this topic. This practice file is located in the *My Documents\Microsoft Press\FrontPage 2003 SBS\ListsTables\FormatTable* folder and can also be accessed by clicking *Start/All Programs/Microsoft Press/FrontPage 2003 Step By Step*.
OPEN the *GardenCo* Web site.

1 In the **Folder List**, double-click **serv02.htm** to open the Carnivorous Plants page in the Page view editing window.

2 Scroll down to the table, and select the three cells of the header row.

3 Right-click the selection, and click **Cell Properties** on the shortcut menu.

The Cell Properties dialog box appears.

4   In the **Cell Properties** dialog box, select the **Header cell** check box.

5   In the **Background** area, click the down arrow to the right of the **Color** box to display the Standard and Theme color palettes.

If you click More Colors, FrontPage displays a dialog box in which you can select from a palette of 127 colors or specify a custom color using the hexadecimal or RGB value. Your options are practically limitless!

6   Select your favorite color from the default set, and then click **OK** to close the **Cell Properties** dialog box and apply your changes.

Tip   When a theme is attached to a Web page, the default colors include those used in the theme. It is generally best to select colors from the theme to maintain a consistent look and feel throughout your Web site.

The background color is applied, and the words inside the header cells become bold and centered.

7   Because the cells are still selected, click away from the table to reveal the actual cell color.

8 In the **Folder List**, double-click **serv01.htm** to open the Spring Splendor page in the Page view editing window.

9 Click anywhere in the table on that page.

10 On the **Tables** toolbar, click the **Table AutoFormat** button.

Table
AutoFormat

The Table AutoFormat dialog box appears.

11 In the **Table AutoFormat** dialog box, use the ⬇ key to scroll through the **Formats** list on the left.

When you select a format, a sample table with that format applied is displayed in the Preview window.

12 Select the **Subtle 1** format.

13 Because this table does not have a special first column, in the **Apply special formats** area, clear the **First Column** check box.

14 Click **OK** to apply the selected format to the table.

15 At the bottom of the Page view editing window, click the **Preview** button to switch to the Preview pane, then scroll down to see the table.

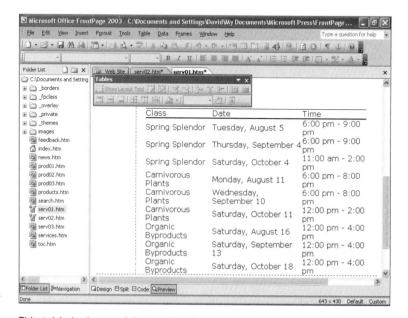

This table looks good, but notice that each class name in the first column is repeated three times. The table would look tidier if each class name appeared only once and spanned three rows.

16 At the bottom of the Page view editing window, click the **Show Design View** button to switch to the Design pane.

17 In the first column, select the three cells containing the words *Spring Splendor*.

Merge Cells

18 On the **Tables** toolbar, click the **Merge Cells** button.

FrontPage merges the three cells into one cell that still contains three instances of *Spring Splendor*.

Tip To split one cell into multiple cells, select the cell, and click the Split Cells button. In the Split Cells dialog box, specify the number of rows or columns you want to split the merged cell into, and click OK.

19 Select and delete two instances of the class name, leaving just one.

The remaining class name is vertically centered within the cell.

20 Repeat steps 17 through 19 for the Carnivorous Plants and Organic Byproducts classes.

21 On the **File** menu, click **Save All** to save the open pages.

CLOSE the *GardenCo* Web site.

Splitting a Table into Separate Tables

In the same way that you can split and merge individual cells, you can split and merge entire tables. You can also nest one table within another. These options might seem pretty complex for presenting straightforward information, but they offer wonderful possibilities, particularly when you want to organize an entire Web page with one table.

In this exercise you will split the Class Schedule table into three separate tables, one for each class, with each class name as the table title.

USE the *GardenCo* Web site in the practice file folder for this topic. This practice file is located in the *My Documents\Microsoft Press\FrontPage 2003 SBS\ListsTables\TableInTable* folder and can also be accessed by clicking *Start/All Programs/Microsoft Press/FrontPage 2003 Step By Step*.
OPEN the *GardenCo* Web site.

1 In the **Folder List**, double-click **serv02.htm** to open the Carnivorous Plants page in the Page view editing window.

2 Scroll down to the table, and click in the first row containing the words *Carnivorous Plants*.

3 On the **Table** menu, click **Split Table**.

FrontPage splits the table into two tables.

4 Click in the first row containing the words *Organic Byproducts*, and split the table again.

You now have three distinct tables.

5 Click in the row containing the words *Class*, *Date*, and *Time*.

6 On the **Table** menu, point to **Select**, and then click **Row**.

7 Right-click the selection, and click **Delete Rows** on the shortcut menu.

The header row is deleted.

8 With the insertion point in the **Spring Splendor** table, on the **Table** menu, point to **Insert**, and then click **Caption**.

A centered caption row is inserted at the top of the table.

9 Type **Autumn Planning for Spring Splendor** as the table caption.

10 Select the caption, and on the Formatting toolbar, click the **Bold** button.

B
Bold

11 Select the first column. Right-click the selection, and click **Delete Columns** on the shortcut menu.

The left column is deleted.

AutoFit to
Contents

12 On the **Tables** toolbar, click the **AutoFit to Contents** button.

13 Repeat steps 8 through 12 for the *Carnivorous Plants* and *Organic Byproducts* tables, using the following class titles as the table captions:

- Carnivorous Plants: Vicious or Delicious?

- Organic Byproducts: Use Them or Lose Them!

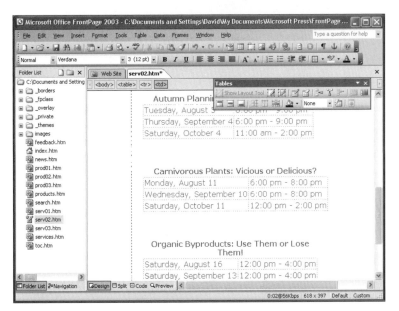

✕
Close [Page]

14 Click the serv02.htm file's **Close** button to close the Carnivorous Plants page, saving your changes when prompted.

CLOSE the *GardenCo* Web site. If you are not continuing on to the next chapter, quit FrontPage.

Key Points

- You can format text as a bulleted or numbered list simply by clicking a button.

- You can convert text to a table, or convert a table to text.

- FrontPage 2003 supplies 38 predefined table formats from which you can choose, or you can format a table by hand.

- After creating a table, you can merge the contents of multiple cells or split individual cells into multiple cells. You can do the same with entire tables.

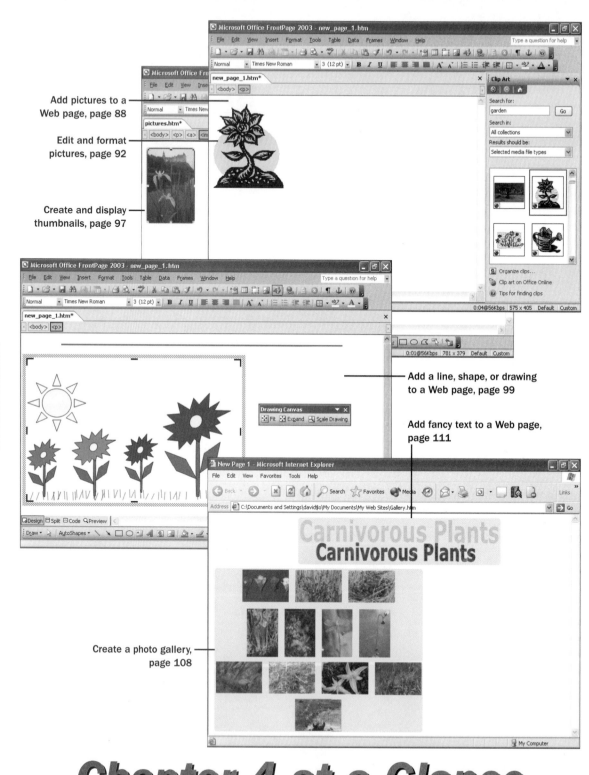

Add pictures to a Web page, page 88

Edit and format pictures, page 92

Create and display thumbnails, page 97

Add a line, shape, or drawing to a Web page, page 99

Add fancy text to a Web page, page 111

Create a photo gallery, page 108

Chapter 4 at a Glance

4 Enhancing Your Web Site with Graphics

In this chapter you will learn to:

✔ Add pictures to a Web page.

✔ Edit and format pictures.

✔ Create and display thumbnails.

✔ Add a line, shape, or drawing to a Web page.

✔ Create a photo gallery.

✔ Add fancy text to a Web page.

You can do a lot to get your message across and increase the appeal of your Web pages by using well-crafted language and by formatting words and paragraphs to good effect. However, there are times when no matter how you format your text, it is not enough to grab the attention of your visitors and to make your Web site stand out from all the others.

At times like these, you need the pizzazz that pictures and other graphic images can add to your pages. With Microsoft Office FrontPage 2003, you can insert a variety of graphic elements, including clip art, picture files, scanned images, drawings, shapes, WordArt objects, and videos.

It is safe to assume that a large part of the appeal of The Garden Company's Web site, which is used as the example for most of the exercises in this book, would be pictures of plants, "idea" shots of gardens to provide inspiration, garden bed designs, and other visually enticing elements. No amount of text will do the trick for a Web site that is about things you have to see to appreciate, just as no amount of text can possibly substitute for a music clip on a site dedicated to a particular band or genre of music.

To make The Garden Company's Web site visually appealing, you would need to use graphics judiciously, carefully selecting an appropriate style and exercising some restraint to avoid a confusing effect. Because you will learn how to add a wide variety of graphic elements in this chapter, you will use the *GardenCo* Web site only when it's appropriate, practicing otherwise on a new page that you can discard when you're through with it.

See Also Do you need only a quick refresher on the topics in this chapter? See the Quick Reference entries on pages xxiv–xxvii.

Important Before you can use the practice files in this chapter, you need to install them from the book's companion CD to their default location. See "Using the Book's CD-ROM" on page xiii for more information.

Adding Pictures to a Web Page

FrontPage makes it easy to add all kinds of *media*, including graphics, photos, videos, and even sound effects, into a Web page. When you're looking for a quick and simple graphic representation that won't cost you a licensing fee, an easy solution is to use *clip art*. A large library of clip art is included with The Microsoft Office System 2003, and a seemingly endless selection is available on the Microsoft Office Design Gallery Live Web site at *dgl.microsoft.com*. If neither of these sources has what you need, you can find hundreds of small clip art galleries on the Web. You can also purchase clip art CD-ROMs, many of which focus on particular themes or on particular styles of clip art.

The Clip Organizer

The Microsoft Office System 2003 stores various clip art elements in different folders, and all of them are available to you in FrontPage 2003.

You can use the Clip Organizer to access and organize media files through an easy-to-use task pane interface. The Clip Organizer contains hundreds of pieces of clip art and makes it easy to find additional digital art on the World Wide Web.

To organize your clips using the Clip Organizer:

1 In the **Clip Art** task pane, click **Organize clips**.

The Add Clips to Organizer dialog box appears.

2 Click the **Now** button.

The Microsoft Clip Organizer takes a few moments to create collections for you based on your media files, and then takes a few moments more to add keywords to your clips so that you can find them later using the keyword search feature.

You can find, access, and insert a variety of media files from the Clip Art task pane. In addition to traditional clip art, which usually consists of cartoon-like drawings, you can choose from photographs, movies, and sounds. This great resource area is a lot of fun to explore!

Where Web pages are concerned, it's worth keeping in mind the well-worn saying "A picture is worth a thousand words." You will often find it beneficial to add photographs to your Web pages to illustrate or enhance the text or to demonstrate a difficult concept. You can obtain Web-ready pictures in a variety of ways: by taking photographs with a digital camera, by scanning existing photographs to create digital files, by buying art files, or by downloading public-domain files from the Internet.

FrontPage 2003 can access picture files that are on your computer, on another computer on your network, or if you have an Internet connection, on a Web site.

For the highest display quality, you should use pictures that have been saved as *Graphics Interchange Format (GIF)* or *Joint Photographic Experts Group (JPG)* files. Both display well over the Web. The GIF file format supports up to 256 colors. The JPG file format was specifically developed for photographs and is the best format to use for photos and other graphics with more than 256 colors. When choosing a graphic format, it is important to remember that smaller files download faster. You might consider saving pictures in both GIF and JPG format to so you can compare file size and picture quality and select the format that best fits your needs.

Tip   When displaying a graphic in FrontPage's Design pane, you can easily convert it to GIF or JPG format. In Page view, right-click the graphic, and then click Picture Properties on the shortcut menu. Click the General tab, and then click the Picture File Type button. In the Picture File Type dialog box, select the GIF or JPG option. The original and changed sizes are shown at the top of the dialog box.

In this exercise, you will insert a piece of clip art and a photograph on a practice page.

USE the *GardenCo* picture in the practice file folder for this topic. This practice file is located in the *My Documents\Microsoft Press\FrontPage 2003 SBS\Pictures\AddPicture* folder and can also be accessed by clicking *Start/All Programs/Microsoft Press/FrontPage 2003 Step By Step.*
BE SURE TO start FrontPage before beginning this exercise.

1   If a new page is not already open, on the Standard toolbar, click the **Create a new normal page** button to open a new blank page to use as a canvas for your artwork.

Create a new
normal page

2   On the **Insert** menu, point to **Picture**, and then click **Clip Art**.

The Clip Art task pane opens.

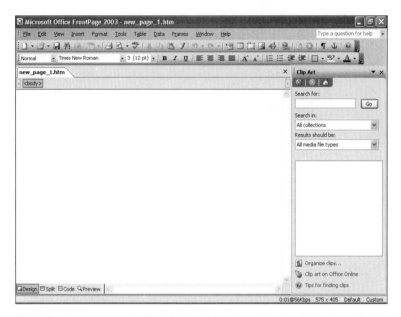

3 Click the down arrow to the right of the **Results should be** box. In the drop-down list, clear the **Photographs**, **Movies**, and **Sounds** check boxes. Make sure the **Clip Art** check box is selected. Then click away from the drop-down list to close it.

4 If you do not have an active Internet connection, click the down arrow to the right of the **Search in** box and clear the **Web Collections** check box. Then click away from the drop-down list to close it.

5 In the **Search for** box, type garden, and then click **Go**.

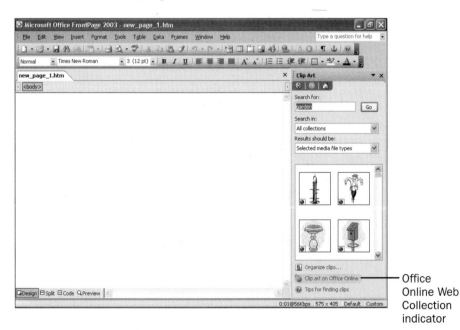

Office
Online Web
Collection
indicator

While FrontPage searches for clip art that matches your search term, the word *(Searching…)* appears above the Results box. When the search is complete, the results are displayed in the Results box.

6 Position the mouse pointer over the first graphic to display its keywords, dimensions, file size, and format.

Tip A vertical bar with a down arrow appears when you position the mouse pointer over a graphic. Clicking the down arrow displays a list of options.

7 Scroll through the search results until you find a graphic you like.

8 Position the mouse pointer over the graphic, and click the down arrow that appears. In the drop-down list, click **Insert**.

FrontPage inserts the selected graphic in your page at the insertion point.

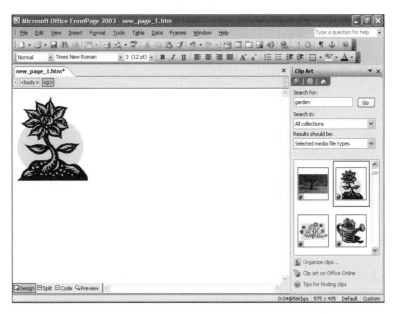

The inserted clip art might not be the right size for your page (sometimes it is very large). Later in the chapter, you will practice resizing graphics.

9 Click the file's **Close** button to close the current file; click **No** when prompted to save your work.

×
Close

10 On the Standard toolbar, click the **Create a new normal page** button to open a new page.

A new, blank page opens in the Page view editing window.

11 On the **Insert** menu, point to **Picture**, and then click **From File** to display the **Picture** dialog box.

12 In the **Picture** dialog box, browse to the practice file folder for this topic, and click (don't double-click) the **GardenCo** file.

Views

13 If you don't see a preview of the picture in the dialog box, on the **Picture** dialog box's toolbar, click the down arrow to the right of the **Views** button, and then click **Preview**.

The dialog box displays a preview of the selected picture, which is The Garden Company's logo.

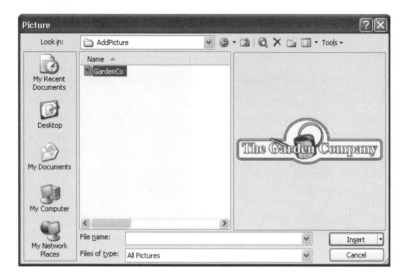

14 Click the **Insert** button to insert the logo on the Web page and close the Clip Art task pane.

CLOSE the practice file without saving your work.

Editing and Formatting Pictures

Sometimes the picture you add to a Web page won't produce exactly the result you are looking for—perhaps it's too large or too small, or perhaps it includes a variety of elements that distract from the thing you're trying to draw the visitor's attention to. For really drastic changes, you will need to manipulate the picture in a graphics-editing program before adding it to the Web page. But for small modifications like sizing, *cropping*, and adding a frame, you can do the job within FrontPage.

The commands used to edit and format pictures are contained on the Pictures toolbar.

- The Insert Picture From File command displays the Picture dialog box, where you can search for and insert a picture.

- The Text command creates a text box in the picture area into which you can insert your own text.

- The Auto Thumbnail command creates a small preview version of your picture, called a *thumbnail*, which is hyperlinked to the original. Viewers can click the thumbnail to view the full-size version.

- The Position Absolutely, Bring Forward, and Send Backward commands control the position of the picture on the page in relation to other elements; whether it is in front of or behind other objects; and whether it moves with the surrounding text.

- You can use the Rotate Left 90°, Rotate Right 90°, Flip Horizontal, and Flip Vertical commands to reverse and rotate your picture.

- You can use the More Contrast, Less Contrast, More Brightness, and Less Brightness commands to adjust the brightness and contrast of the selected picture.

- You can use the Crop command to cut the picture down to a smaller size. This will not shrink the picture, but will instead trim the edges of the picture as you indicate.

- You can use the Line Style command to display a menu of line widths and styles. By clicking More Lines on the menu, you can access the Format AutoShape dialog box, where you can change the width, length, color, and pattern of lines.

- You can use the Set Transparent Color command to select a particular color that will be transparent when the graphic is viewed on a Web page. This is ideal when you want to display an irregularly shaped object (one without straight borders).

- You can use the Color command to create a black and white, grayscale (black, white, and shades of gray), or washed out version of the original picture.

- You can use the Bevel command to apply a beveled edge to the selected picture, creating a self-framing effect.

- You can use the Resample command to refine the focus of a picture that has been enlarged or reduced.

■ You can use the Select command to change the insertion point to a pointer so that you can select a picture for editing. This button is selected by default when the Pictures toolbar is opened.

■ You can use the Rectangular Hotspot, Circular Hotspot, Polygonal Hotspot, and Highlight Hotspots commands to select and view hotspots, or image maps, on your picture. These are areas that can be hyperlinked to jump to other graphics, other Web pages, or other Web sites. They can even generate e-mail messages!

■ You can use the Restore command to undo all changes made to the picture since the Pictures toolbar was opened.

If the Pictures toolbar does not open automatically when you select a picture for editing, you can open it at any time by right-clicking the toolbar area and then clicking Pictures on the shortcut menu.

In this exercise, you will work with a photograph to practice using some of FrontPage's picture-editing and formatting capabilities. First you will size the picture and crop away the parts you don't want; then you will convert the picture to black-and-white and give it a beveled frame.

USE the *GardenView* picture in the practice file folder for this topic. This practice file is located in the *My Documents\Microsoft Press\FrontPage 2003 SBS\Pictures\CropPicture* folder and can also be accessed by clicking *Start/All Programs/Microsoft Press/FrontPage 2003 Step By Step*.

Create a new
normal page

1 On the Standard toolbar, click the **Create a new normal page** button to create a new page.

2 On the **Insert** menu, point to **Picture**, and then click **From File**.

The Picture dialog box appears.

3 Navigate to the **GardenView** image, select it, and click **Insert**.

The image is inserted into the Web page.

4 On the **View** menu, point to **Toolbars**, and then click **Pictures** to open the Pictures toolbar.

Tip By default, the Pictures toolbar opens as a floating toolbar. If you prefer, you can dock it at the top, the bottom, or either side of the window.

5 Drag the Pictures toolbar to the bottom of the window to dock it out of the way.

Crop

6 Click the picture to select it, and on the Pictures toolbar, click the **Crop** button.

A dashed box appears in the picture, defining the edges of the area to be cropped.

7 Drag the handles of the crop box until the box frames the collection of spheres.

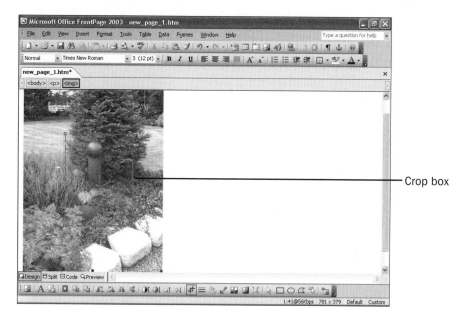

— Crop box

8 Press [Enter] or click the **Crop** button again to crop the picture to the specified shape and size.

9 Double-click the picture to display the **Picture Properties** dialog box.

10 On the **Appearance** tab, make sure the **Specify size** check box is selected.

11 To prevent distortion, ensure that the **Keep aspect ratio** check box is selected.

12 Set the **Width** to 165 pixels.

The height setting automatically changes to match the new width.

13 Click **OK** to close the dialog box and apply your changes.

FrontPage resizes the graphic to your specified dimensions.

Color

14 On the Pictures toolbar, click the **Color** button.

15 In the **Color** drop-down list, click **Grayscale**.

The picture is converted to shades of gray, but retains the original quality of detail.

Bevel

16 On the Pictures toolbar, click the **Bevel** button.

The colors at the edges of the picture change to make it appear that the center is raised.

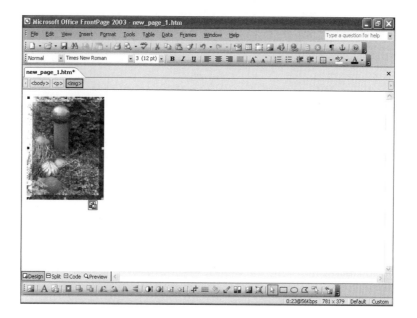

CLOSE the practice file without saving your work.

Creating and Displaying Thumbnails

Thumbnails are small versions of graphics that are hyperlinked to full-size versions. Thumbnails are often used on Web pages that contain many graphics that Web visitors might want to see (catalog items, for example). Because thumbnails are small, they download faster, so visitors are less likely to get impatient and move to another site.

In this exercise, you create a thumbnail of a picture and test it in FrontPage.

USE the *pictures* Web page in the practice file folder for this topic. This practice file is located in the *My Documents\Microsoft Press\FrontPage 2003 SBS\Pictures\Thumbnail* folder and can also be accessed by clicking *Start/All Programs/Microsoft Press/FrontPage 2003 Step By Step*.

1   On the **File** menu, click **Open**.

2   In the **Open File** dialog box, browse to the practice file folder for this topic, and double-click the **pictures** Web page.

3   Click the picture on the page to select it and activate the Pictures toolbar.

4   On the Pictures toolbar, click the **Auto Thumbnail** button.

Auto Thumbnail

The picture shrinks to thumbnail size and is surrounded by a blue border that indicates the presence of a hyperlink.

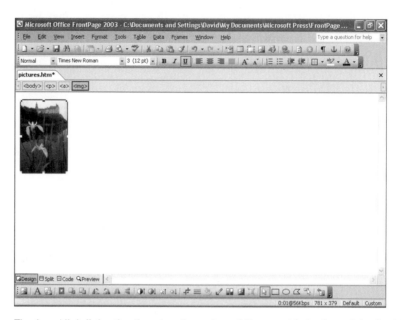

The hyperlink links the thumbnail version of the graphic to the original, which is no longer displayed on the page.

Split

Show Split View

5 At the bottom of the Page view editing window, click the **Show Split View** button to display the HTML code that links the thumbnail to the original graphic.

The code looks something like this:

```
<p><a href="PH01245J[1].jpg">

<img border="2" src="file:///C:/Documents%20and%20Settings/Joan/
Local%20Settings/Temporary%20Internet%20Files/FrontPageTempDir/
PH01245J[1]_small.jpg" xthumbnail-orig-image="PH01245J[1].jpg"></a></p>
```

Design

Show Design View

6 At the bottom of the Page view editing window, click the **Show Design View** button to return to the Design pane.

7 Drag the handles surrounding the selected thumbnail to make it bigger.

The thumbnail becomes blurry and grainy when you make it bigger because it is not as detailed as the original picture.

Undo

8 After you have seen the effect of enlarging the thumbnail, on the Standard toolbar, click the **Undo** button to return the thumbnail to its original size.

Preview in Browser

9 To experience the thumbnail link as your Web visitors will, on the Standard toolbar, click the **Preview in Browser** button. Save the page and embedded graphics when prompted to do so.

Your Web page opens in your browser, displaying the hyperlinked thumbnail.

10 Click the thumbnail to display the full-size graphic, and then click the browser's **Back** button to return to the thumbnail.

CLOSE the browser, and then close the practice file.
BE SURE TO close the Pictures toolbar if you don't want to display it.

Adding a Line, Shape, or Drawing to a Web Page

When it comes to dressing up your pages with graphic elements, you are not limited to clip art, pictures, and photographs. You can also create designs with lines, squares, circles, and other shapes, and if you are artistically inclined, you can even create entire drawings from within FrontPage. For professional-quality art, you should use a dedicated graphics program, but you can use FrontPage to turn out simple, Web-ready artwork.

FrontPage 2003 includes drawing tools that make it easy to incorporate specially formatted lines, a wide variety of preformed shapes, WordArt objects, text boxes, and shadows. These tools are similar to those in Microsoft Office Word and Microsoft Office PowerPoint. You can also copy drawings from other Microsoft Office System applications and paste them directly into your FrontPage-based Web site.

The commands you use to work with most graphics are represented as buttons on the Drawing toolbar and on the Drawing Canvas toolbar. Both of these toolbars can be opened at any time by right-clicking the toolbar area and clicking their names on the toolbar shortcut menu. The Drawing toolbar contains these commands:

- The commands on the Draw menu control the grouping, position, and movement of objects.

- You can use the Select Objects command to change the insertion point to a pointer so that you can select a drawing object for editing.

- You can use the AutoShapes command to display a menu from which you can choose any of 130 shapes, ranging from basic geometric shapes and arrows to fully formed weather indicators. Special flowchart, banner, and call-out symbols are also included. Clicking More AutoShapes at the bottom of the menu displays an additional 73 basic clip art items that you can build on. You can drag the AutoShapes menu or any of its submenus away from the Drawing toolbar so that they become floating toolbars.

- You can use the Line, Arrow, Rectangle, and Oval commands to draw these basic shapes in any size by clicking and dragging the shape onto the page.

- You can use the Text Box command to insert a text frame within a drawing.

- You can use the Insert WordArt, Insert Clip Art, and Insert Picture From File commands to insert existing graphic elements from your local computer or the Internet into your drawing.

- You can use the Fill Color, Line Color, and Font Color commands to control the colors of their respective elements.

- You can use the Line Style, Dash Style, and Arrow Style commands to format the thickness, color, solidity, and end caps of line elements.

- You can use the Shadow Style command to apply a variety of shadows to graphic elements. Clicking Shadow Settings opens a separate toolbar with which you can move an existing shadow or change its color.

- You can use the 3-D Style command to give graphic elements a three-dimensional look.

You can *group* several drawing elements together so that you can treat them as one. In this way, you can create a drawing out of several shapes, and then copy and paste the entire drawing, or reduce or enlarge it. If you want to treat the drawing as individual elements again, you can *ungroup* them at any time.

The "frame" in which drawings are created in FrontPage is called the *drawing canvas.* You can use the drawing canvas as an actual frame by formatting it with visible borders and background colors, but its main purpose is to contain all the elements of the drawing, so that the underlying HTML code for the drawing can be selected and treated as a unit. The formatting of the drawing canvas also determines the way in which text wraps around the drawing and the position of the drawing in relation to other objects on the page.

The Drawing Canvas toolbar opens when you insert a new drawing.

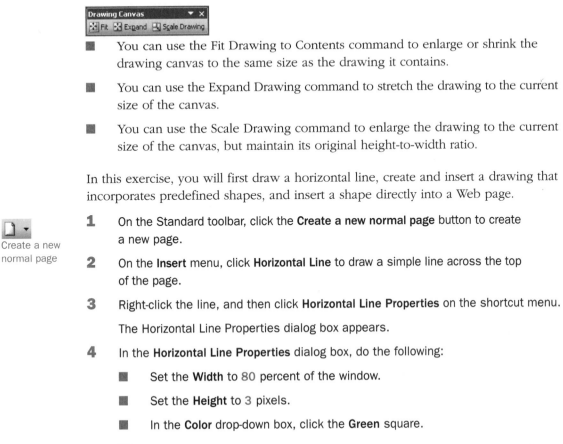

- You can use the Fit Drawing to Contents command to enlarge or shrink the drawing canvas to the same size as the drawing it contains.

- You can use the Expand Drawing command to stretch the drawing to the current size of the canvas.

- You can use the Scale Drawing command to enlarge the drawing to the current size of the canvas, but maintain its original height-to-width ratio.

In this exercise, you will first draw a horizontal line, create and insert a drawing that incorporates predefined shapes, and insert a shape directly into a Web page.

1 On the Standard toolbar, click the **Create a new normal page** button to create a new page.

Create a new normal page

2 On the **Insert** menu, click **Horizontal Line** to draw a simple line across the top of the page.

3 Right-click the line, and then click **Horizontal Line Properties** on the shortcut menu.

The Horizontal Line Properties dialog box appears.

4 In the **Horizontal Line Properties** dialog box, do the following:

- Set the **Width** to **80** percent of the window.

- Set the **Height** to 3 pixels.

- In the **Color** drop-down box, click the **Green** square.

Tip Move the mouse over the colors in the Color drop-down list to see each color's name displayed as a ScreenTip.

- Click **OK** to close the dialog box and apply your settings, and then click anywhere on the page to deselect the horizontal line.

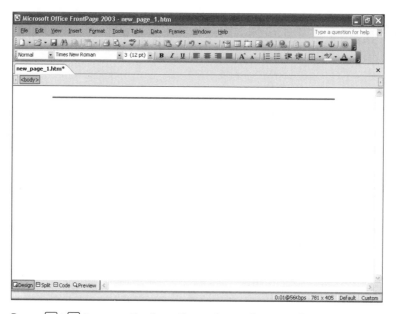

5 Press Ctrl+End to move the insertion point to the end of the page.

6 On the **Insert** menu, point to **Picture**, and then click **New Drawing**.

FrontPage displays an empty drawing canvas, the Drawing Canvas toolbar, and the Drawing toolbar.

The drawing canvas

The Drawing Canvas toolbar

Tip Depending on your previous actions, the Drawing toolbar might open as floating or docked. If it opens as a floating toolbar, you can dock it to keep it out of the way while you're working.

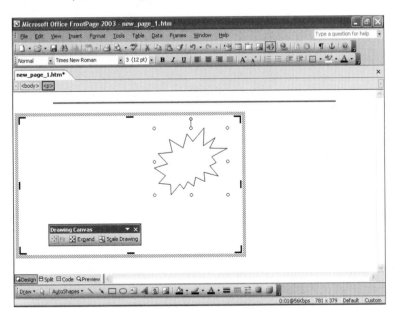

7 On the Drawing toolbar, click the **AutoShapes** button to display the menu of available shapes.

Tip When you see a drop-down list with a "handle" on it (horizontal lines in a shaded stripe), you can drag the menu onto the work area, and it will float there as a toolbar until you click its Close button. Alternatively, you can dock it at the left, right, or bottom edge of the window.

8 Point to **Stars and Banners**, and then click the **Explosion 2** symbol (the second symbol in the top row).

Tip Move the pointer over a symbol to see the symbol's name displayed as a ScreenTip.

9 Point to the upper-right corner of the drawing canvas, and drag downward to create a small "explosion" shape.

This shape will become the head of a flower.

10 Use the **Terminator** and **Decision** shapes available on the **AutoShapes Flowchart** menu to create a stem and leaves for your flower.

The Explosion 2 shape from the Stars and Banners menu

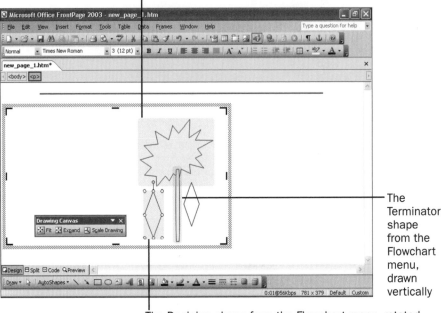

The Terminator shape from the Flowchart menu, drawn vertically

The Decision shape from the Flowchart menu, rotated

11 To rotate the "leaves" to appropriate angles, click each in turn, and drag its rotate handle (the green dot) in a clockwise or counterclockwise circle.

12 After the "leaves" are rotated, drag them into position against the "stem."

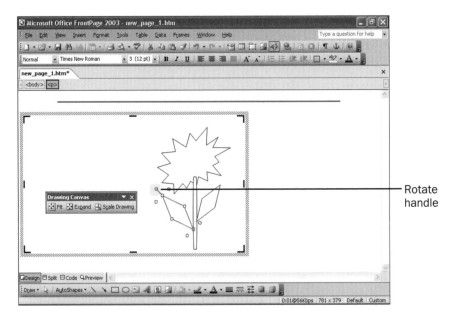

Rotate handle

13 Right-click the explosion, and on the shortcut menu, point to **Order**, and then click **Bring to Front**.

The head of the flower now appears in front of the stem. Depending on how closely you overlapped your stem and flower head, this repositioning might be difficult to see.

14 Experiment with the available shapes to create a garden scene.

The Sun shape from the Basic Shapes menu

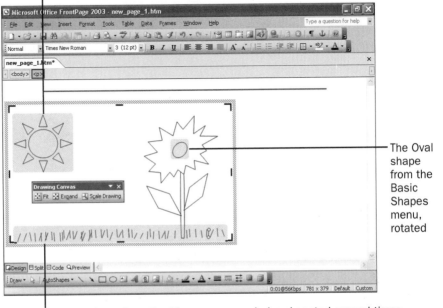

The Oval shape from the Basic Shapes menu, rotated

The Line shape from the Lines menu, copied and pasted several times

15 Click the head of the flower to select it, hold down the [shift] key, and click the stem and each of the leaves so that they are all selected.

16 Right-click the selected elements, and on the shortcut menu, point to **Grouping**, and then click **Group**.

The elements are grouped so that you can work with the flower as a whole.

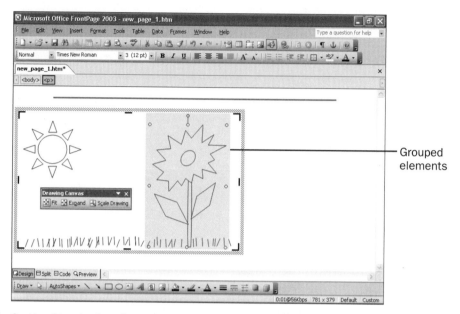

Grouped elements

17 On the Standard toolbar, click the **Copy** button to copy the picture to the Office Clipboard.

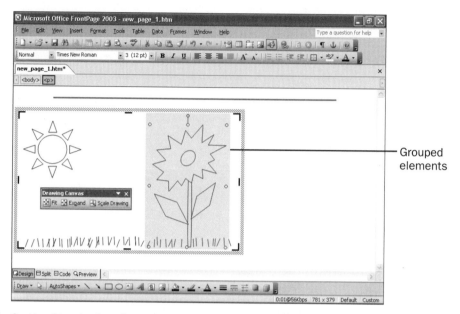
Copy

18 On the Standard toolbar, click the **Paste** button several times to paste multiple copies of the flower into your drawing to create an entire field.

Paste

Troubleshooting If you find that you are pasting copies of the flower outside the drawing canvas, delete those flowers, click inside the drawing canvas, and paste again.

19 Drag each flower's sizing handles to move the flowers and make a field of flowers of different sizes.

20 Right-click each flower, point to **Grouping** on the shortcut menu, and click **Ungroup** to separate the elements so that they can be individually colored.

21 Right-click the sun in your picture, and click **Format AutoShape** on the shortcut menu to display the **Format AutoShape** dialog box.

22 In the **Format AutoShape** dialog box, do the following:

- On the **Colors and Lines** tab, set the **Fill Color** to **Yellow**.

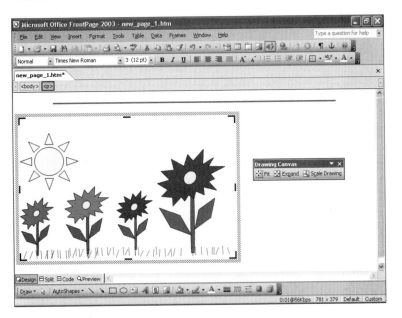

- Click **OK** to close the dialog box and apply your settings.

23 Color the flower elements to create a cheerful garden scene.

CLOSE the Drawing toolbar, and then close the practice file, saving your work if you want.

Creating a Photo Gallery

Companies like The Garden Company often want to include photo galleries in their Web sites—sometimes of products, sometimes of offices or other company buildings, or sometimes of key people whom Web visitors will deal with. To create a photo gallery by hand, you can simply add your pictures to a page, format them as thumbnails, and arrange them the way you want them.

FrontPage offers an even easier method. You can use the Photo Gallery Web component to quickly and easily create an attractive display of personal or business photos or images. You can choose from four styles, arranging your pictures either horizontally, vertically, in a tableau-style montage, or in a slideshow. With the Photo Gallery Web component, you can add captions and descriptions to your images and update the layout and content in seconds.

About Web Components

FrontPage 2003 offers many exciting, ready-made Web components that can be added to a Web page to give your site extra zing with very little effort.

FrontPage Web components range from decorative to informative to downright useful, and they are one of the most appealing aspects of the program. Any FrontPage-savvy designer can use Web components, such as *hit counters*, photo galleries, and link bars, to create a well-programmed, fully functional site without ever having to do any actual programming.

In this exercise, you will create a photo gallery in an existing Web site using the Photo Gallery Web component. The photos used in this exercise are from the Carnivorous Plant Database at *www.omnisterra.com/bot/cp_home.cgi* and are used by permission of the database owner.

USE the *plant1* through *plant12* photographs in the practice file folder for this topic. These practice files are located in the *My Documents\Microsoft Press\FrontPage 2003 SBS\Pictures\PhotoGallery* folder and can also be accessed by clicking *Start/All Programs/Microsoft Press/FrontPage 2003 Step By Step.*
OPEN the *GardenCo* Web site.

Create a new
normal page

1 On the Standard toolbar, click the **Create a new normal page** button to open a new page.

2 On the **Insert** menu, click **Web Component**.

The Insert Web Component dialog box appears.

3 In the **Insert Web Component** dialog box, click **Photo Gallery**.

The photo gallery options appear in the display window.

4 In the **Choose a Photo Gallery Option** box, click each of the four options, and read the description that appears in the pane.

5 Select the **Montage Layout** option (the second option in the top row), and click **Finish**.

The Photo Gallery Properties dialog box appears so you can add photos to the photo gallery.

Tip If you later change your mind about the layout of your photo gallery, simply right-click the Photo Gallery Web component in Page view, and click Photo Gallery Properties on the shortcut menu to display the Photo Gallery Properties dialog box. On the Layout tab, select a different layout option, and click OK to reformat your photo gallery.

6 Click **Add**, and then click **Pictures from Files**.

7 Browse to the *My Documents\Microsoft Press\FrontPage 2003 SBS\Pictures\PhotoGallery* folder, where you'll find 12 photos of carnivorous plants.

8 Click the **plant1** file, hold down the Shift key, and then click the **plant12** file.

All 12 photos are selected.

9 Click the **Open** button.

FrontPage imports the pictures into the photo gallery and displays them in the Photo Gallery Properties dialog box.

10 In the file list, click **plant1.jpg**.

11 In the **Caption** box, type Four Deadly Beauties.

12 Select the **Override and use custom font formatting** option.

13 Select the text in the **Caption** box.

Times New Roman
Font

14 In the **Font** drop-down list, click **Georgia**.

3 (12 pt)
Font Size

15 In the **Font Size** drop-down list, click **2 (10 pt)**.

Font Color

16 In the **Font Color** drop-down list, click the **Purple** square.

B
Bold

17 Click the **Bold** button.

18 Click **OK** to close the **Photo Gallery Properties** dialog box and generate the photo gallery.

Preview in
Browser

19 On the Standard toolbar, click the **Preview in Browser** button to preview the file in your default browser and window size. When prompted to do so, save the page file with the name Gallery.htm and the embedded graphics with their default names.

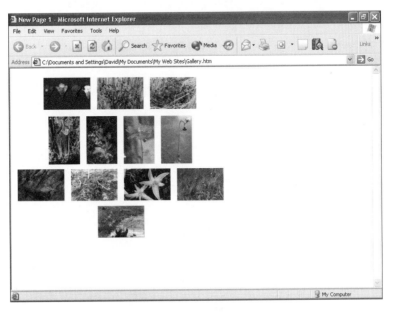

Pretty impressive for a few minutes' work!

20 Click the thumbnail graphics to open the full-size version, and then click the browser's **Back** button to return to the photo gallery.

21 When you're done admiring your work, close the browser to return to FrontPage.

CLOSE the practice file, saving your work if you want, and then close the *GardenCo* Web site.

Adding Fancy Text to a Web Page

WordArt objects are text objects with special formatting applied, for example to make them bend, slant, or appear in fancy colors. You can choose from 30 basic formatting options, and then make further changes from the WordArt toolbar. This toolbar opens automatically when you insert a WordArt object.

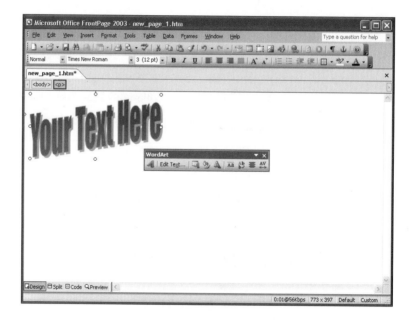

- You can use the Insert WordArt command to display the WordArt Gallery dialog box so that you can create a new WordArt object.

- You can use the Edit Text command to display the Edit WordArt Text dialog box, in which you can change the text, font, font size, and font formatting of your WordArt object.

- You can use the WordArt Gallery command to choose from 30 different WordArt styles.

- You can use the Format WordArt command to change the colors and lines, size, layout, and alternate Web text of your WordArt object.

- You can use the WordArt Shape command to build your WordArt around any of 40 basic shapes, curves, and angles.

- You can use the WordArt Same Letter Heights command to make uppercase and lowercase letters the same height.

- You can use the WordArt Vertical Text command to change text from the default horizontal alignment to vertical alignment.

- You can use the WordArt Alignment command to specify that the WordArt text is aligned to the left, center, or right within the available space, or that it be word-justified or stretched to fill the space.

- You can use the WordArt Character Spacing command to control the *kerning* between letters.

If you have already used WordArt to create fancy headings in Word documents, you know how easy it is to create effects that would be very hard, if not impossible, to replicate with regular formatting. For those times when ordinary formatting simply won't do the trick, you can use WordArt in FrontPage to create headings for your Web pages.

In this exercise, you will create an eye-catching WordArt page title.

Create a new
normal page

1 On the Standard toolbar, click the **Create a new normal page** button to create a new page.

A new page opens in the Page view editing window with the insertion point positioned at the top of the page.

2 On the **Insert** menu, point to **Picture**, and then click **WordArt**.

3 In the **Word Art Gallery** dialog box, click your favorite style.

This style is
used in this
exercise.

4 After you select a style, click **OK**.

The Edit WordArt Text dialog box appears.

5 In the **Text** box, type Carnivorous Plants.

6 In the **Font** drop-down list, click **Verdana**.

7 In the **Size** drop-down list, click **24**.

B

Bold

8 Click the **Bold** button.

9 Click **OK** to close the dialog box and apply your settings.

FrontPage creates the page title according to your specifications, inserts it in the Web page at the insertion point, and displays the WordArt toolbar.

✕

Close (Toolbar)

10 Click the WordArt toolbar's **Close** button to close the toolbar.

11 Click to the right of the WordArt object to deselect it.

12 On the **Format** menu, click **Paragraph**.

The Paragraph dialog box appears.

13 In the **Alignment** drop-down list, click **Center**. Then click **OK** to close the dialog box and apply your changes.

The WordArt title is centered on the page.

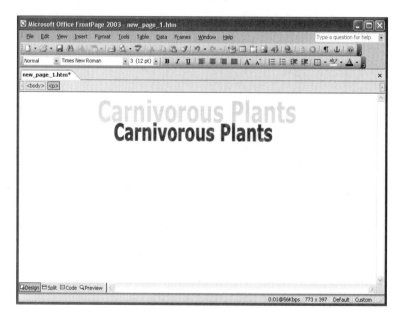

CLOSE the page file without saving your changes. If you are not continuing on to the next chapter, quit FrontPage.

Key Points

- You can add pictures of all kinds to your Web page. If you don't have a picture you want to use, you can select from the variety of clip art that comes with The Microsoft Office System 2003.

- If you have an active Internet connection, you can select from an extensive collection of clip art in the Office Online clip art gallery.

- You can create drawings from a variety of basic shapes directly in FrontPage, or paste in drawings from another Microsoft Office System application.

- You can easily create a functioning photo gallery by using the Photo Gallery Web component.

- You can add pizzazz to your Web page with fancy WordArt text.

Create an empty Web site, page 118

Add a new Web page to a Web site, page 121

Change a Web page title, page 123

Set Page Title

Page title:

Welcome to The Garden Company

The title of the page is displayed in the title bar of the browser.

OK   Cancel

Welcome to The Garden Company!

The Garden Company

Format a Web page background, page 126

Format a Web page with borders and shading, page 130

Use page banners and shared borders, page 133

Class Offerings

The Garden Company offers a variety of classes on plant selection for your geographical area, general and seasonal plant care, and garden-related craft activities.

Autumn Planning for Spring Splendor

It's never too early to get s garden!

This class is taught by Davi native and local gardening interactive discussion forur to bring examples of favor

Format an entire Web site, page 138

Theme

Current theme: Nature

Select a theme

Iris

Customize Theme

Color Schemes | Color Wheel | Custom

Preview of: Nature

Banner

Horizontal Navigation

Bullet List

🌸 Bullet 1
🍃 Bullet 2
Bullet 3

Colors in this scheme:

Brightness:

Theme color set: ○ Normal colors   ● Vivid colors   OK   Cancel

Create a custom FrontPage theme, page 142

Chapter 5 at a Glance

5 Creating a Web Site from Scratch

In this chapter you will learn to:

✔ Create an empty Web site.

✔ Add a new Web page to a Web site.

✔ Change a Web page title.

✔ Format a Web page background.

✔ Format a Web page with borders and shading.

✔ Use page banners and shared borders.

✔ Format an entire Web site.

✔ Create a custom FrontPage theme.

Microsoft Office FrontPage 2003 includes many handy wizards and templates that you can use to create complex Web sites with very little effort. But what if none of these options fits your needs? It's then that you need to know how to create a Web site from scratch.

Building a custom Web site from the ground up also gives you a better understanding of how Web sites created with templates and wizards work. For example, although you don't need to know the intricacies of a FrontPage-based Web site's navigational structure, a basic understanding of how pages are linked will help you determine how to go about making changes without breaking anything. The simplest way to learn how a template-based Web site is constructed is to build one piece by piece, and that's what this chapter is all about.

See Also Do you need only a quick refresher on the topics in this chapter? See the Quick Reference entries on pages xxvii–xxix.

Important Before you can use the practice files in this chapter, you need to install them from the book's companion CD to their default location. See "Using the Book's CD-ROM" on page xiii for more information.

Creating an Empty Web Site

Suppose you have tried creating a Web site by using a wizard but you aren't satisfied with the results. Perhaps the wizard created pages you don't need and didn't create pages you do need. You could modify the existing Web site, but you are not sure how to go about it and you are nervous about messing things up. You want to try your hand at creating a Web site from scratch so that you can become more familiar with what's involved.

With very little effort, you can create the framework upon which to build a new FrontPage-based Web site. Using the empty Web site as a foundation, you can then add pages and link them in any way you want. But the important thing is to get the basic structure of a FrontPage-based Web site in place first.

In this exercise, you will use the Empty Web template to create the structure required for a FrontPage-based Web site.

BE SURE TO start FrontPage before beginning this exercise.

1 If the **New** task pane is not displayed, on the **File** menu, click **New.**

2 In the **New Web site** area of the **New** task pane, click **More Web site templates.**

The Web Site Templates dialog box appears.

3 Click (don't double-click) the **Empty Web Site** icon.

Tip   You need to specify the location and name of the new Web site. FrontPage provides a special folder in which you can store your Web sites, called My Web Sites. This folder is located in your My Documents folder.

4   In the **Options** area, click the **Browse** button to browse to the Web site location.

The New Web Site Location dialog box opens.

Tip   When specifying a Web site location by typing rather than browsing, precede the location with a drive letter for disk-based sites or with *http://* for server-based sites.

5   On the Places bar, click **My Documents**, and then in the file list, double-click **My Web Sites**.

6   On the dialog box toolbar, click the **Create New Folder** button.

Create
New Folder

7   In the **New Folder** dialog box, type **EmptyWeb** in the **Name** text box, and then click **OK**.

8   In the **New Web Site Location** dialog box, click the **Open** button.

9   In the **Web Site Templates** dialog box, click **OK**.

In about three seconds, FrontPage displays the structure of your newly created empty Web site.

Tip FrontPage opens your new Web site in the view that was last active. If your screen doesn't look like our graphic, you might need to open the Folder List or change the view to make your screen look the same as ours.

In FrontPage, your new Web site appears to consist of two empty folders called *_private* and *images*.

Tip The _private and images folders might initially appear with plus signs (signifying that they contain subfolders) next to their names. The plus signs disappear the first time you click them.

10 Open Windows Explorer, and browse to the new *EmptyWeb* Web site in your My Web Sites folder.

If your folder options are set to view hidden files and folders in Windows Explorer, you can see that your site consists of four folders and several files, many of which are hidden. If the hidden files and folders are visible, they are indicated by faded icons.

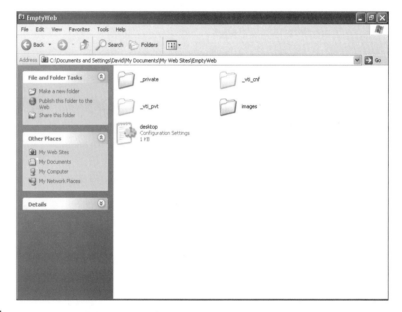

Close

11 In the upper-right corner of the window, click the **Close** button to close Windows Explorer.

12 On the **File** menu, click **Close Site** to close the Web site.

Adding a New Web Page to a Web Site

Adding pages to a Web site is very easy. The first (and only) page that is required for any Web site is the home page. This page appears when a visitor types in the site's Universal Resource Locator (*URL*). The home page file is named either *default.htm* for server-based Web sites or *index.htm* for disk-based Web sites. When you create a FrontPage-based Web site, FrontPage suggests an appropriate file name for your home page depending on the type of site you are creating. If you initially create a disk-based site with a home page file named *index.htm* and then publish the site to a server, FrontPage will rename the home page file during the publishing process.

Tip   A new page is not actually part of a Web site until you save it as part of the site.

In this exercise, you will create a blank Web page and save it as the home page of the currently empty *GardenCo* Web site.

USE the *GardenCo* Web site in the practice file folder for this topic. This practice file is located in the *My Documents\Microsoft Press\FrontPage 2003 SBS\FromScratch\NewPage* folder and can also be accessed by clicking *Start/All Programs/Microsoft Press/FrontPage 2003 Step By Step*.
BE SURE TO start FrontPage before beginning this exercise.

1   On the **File** menu, click **Open Site**.

2   In the **Open Site** dialog box, browse to the practice file folder for this topic.

3   Double-click **GardenCo**, and then click the **Open** button.

The *GardenCo* Web site opens. This version of the Web site consists of only the basic site structure.

Create a new
normal page

4   On the Standard toolbar, click the **Create a new normal page** button.

A new, blank page called *new_page_1.htm* opens with the insertion point positioned at the top of the page. The page is not displayed in the Folder List because it hasn't yet been saved as part of your Web site.

5   Type Welcome to The Garden Company!

As you begin typing, an asterisk appears next to the file name on the page tab.

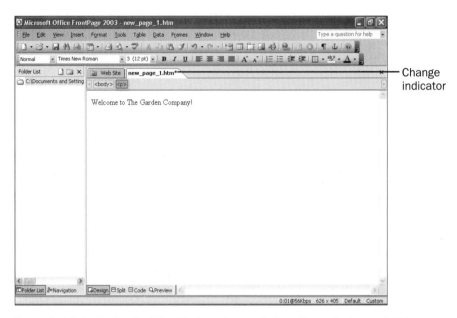

Change indicator

The asterisk indicates that the file has changed since it was last saved (this particular file has never been saved).

6 On the **File** menu, click **Save As** to open the **Save As** dialog box.

In the Save in drop-down list, the *GardenCo* Web site is already selected. Because this Web site's folder contains no home page, FrontPage suggests *index* as the Web page's file name. The suggested page title, *Welcome to The Garden Company*, is appropriate for a home page, so you can leave it as is.

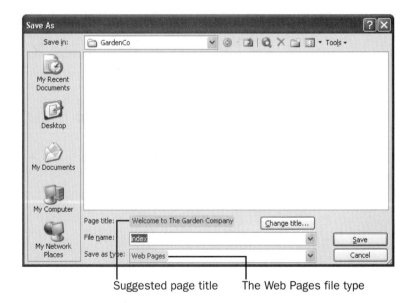

Suggested page title   The Web Pages file type

7   Accept the suggested settings by clicking the **Save** button.

FrontPage saves the file as part of the *GardenCo* Web site and displays it in the Folder List. The file name is preceded by the Home page icon.

Troubleshooting   If you don't see the index.htm file in the Folder List, double-click the Folder icon.

The Home page icon indicates the page that
is displayed when you first open the Web site.

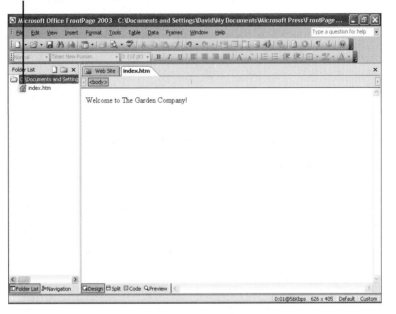

✕
Close

8   Click the new home page's **Close** button to close the file.

CLOSE the *GardenCo* Web site (don't close FrontPage).

Changing a Web Page Title

Each page in a Web site represents one or more individual files. While you are building a Web site, you will become very familiar with its structure and have little difficulty identifying pages from their file names. However, visitors to your Web site will expect your pages to have more intuitive names, and that's where page titles come into play.

The *page title* is the text that visitors see on the title bar when a Web page is open in an Internet browser. If you use *page banners* on your site, the page title is also the title that visitors see at the top of the page. The page title does not have to be the same as the file name; it doesn't even have to be similar, although many Web developers use subject-related names that will help them to remember which file is which.

When you save a new page, FrontPage suggests a page title that reflects the first line of text in the page. If this suggestion is not appropriate, changing the page title while you are saving the page for the first time is a simple matter of replacing the suggested title with a different one. If you want to change an existing page title after the page has been saved, you can do it in the Save As dialog box; in the Folder List; or in Page, Navigation, or Hyperlinks view.

In this exercise, you will experiment with different methods of changing a Web page title.

USE the *GardenCo* Web site in the practice file folder for this topic. This practice file is located in the *My Documents\Microsoft Press\FrontPage 2003 SBS\FromScratch\PageTitle* folder and can also be accessed by clicking *Start/All Programs/Microsoft Press/FrontPage 2003 Step By Step.*
OPEN the *GardenCo* Web site.

1   In the **Folder List**, double-click **index.htm** to open it in the Page view editing window.

2   On the **File** menu, click **Save As**.

The Save As dialog box appears.

The current page title

3   In the **Save As** dialog box, click the **Change title** button.

The Set Page Title dialog box appears, displaying the current page title in an editable format.

4 Replace the page title with Glorious Gardens, and click **OK** to close the **Set Page Title** dialog box.

5 Click **Save** to close the **Save As** dialog box and save your change.

Because a file by this name already exists, you are prompted to overwrite the existing file.

6 Click **Yes** to continue.

7 On the **View** menu, click **Folders** to switch to Folders view.

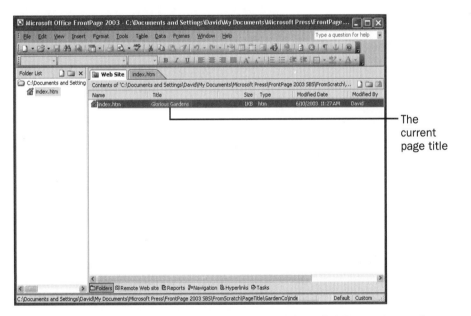

The current page title

8 In the **Folder List**, right-click the **index.htm** file, and then click **Properties** on the shortcut menu.

The General tab of the index.htm Properties dialog box appears with the current page title in the Title box.

---

index.htm Properties [X]

General | Summary | Workgroup

Filename: index.htm

Title: [Glorious Gardens] ——————————— The current page title

Type: HTML Document

Location: C:\Documents and Settings\David\My Documents\Mi

Size: 380 bytes

[OK]   [Cancel]   [Apply]

---

9   Change the title to Welcome to The Garden Company, and click **OK** to save
the change.

The change is reflected in the Title column of the list.

10   Click the **index.htm** page tab to switch back to Page view.

CLOSE the open file and the *GardenCo* Web site.

Formatting a Web Page Background

Any newly created blank Web page looks a little...blank. And although black text
on a white background is certainly legible, and legibility is essential if you want to
convey information using text, it is neither very attractive nor very exciting.

The simplest way of adding pizzazz to a Web page is to apply a background color.
You can also associate the look of a page with the subject of the Web site by using a
graphic as a background image. For example, you might choose to use your company
logo as the background graphic of your business Web site.

Although a background image can give a Web page a more interesting look, remember
that depending on your Web visitor's connection speed and browser, the image might
not be displayed as beautifully or as quickly as you would like. When using a background image, it is a good idea to also set the background to a similar color, preferably
one from the standard Web palette. That way, when your visitors access your site, they
won't have to wait while a series of changes or errors is displayed, and they will still
see the planned color scheme while the graphic is loading on their computer.

You will usually want to display text over a background image. To make the text
legible, you must set the font of all the text elements on the page to a color that is
easily seen against the background. It isn't a good idea to set the font color to white

unless you set a contrasting background color. Otherwise, if the background image doesn't load and the text font is white, your Web visitor will not be able to see the text. You can get around this problem by setting the background to one of the colors used in the background image. Then if the background image doesn't load, the text will be visible against the background color.

It's important to select a background color that is light enough so that the text of the page will be legible. You can experiment with various combinations, but dark text on a light background will almost always work best.

In this exercise you will experiment with background colors and images. You will also learn different methods of applying and removing page formatting.

USE the *GardenCo* Web site and the *tgc_bkgrnd* and *bgimage* graphics in the practice file folder for this topic. These practice files are located in the *My Documents\Microsoft Press\FrontPage 2003 SBS\FromScratch \Backgrounds* folder and can also be accessed by clicking *Start/All Programs/Microsoft Press/FrontPage 2003 Step By Step.*
OPEN the *GardenCo* Web site.

1   In the **Folder List,** double-click the **index.htm** file to open it in the Page view editing window.

2   On the **Format** menu, click **Background**.

The Page Properties dialog box appears with the Formatting tab displayed.

3   In the **Colors** area, click the down arrow to the right of the **Background** box.

The drop-down list displays 16 colors and a link to additional colors.

4 Click **More Colors**.

The More Colors dialog box appears.

5 In the color palette, select a pale shade of green that conveys the idea of gardening, yet is still light enough for text to show up well.

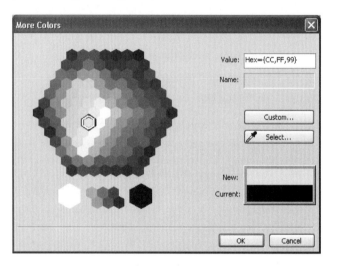

When you click a color, FrontPage enters the hexadecimal code of the color in the Value box and displays a swatch of the color in the lower-right corner of the dialog box.

6 Click **OK** to close the **More Colors** dialog box, and then click **OK** to close the **Page Properties** dialog box and apply the selected background color to the Web page.

7 On the **Format** menu, click **Background** again.

8 On the **Formatting** tab of the **Page Properties** dialog box, select the **Background picture** check box.

9 Click the **Browse** button, browse to the practice file folder for this exercise, click **bgimage**, and click **Open**.

The relative file location is saved in the text box.

10 Select the **Make it a watermark** check box to keep the background image stationary when the page scrolls, and then click **OK**.

In addition to the background color, your page now features a large, tiled background graphic. The results might seem overwhelming.

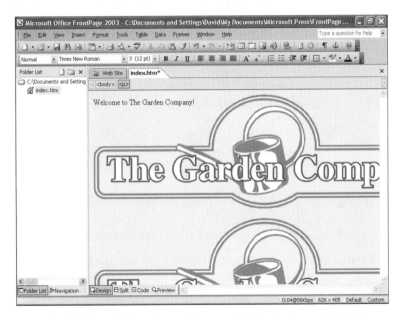

This could be considered a good example of a bad graphic to choose as a background image.

Troubleshooting If you make changes to a graphic while it is open in FrontPage, you might have to close and reopen FrontPage to view the effects of your changes in the Normal pane. To view the changes without restarting FrontPage, switch to the Preview pane.

11 For a more suitable background image, repeat steps 7 through 10 using the *tgc_bkgrnd* graphic from the practice file folder for this exercise.

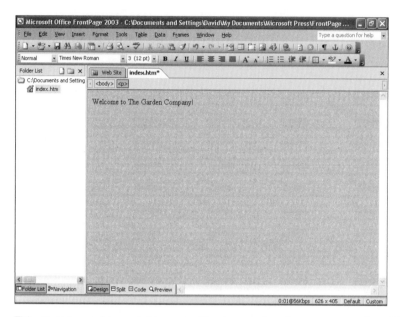

This graphic provides a fairly neutral background and some texture for added interest.

Tip To remove background formatting from a Web page, open the Page Properties dialog box, in the Background area of the Formatting tab, clear the check boxes, and set the background color to Automatic.

CLOSE the open file and the *GardenCo* Web site without saving your changes.

Formatting a Web Page with Borders and Shading

Another method of formatting a Web page background is to use *borders* and *shading*. FrontPage gives you a wide variety of page border options—you can control the color, width, and pattern of your border, how much space is left around it, and which borders are affected. The shading options are nearly as varied—you can choose from a practically limitless number of background and foreground colors.

In this exercise you will experiment with different methods of making Web pages distinctive by adding borders and shading.

USE the *GardenCo* Web site and the *bgimage_small* file in the practice file folder for this topic. This practice file is located in the *My Documents\Microsoft Press\FrontPage 2003 SBS\FromScratch\Borders* folder and can also be accessed by clicking *Start/All Programs/Microsoft Press/FrontPage 2003 Step By Step*. OPEN the *GardenCo* Web site.

1 In the **Folder List**, double-click the **index.htm** file to open it in the Page view editing window.

2 Click the line below the heading, and press [Enter] several times to insert enough new blank paragraphs under the heading to fill the page.

3 Press [Ctrl]+[A] to select the entire page.

4 On the **Format** menu, click **Borders and Shading**.

The Borders and Shading dialog box appears, showing a variety of options similar to those available in Microsoft Office Word.

5 In the **Borders and Shading** dialog box, click the **Borders** tab.

6 In the **Setting** area, click the illustration to the left of **Custom** to create a custom border.

7 In the **Style** list, click **outset**.

8 In the **Color** drop-down list, click the **Maroon** square (the fourth square from the left on the top row of the **Standard Colors** area).

Tip Point to the colors in the color selection box to see the name of each color displayed as a ScreenTip.

9 Set the **Width** to **2**, and leave the **Padding** settings at **0**.

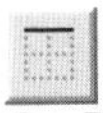

10 In the **Preview** area, click the **Top Border** button to apply the settings to this area.

The Preview box displays your selections.

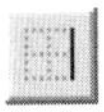

Top Border

11 In the **Preview** area, click the **Right Border** button.

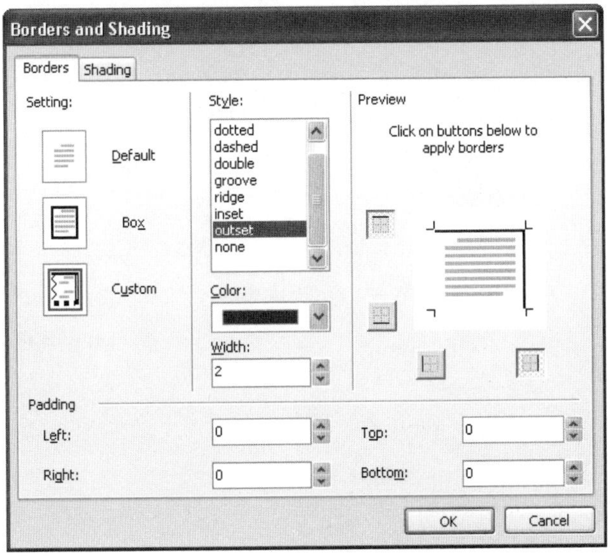

Right Border

12 In the **Borders and Shading** dialog box, click the **Shading** tab.

13 In the **Background color** drop-down list, click **More Colors**, choose a pale green, and then click **OK**.

14 In the **Foreground color** drop-down list, click the maroon square.

15 Click the **Browse** button to the right of the **Background picture** box. In the **Select Background Picture** dialog box, browse to the *My Documents\Microsoft Press \FrontPage 2003 SBS\FromScratch\Borders* folder, click **bgimage_small**, and then click **Open**.

16 In the **Vertical position** drop-down list, click **center**.

17 In the **Horizontal position** drop-down list, click **center**.

18 In the **Repeat** drop-down list, click **no-repeat**.

19 In the **Attachment** drop-down list, click **scroll**.

Borders and Shading

Borders | Shading

Fill

Background color:

Foreground color:

Preview

Patterns

Background picture: ../bgimage_small.gif   Browse...

Vertical position: center   Repeat: no-repeat

Horizontal position: center   Attachment: scroll

OK   Cancel

20 Click **OK** to close the **Borders and Shading** dialog box and apply your settings.

21 Press the [Home] key to release the selection so you can see the results of your work.

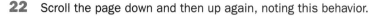

FrontPage centers the logo on the page and will move it with the surrounding text as the page is scrolled.

22 Scroll the page down and then up again, noting this behavior.

CLOSE the open file and the *GardenCo* Web site without saving your changes.

Using Page Banners and Shared Borders

Page banners are a quick way to display titles on Web pages. If a *theme* is applied to the current page, the page banner uses the font and graphics of the theme; otherwise the page banner displays only text, which you can format manually. The page banner displays the page title of each page.

Your pages can also have *shared borders*, which are areas at the top, bottom, left, or right of all or some of the pages in a Web site. The advantage of using shared borders is that you can update the information on every page by updating it in only one place. For example, if The Garden Company's corporate logo appears at the top of each page in the *GardenCo* Web site and a copyright notice appears at the bottom, you can update the logo and copyright notice on one page and have the change instantly reflected on all the other pages. Shared borders ensure that information is presented consistently and correctly throughout the site.

Troubleshooting   In FrontPage 2003, shared borders are disabled by default and must be enabled before you can use them.

Using a page banner inside a shared border is a way to quickly add or update titles on multiple pages in a Web site. Many developers insert automatically updating date components in bottom shared page borders to indicate the date that the information on the page was last updated. This helps visitors to know that your site is fresh and that they can count on the information given there.

In this exercise, you will enable shared borders and create top and bottom shared borders on the pages of the *GardenCo* Web site. You will then insert a page banner in the top shared border, and finish by inserting a date stamp in the bottom shared border.

USE the *GardenCo* Web site in the practice file folder for this topic. This practice file is located in the
My Documents\Microsoft Press\FrontPage 2003 SBS\FromScratch\Banners folder and can also be accessed
by clicking *Start/All Programs/Microsoft Press/FrontPage 2003 Step By Step*.
OPEN the *GardenCo* Web site.

1 In the **Folder List**, double-click the **index.htm** file and then the **classes.htm** file to open them in the Page view editing window.

2 On the **Tools** menu, click **Page Options**.

3 In the **Page Options** dialog box, click the **Authoring** tab.

4 In the **FrontPage and SharePoint technologies** area of the **Authoring** tab, select the **Shared Borders** check box, and then click **OK**.

5 On the **Format** menu, click **Shared Borders**.

6 In the **Shared Borders** dialog box, select the **All pages** option, and select the **Top** and **Bottom** check boxes.

Your selections are reflected in the preview window.

7   Click the **Border Properties** button to open the **Border Properties** dialog box.

8   In the **Border** drop-down list, click **Top**.

9   Select the **Color** check box, and then in the **Color** drop-down list, click **More Colors**.

10   In the **More Colors** dialog box, click the pale green color to the left of the center, and then click **OK**.

11   Repeat steps 8 through 10 to set the color of the bottom shared border to the same pale green, and then click **OK** to close the **Border Properties** dialog box.

12   Click **OK** to close the **Shared Borders** dialog box and apply the new border settings.

> **Troubleshooting**   If your file contains previously formatted content, a message box warns you that changing the settings for the top or left shared borders will overwrite your content. Click Yes to continue.

The shared borders appear above and below the rest of the content on each page of the Web site, with a comment identifying each border.

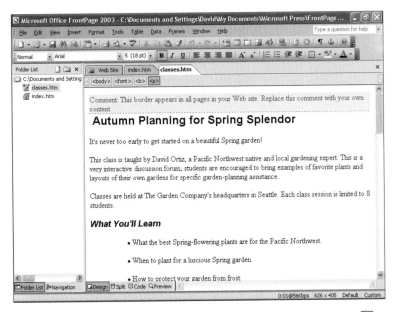

13   Click the comment in the top border to select it, and press the ⌦ key to delete the comment and leave the empty top border.

14   On the **Insert** menu, click **Page Banner**.

The Page Banner Properties dialog box appears, displaying the current page title.

Page Banner Properties

Properties
- ⊙ Picture
- ○ Text

Page banner text

Class Offerings

OK　Cancel

15　With the **Picture** option selected, click **OK**.

The page banner is inserted. Because there is no graphic theme applied to the Web site, the page banner is currently unformatted and looks just like normal text.

16　Click the new page banner to select it.

Normal ▾

Style

17　On the Formatting toolbar, in the **Style** drop-down list, click **Heading 1**.

Center

18　On the Formatting toolbar, click the **Center** button.

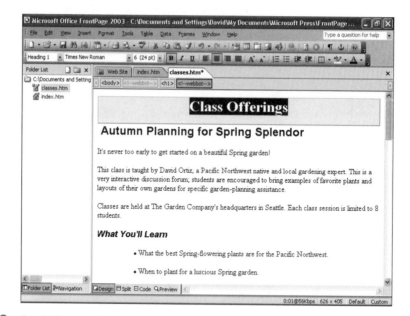

19　Scroll down to the bottom shared border.

20　Select and delete the comment text.

21　On the **Insert** menu, click **Horizontal Line** to insert a line that separates the page content from the bottom border.

22 Under the line, type **Last Updated:** and a space.

23 On the **Insert** menu, click **Date and Time**.

The Date and Time dialog box appears.

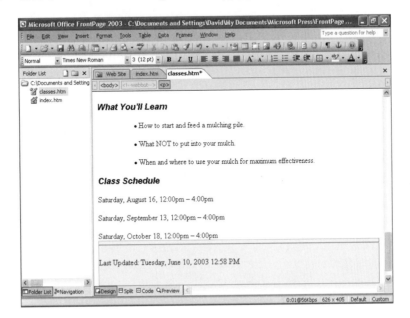

24 In the **Display** area of the **Date and Time** dialog box, leave the **Date this page was last edited** option selected.

25 In the **Date format** drop-down list, select the format that expresses the date as *Weekday, Month Day, Year*—for example, *Thursday, January 01, 2004*.

26 In the **Time format** drop-down list, select the format that expresses the time as *HH:MM AM/PM*—for example, *12:00 PM*.

27 Click **OK** to close the dialog box and apply your settings.

28 Click the page tab to switch to the index.htm file.

29 Click the **Show Preview View** button at the bottom of the Page view editing window to view the page in the Preview pane.

The shared borders have been added to this page, with the date in the bottom border.

CLOSE the open files and the *GardenCo* Web site without saving your changes.

Formatting an Entire Web Site

New In Office 2003

Improved themes

FrontPage 2003 uses cascading style sheets to apply themes, so files with applied themes are smaller than those created in previous versions of FrontPage, which used HTML themes by default. HTML themes involve a lot more code in each file. If you're working with files created in a previous version of FrontPage that had HTML themes applied, those themes will still work.

Formatting pages one at a time is fine if you have a very small Web site, but it would obviously be tedious and inefficient to have to apply page formatting to every page of a Web site of 20, 50, or 100 pages. With FrontPage, you can format an entire site in one fell swoop—backgrounds, headings, fonts, colors, and all—by applying a *theme* to it.

Themes are predefined packages of colors, graphics, fonts, and styles that you can apply to a single page or an entire site. FrontPage comes with 42 standard themes, and additional themes can be installed from the Microsoft Office System 2003 CD-ROM. Use these themes as they are, modify them, or create your own.

In addition to the styles and fonts associate with each theme, you have the option of using vivid colors, active graphics, and a background picture.

- The Vivid colors option displays the color scheme in brighter colors.

- The Active graphics option displays a livelier set of banners, buttons, bullets, and other graphic elements, some with animation effects.

- The Background picture option displays the background image shown as part of the theme. If you don't use the background picture, the background is set to a solid color that corresponds to the theme. Many Web designers prefer to use a solid background to avoid possible download delays with background graphics.

In this exercise, you will work with a version of The Garden Company's corporate Web site consisting of a home page and four second-level pages: Products, Class Offerings, Press Releases, and Contact Us. The site has top and bottom shared borders and only minimal formatting. The top shared border contains a page banner. The bottom shared border contains a horizontal line and text.

You begin by opening and exploring the Web site to see what you are working with. You then apply a garden-appropriate graphic theme, first to one page of the site and then to the entire site. You also learn how to remove a theme from a Web site.

USE the *GardenCo* Web site in the practice file folder for this topic. This practice file is located in the *My Documents\Microsoft Press\FrontPage 2003 SBS\FromScratch\Themes* folder and can also be accessed by clicking *Start/All Programs/Microsoft Press/FrontPage 2003 Step By Step*.
OPEN the *GardenCo* Web site.

1   In the **Folder List**, click **classes.htm**, press [Shift], and click **products.htm** to select the five pages of the site. Press [Enter] to open them all in the Page view editing window.

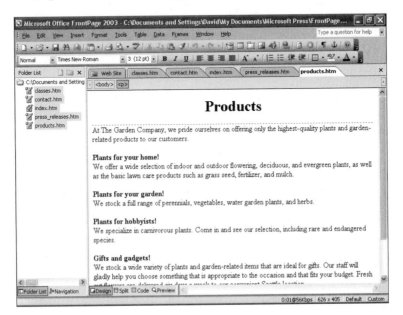

2   At the top of the Page view editing window, click the **Web Site** tab.

3   Familiarize yourself with the Web site as a whole by looking at the Folders, Reports, and Navigation views.

> **Tip**   Use the buttons at the bottom of the Web Site page to change views.

4   Familiarize yourself with the individual Web pages by looking at them in Page view and Hyperlinks view.

You will notice that there are currently no navigational links between the pages.

5   When you are done looking at the site as a whole, click the **classes.htm** page tab to switch to that file.

6   On the **Format** menu, click **Theme**.

The Theme task pane appears.

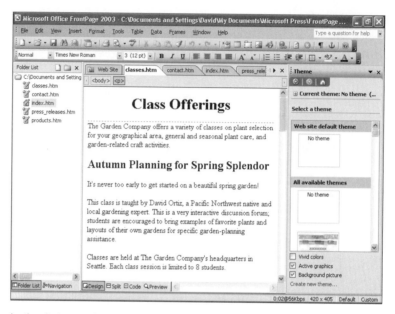

7 In the **Select a theme** box, scroll through the list of available themes until you can see the *Nature* theme.

A preview of each theme is shown in the box.

Tip To install additional themes, scroll to the bottom of the "Select a theme" box and click "Install additional themes." You will need to have your Microsoft Office System 2003 CD-ROM handy or be connected to your installation location to install the additional themes.

8 At the bottom of the task pane, the **Active graphics** and **Background picture** check boxes are selected by default. Select the **Vivid colors** check box.

Note that the colors in the theme previews change. If you missed this, clear the check box and then select it again while watching the previews to see the changes.

9 Position the mouse pointer over the **Nature** theme.

A down arrow appears to the right of the theme preview.

10 Click the down arrow to display the list of options.

11 In the drop-down list, click **Apply to selected page(s)**.

The Nature theme is applied to the Class Offerings page, immediately changing the presentation of the page.

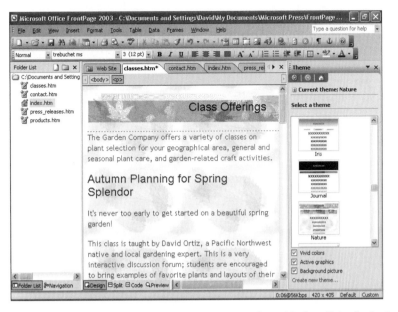

The page has gone from very ordinary to very nice with the click of a button. Obvious changes include the fonts, font colors, and background graphics. Graphic elements include the page banner background, content area background, bullets, and lines.

Q Preview

Show
Preview View

12 To see the effect of the active graphics, click the **Show Preview View** button at the bottom of the Page view editing window.

Notice that the bullets cycle through a series of colors.

13 Click the **contact.htm** page tab to switch to that file.

The theme has not been applied to this page, and what a difference it makes!

14 Click the **classes.htm** page tab to return to the Class Offerings page.

15 In the **Theme** task pane, scroll to the top of the **Select a theme** box, and click **No theme**.

The Nature theme is removed from the page.

Important In this exercise, you are removing the theme only to practice doing so. It is not necessary to remove a theme before applying another. Note that removing a theme from a Web page or Web site does not restore any special formatting that was removed when the theme was applied.

16 Now that you've checked the theme on a single page, you will apply it to the entire site. In the **Select a theme** box, click the down arrow that appears to the right of the **Nature** theme.

17 On the shortcut menu, click **Apply as default theme**.

Troubleshooting   If a message box warns you that individual page formatting will be permanently replaced, click Yes to continue.

The Nature theme is applied to the entire site.

18 Use the page tabs to switch between the open pages and examine the results of the application of the theme.

Notice how page elements such as buttons and bullets are formatted.

19 Click the **Close** button in the upper-right corner of the **Theme** task pane.

☒
Close

CLOSE the open files and the *GardenCo* Web site without saving your changes.

Creating a Custom FrontPage Theme

You are not limited to the themes that are supplied by FrontPage and The Microsoft Office System 2003. You can create custom themes from scratch or modify any of the available themes. Because of the number of elements that are controlled by the theme, it is much easier to modify a theme than to start from scratch.

Almost any element of a theme can be modified:

- You can change the graphics associated with the background picture, banner, bulleted lists, buttons, bars, and horizontal rules.

- You can change the artwork by simply selecting another file for most graphic elements.

- You can change the typeface, style, size, and alignment of the font used.

- You can change the graphics associated with the body of the page or with the individual heading levels.

- You can change the default screen font or stipulate more than one font for each element. The visitor's browser will display the element with the first named font that is available on his or her computer. If you want to use an unusual font, it is a good idea to back it up with another font that you know will be generally available.

Important   To create a custom theme, at the bottom of the Theme task pane, click the "Create new theme" link. Then customize the colors, graphics, and text of the theme until you like the way it looks in the preview window. To save your new theme, click the Save As button.

Custom themes can be created independently of a Web site. After you have created the theme, it is stored on your computer with the other installed themes and is always available to you.

In this exercise, you will create an alternate version of the Nature theme.

BE SURE TO start FrontPage before beginning this exercise.

1 Create a new normal page.

2 On the **Format** menu, click **Theme** to open the **Theme** task pane.

> **Tip**   If a task pane is already open, click Theme in the drop-down title bar to switch to the Theme task pane.

3 In the **Select a theme** box, click the down arrow to the right of the **Nature** theme.

4 In the drop-down list, click **Customize**.

The Customize Theme dialog box appears with the default Nature theme shown in the preview window.

5 Click the **Colors** button.

The Customize Theme dialog box displays the changeable color information.

On the Color Schemes tab, you can choose a color scheme from any of the installed themes. If you don't want to use a predefined color scheme, you can select colors on the Color Wheel tab or on the Custom tab.

6 On the **Color Schemes** tab, click **Construction Zone**.

The background and text colors displayed in the preview window change to reflect the selected color scheme.

7 On the **Color Schemes** tab, click **Downtown**.

The preview window changes again.

8 In this case, the current theme uses a custom color scheme. Scroll down through the preview box to see how each of the colors is applied.

9 Click the **Color Wheel** tab, and experiment with moving the locator on the color wheel and adjusting the brightness.

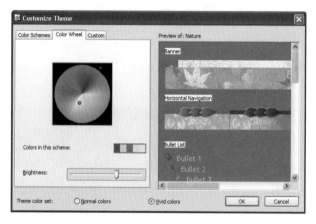

Your changes are reflected in the text and horizontal rule colors shown in the preview window.

10 Click the **Custom** tab.

11 Click the down arrow to the right of the **Item** box.

The list includes each of the elements for which you can specify a color.

Important   The background color is applied behind any background graphic that you choose, and it is displayed until the background graphic is loaded. If your visitors' browser settings do not allow background graphics, or if they are using a slow connection, the background color will be displayed instead of the background graphic.

12 Return to the **Color Schemes** tab.

Notice that the highlighted Custom color scheme has been updated to reflect your choices.

13 Click **OK**, or click **Cancel** to retain the original color scheme.

14 In the **Customize Theme** dialog box, click the **Graphics** button.

The Customize Theme dialog box displays the changeable graphic elements.

15 Click the down arrow to the right of the **Item** box to see a list of the individual graphic elements you can change.

16 Select various elements, and notice the changes that occur on the **Picture** tab and on the **Font** tab.

17 Experiment with making graphic changes. When you are done, click **OK** to confirm your choices, or click **Cancel** to retain the original graphic theme.

18 In the **Customize Theme** dialog box, click the **Text** button.

The Customize Theme dialog box displays the changeable text elements.

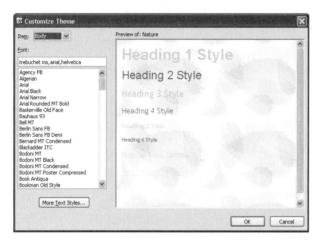

Tip To call out multiple fonts for an element, select the element from the Item drop-down list. In the Font list, select your first choice for the selected element. Position the insertion point at the end of the element's name in the Font box, and type the names of the backup fonts, separating all the font names with commas.

19 Experiment with making changes. When you are done, click **OK** to confirm your choices.

20 In the **Customize Theme** dialog box, click the **Save As** button.

The Save Theme dialog box appears.

21 Type Customized Nature Theme as the name of your new theme, and then click **OK**.

22 Click **OK** again to close the **Customize Theme** dialog box.

The customized theme is now available from the Select a theme box in the Theme task pane, with the same options as the standard FrontPage themes.

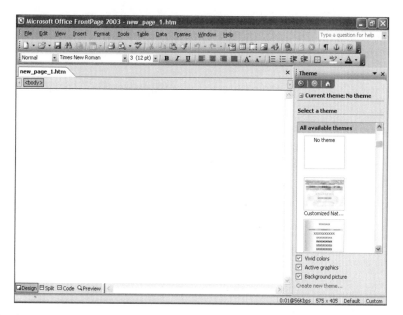

23 Close the **Theme** task pane.

CLOSE the practice file. If you are not continuing on to the next chapter, quit FrontPage.

Key Points

■ You can create an empty Web site from scratch and populate it with only the pages you want.

■ Each page of a Web site has a page title that is displayed to the visitor. It is important to assign an appropriate and meaningful title to each page.

■ You can format Web pages by using background colors and graphics, borders, shading, page banners, and shared borders.

■ You can quickly format the background, colors, and fonts of an entire Web site by applying a FrontPage theme. If you don't like the available themes, you can customize an existing theme or create your own.

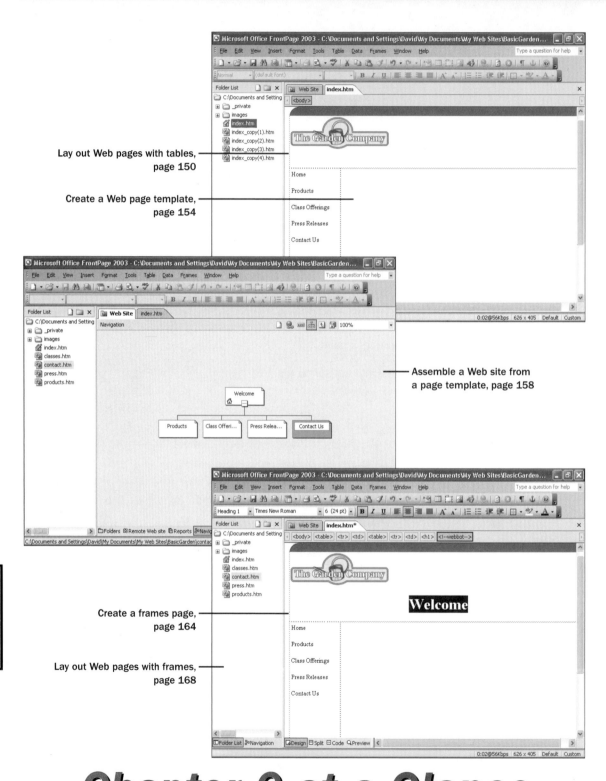

Lay out Web pages with tables, page 150

Create a Web page template, page 154

Assemble a Web site from a page template, page 158

Create a frames page, page 164

Lay out Web pages with frames, page 168

Chapter 6 at a Glance

6 Changing Web Page Layout

In this chapter you will learn to:

✔ Lay out Web pages with tables.

✔ Create a Web page template.

✔ Assemble a Web site from a page template.

✔ Create a frames page.

✔ Lay out Web pages with frames.

Microsoft Office FrontPage 2003 includes a variety of templates and wizards that produce Web sites of varying complexity and sophistication. When you are anxious to quickly establish a Web presence for yourself, your business, or your group or organization, you can use these ready-made sites to launch a site that will do a creditable job.

If the layout of a predefined site does not quite meet your needs, you can customize it in a few simple ways to make it appropriate. However, without deeper knowledge of how the site is put together, you risk "breaking" the site if you attempt more fundamental structural changes. To allow you to create sophisticated-looking sites with apparent ease, FrontPage shields you from a lot of the complex underpinnings that make the site work correctly. Making a structural change without understanding its implications might cause unexpected results.

To give you a better understanding of the way many professional Web sites are put together, in this chapter you will look at a couple of the more sophisticated techniques used for laying out pages. First you will work with tables to provide page structure, and then you will explore the use of frames.

See Also Do you need only a quick refresher on the topics in this chapter? See the Quick Reference entries on pages xxix–xxx.

Important Before you can use the practice files in this chapter, you need to install them from the book's companion CD to their default location. See "Using the Book's CD-ROM" on page xiii for more information.

Laying Out Web Pages with Tables

The use of *tables* in Web design is quite different from the use of tables in other areas of document design. Web site tables are made up of *rows* and *columns* and they can be used to convey structured information just like other tables. But the real purpose of tables in Web design is to break the page into specific boxes, measured either in an absolute number of *pixels* or in the relative percentage of the available *screen real estate*. When you structure a Web page using a table, you can control the layout much more precisely. And you can create interesting, magazine-type layouts by filling some *cells* with content and leaving other cells empty. To make things even more interesting, you can *nest* tables inside of other tables to gain tighter control over some areas of the page.

New in Office 2003
Layout tables and cells task pane

The new Layout Tables and Cells task pane includes all the tools you need to design your table-based page layout in one central location. From this task pane, you can:

■ Draw a layout table or insert a layout cell.

■ Set the width and height of a new or selected table or cell.

■ Align your table with the left margin, center, or right margin of the page.

■ Adjust the margins of the Web page.

■ Choose from 12 predefined table-based page layout options.

You can also choose to display the new FrontPage Layout Tool, a guide that appears on your Web page to indicate various aspects of the table you're creating, such as the width and height of tables and cells. You can use this on-screen tool to quickly change table dimensions and see the results of your changes. Using the Layout Tool, you can easily adapt any of the predefined table layouts to fit your needs.

Generally, you should use only one page layout throughout the entire site, although some sites use a different layout for the home page. When planning Web page layout, you need to consider in advance the various elements that will be important for each page so that you can come up with an overall design that is appropriate for all the pages. You should then create and test one template page first. When you have all the elements the way you want them, you can then create your content within the framework, or move existing content into the framework. When you plan your Web site this way, you avoid having to replicate changes across several pages every time you discover something you missed or something new you'd like to add.

In this exercise, you will create a basic page layout *template* with areas for a logo, page title, table of contents, and site information, as well as an area for specific page contents. You will do this by adapting one of the predefined layout tables.

BE SURE TO start FrontPage and close any open task panes before beginning this exercise.

Create a new
normal page

1 Click the **Create a new normal page** button to create a new page.

A new file called *new_page_1.htm* opens.

Tip To display more precise ScreenTips and keyboard shortcuts for toolbar buttons, on the Tools menu, click Customize, and then select the "Show shortcut keys in ScreenTips" check box.

Save

2 Click the **Save** button.

The Save As dialog box appears with *My Web Sites* selected in the "Save in" box.

3 In the **File name** box, type table_template.

4 Click the **Change title** button to open the **Set Page Title** dialog box.

5 In the **Page title** box, type Table Layout Template.

> **Set Page Title** ✕
>
> Page title:
>
> Table Layout Template
>
> The title of the page is displayed in the title bar of the browser.
>
> [OK] [Cancel]

6 Click **OK** to close the **Set Page Title** dialog box, and then click **Save** to close the **Save As** dialog box and save your file.

7 If the **Folder List** appears, close it so you can see more of your Web page.

8 Click in the body of the table_template page.

9 On the **Table** menu, click **Layout Tables and Cells**.

Scroll bar

The Layout Tables and Cells task pane appears.

10 In the **New tables and cells** area, click **Insert Layout Table**.

Table markers appear in the page body, designating a table 450 pixels wide by 450 pixels high.

11 In the **Table properties** area, in the **Width** box, type 640.

Align Center

12 Still in the **Table properties** area, click the **Align Center** button.

13 At the bottom of the **Layout Tables and Cells** task pane, position the mouse pointer over the scroll bar to scroll to the bottom of the task pane.

14 In the **Table layout** area, scroll through the predefined layout options. Click the **Header, Body, Footer, and Left** layout (the fourth option on left side), which includes a horizontal header cell at the top, a vertical cell on the left, a horizontal footer cell at the bottom, and the main page body at the center right.

The page changes to reflect the selected layout. The width and height of each cell is indicated by the Layout Tool.

Green lines indicate the outer edges of the table.

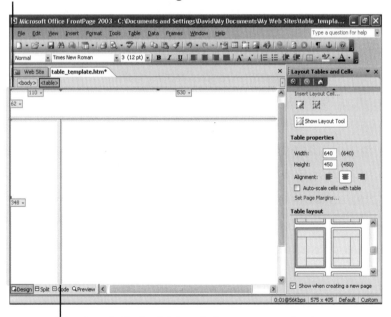

Blue lines indicate divisions between rows and columns.

15 Close the **Layout Tables and Cells** task pane.

The Layout Tool indicates the outlines of the header, body, and left pane.

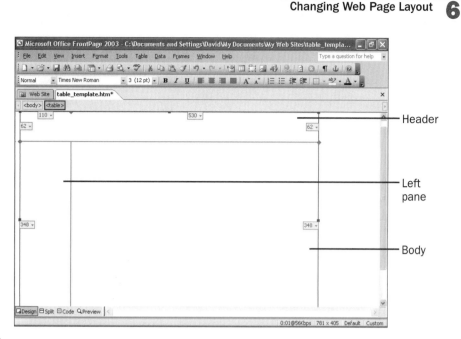

Header

Left pane

Body

16 Scroll to the bottom of the Page view editing window so you can see the footer, body, and left pane.

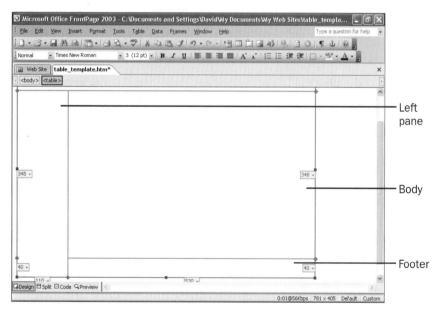

Left pane

Body

Footer

17 Click the line at the bottom of the left pane to select that cell.

The selected cell is indicated by square handles at each corner and at the center of each side.

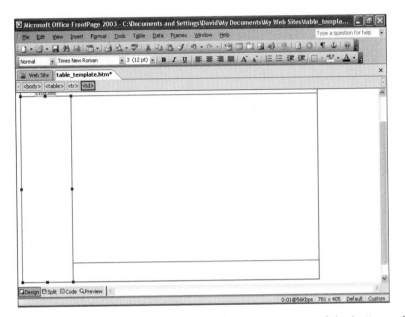

18 Position the mouse pointer over the handle at the center of the bottom edge of the selected cell.

The mouse pointer changes to a T shape.

19 Drag the bottom edge of the cell upward until it aligns with the top of the footer.

The new cell created in the lower-left corner of the table is shaded gray.

20 Click the line at the bottom of the footer to select that cell.

21 Drag the left edge of the cell to the left until it aligns with the left edge of the table.

The footer now extends across the entire bottom of the table.

CLOSE the file, saving your work if you want.

Creating a Web Page Template

You can think of Web sites as consisting of two kinds of information: the elements that appear on every page in the site, and the elements that are unique to a particular page. When creating a page template, you should include all the information that is common to every page in the site in the template so that you have to create it only once. You can keep any areas in which information will change on every page separate from the static areas by designating separate cells for the changing information.

In this exercise, you will add site-wide information to a Web page to create a template from which you can create other Web pages.

USE the *table_template* Web page and the *tgclogo_sm* graphic in the practice file folder for this topic. This practice file is located in the *My Documents\Microsoft Press\FrontPage 2003 SBS\PageLayout \Template* folder and can also be accessed by clicking *Start/All Programs/Microsoft Press/FrontPage 2003 Step By Step.*
BE SURE TO start FrontPage before beginning this exercise.

1 On the **File** menu, click **Open**.

2 Browse to the *My Documents\Microsoft Press\FrontPage 2003 SBS\PageLayout \Template* folder. Click **table_template**, and then click **Open**.

A basic table outline appears, consisting of a header, left pane, body, and footer.

3 Scroll down to see the table footer, and then scroll up to the top again.

4 Move the mouse pointer over the cells of the table.

As the mouse pointer moves over each dotted line, a different cell of the table is outlined. The table outline appears in green; the individual cell outlines appear in blue.

5 Click the dotted line at the top of the table.

The table and cell outlines are displayed.

6 Right-click in the table header cell and on the shortcut menu, click **Cell Formatting**.

The Cell Formatting task pane appears.

7 On the **Cell Formatting** task pane, click **Cell Corners and Shadows**.

The task pane contents change to reflect your selection.

8 In the **Corners** area, click the down arrow to the right of the **Color** box, and in the drop-down list, click the **Teal** square (the last square in the second row).

Top Left
Corner

9 In the **Corners** area, in the **Apply** list, click the **Top Left Corner** button.

A bar appears across the top of the header, with a rounded left corner.

10 Scroll to the right to see the right end of the bar, which still has a straight corner.

Top Right
Corner

11 On the **Cell Formatting** task pane, in the **Corners** area, click the **Top Right Corner** button.

The corner changes from straight to rounded.

12 Position the insertion point in the header cell.

13 On the **Insert** menu, point to **Picture**, and click **From File**. Browse to the *My Documents \Microsoft Press\FrontPage 2003 SBS\PageLayout\Template* folder, click **tgclogo_sm**, and then click **Insert**.

The Garden Company's logo is inserted in the table header beneath the curved border.

14 Press [Enter] to move the insertion point to a new line after the logo.

After the page is added to a Web site structure, the page banner will go here.

15 Position the insertion point in the contents cell of the table (the middle left cell), and type the following words (without the bullets), pressing [Enter] after each line:

- Home
- Products
- Class Offerings
- Press Releases
- Contact Us

This table cell will contain the navigation links to each page of your site. This is commonly referred to as a *TOC* because it functions like a table of contents for your Web visitors.

16 On the **Cell Formatting** task pane, click **Cell Properties and Borders**.

The task pane changes to reflect your selection.

17 In the **Layout cell properties** area, click the down arrow to the right of the **VAlign** box and in the drop-down list, click **Top**.

The cell contents move to vertically align at the top of the cell.

18 Select the number in the **Padding** box, type 5, and then press ⌷Enter⌷.

The cell contents move down and to the right 5 pixels.

19 Click the right border of the contents cell to select all the text inside.

20 On the Formatting toolbar, click the **Decrease Font Size** button.

The font of the content list decreases from 12 points to 10 points.

Decrease
Font Size

21 On the Formatting toolbar, click the **Bold** button.

Each of the content list items changes to bold font.

Bold

22 Scroll to the bottom of the page, and click the top border of the footer cell to select it. (If the page body cell is selected instead, try again, clicking slightly lower.)

23 On the **Cell Formatting** task pane, click **Cell Corners and Shadows**.

24 In the **Corners** area, click the **Bottom Left Corner** button.

The rounded border is applied in teal, because the color is still set from your previous action.

Bottom
Left Corner

25 Click the **Bottom Right Corner** button to complete the rounded borders.

26 Click to position the insertion point at the top of the footer cell.

Bottom
Right Corner

27 Type E-mail the Webmaster with questions or comments about this Web site.

Web visitors expect to see site contact information at the very end of a Web page.

28 Triple-click the sentence to select it, and on the Formatting toolbar, click the **Decrease Font Size** button to decrease the font from 12 points to 10 points.

29 On the **Cell Formatting** task pane, click **Cell Properties and Borders**.

30 In the **Padding** box, type 5, and then press [Enter].

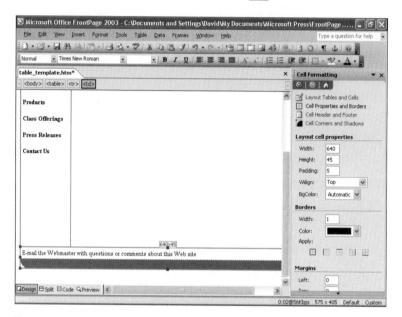

The cell contents move down and to the right 5 pixels.

CLOSE the Cell Formatting task pane and the open file, saving your work if you want.

Assembling a Web Site from a Page Template

After you have created your basic page template, you need to create each page of your Web site from the template, add each page to the site navigation, and add page banners and navigation links as appropriate.

In this exercise, you will copy a Web page template and rename and link the copies to create an entire Web site.

USE the *table_template* Web page in the practice file folder for this topic. This practice file is located in the *My Documents\Microsoft Press\FrontPage 2003 SBS\PageLayout\Assembly* folder and can also be accessed by clicking *Start/All Programs/Microsoft Press/FrontPage 2003 Step By Step*.
BE SURE TO start FrontPage before beginning this exercise.

1 Create a one page Web site called BasicGarden.

Troubleshooting For step-by-step instructions on how to create a one page Web site, refer to "Creating a New Web Site by Using a Template" in Chapter 2.

2 If the **Folder List** is not open, on the **View** menu, click **Folder List**.

3 On the **File** menu, click **Open**.

4 In the **Open File** dialog box, browse to the *My Documents\Microsoft Press \FrontPage 2003 SBS\PageLayout\Assembly* folder and double-click the **table_template** file.

The template page opens in the Page view editing window.

5 On the **File** menu, click **Save As**.

6 In the **Save As** dialog box, browse to the *My Documents\My Web Sites\BasicGarden* folder and double-click the **index** file. When prompted to replace the existing file, click **Yes**.

The Save Embedded Files dialog box appears, listing the files that need to be saved along with the page template.

7 With all five files selected, click **Change Folder**.

8 In the **Change Folder** dialog box, double-click the images folder, click **OK**, and then click **OK** to save the embedded files in the images folder of the BasicGarden site.

The page template is now saved as the home page of your new Web site.

9 In the **Folder List**, right-click the **index.htm** file, and on the shortcut menu, click **Copy**.

10 Right-click an empty area of the **Folder List** and on the shortcut menu, click **Paste**. Repeat three times to create four copies of the page.

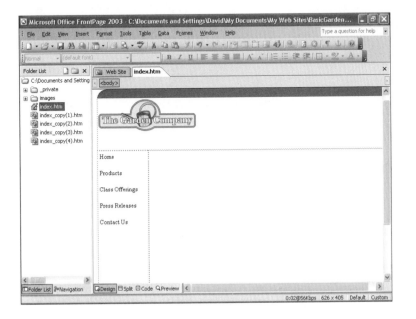

11 Right-click the **index_copy(1).htm** file, and on the shortcut menu, click **Rename**. Rename the file classes.htm.

12 Repeat step 11 for the other copies, renaming them contact.htm, press.htm, and products.htm.

13 For each of the five files, in the **Folder List**, right-click the file, and then click **Properties**. In the **Title** box, change the page titles as follows, and then click **OK**.

File name	Page title
index.htm	Welcome
classes.htm	Class Offerings
contact.htm	Contact Us
press.htm	Press Releases
products.htm	Products

⌐ᵃNavigation

Navigation View

14 Click the **Web Site** tab, and then click the **Navigation View** button.

15 Drag the **products.htm**, **classes.htm**, **press.htm**, and **contact.htm** files from the **Folder List** to the Navigation view window, and drop them in that order as sub-pages of the home page.

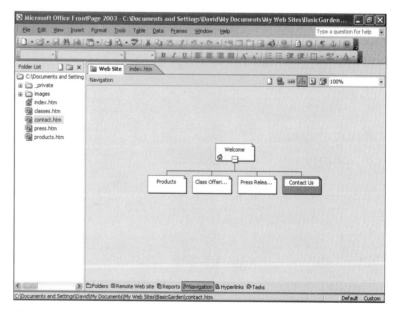

16 Click the **index.htm** page tab.

17 Position the insertion point in the space below The Garden Company's logo. The easiest way to do this is to click the logo, and then press the **Right Arrow** button twice.

18 On the **Insert** menu, click **Page Banner**, and then click **OK**.

19 Select the inserted placeholder, and do the following:

- In the **Style** drop-down list, click **Heading 1**.

Normal ▾
Style

- On the Formatting toolbar, click the **Center** button to center the heading within the header cell.

≡
Center

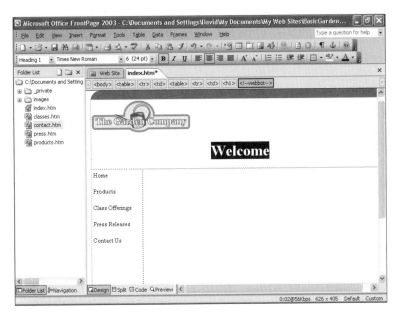

20 In the contents cell, double-click the word **Home**.

21 On the Standard toolbar, click the **Insert Hyperlink** button to open the **Insert Hyperlink** dialog box.

Insert Hyperlink

22 In the file list, click **index** and then click **OK**.

FrontPage inserts a hyperlink from the word *Home* to the home page of the site and closes the dialog box.

23 Repeat steps 20 through 22 for each of the remaining entries in the contents cell, linking each to its corresponding Web page, as follows:

TOC entry	File name
Products	products
Class Offerings	classes
Press Releases	press
Contact Us	contact

24 In the footer cell, double-click the word *Webmaster* to select it, and on the Standard toolbar, click the **Insert Hyperlink** button.

25 In the **Insert Hyperlink** dialog box, on the **Link to** bar, click **E-mail Address**.

26 Do the following:

- In the **E-mail address** box, type Webmaster@gardenco.msn.com.

  The word *mailto:* is inserted at the beginning of the line as you type.

- In the **Subject** box, type Web site feedback to set the subject line of each e-mail message generated from the link so that you can easily identify the source of these messages.

- Click the **ScreenTip** button, type E-mail the Webmaster! in the **ScreenTip text** box, and then click **OK** to set the ScreenTip text.

■ In the **Insert Hyperlink** dialog box, click **OK** to insert the e-mail link and close the dialog box.

27 Close the index.htm page, saving your work when prompted.

28 To check your links, on the **Web Site** tab, click the **Hyperlinks View** button.

The links from the home page to the child pages and the e-mail link are all shown.

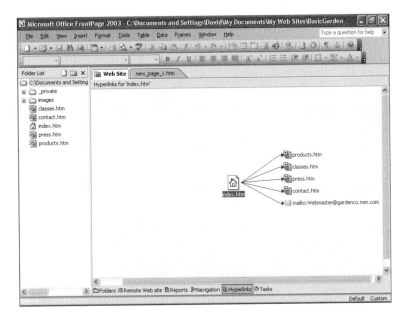

CLOSE the Web site.

Linking to Bookmarks

You can insert placeholders called *bookmarks* in your Web pages so that visitors can jump directly to a certain place on the page, rather than just to that particular file. Bookmarks are useful when you have long pages that are divided into logical sections, or when you want to jump from one central list of links to multiple locations on a page. For instance, bookmarks are often used on Frequently Asked Questions pages, in which a list of questions at the top of the page is followed by a list of answers. Clicking each question jumps to the corresponding answer.

In HTML code, a bookmark is a variation on an *anchor tag*, or <a> tag. Creating a bookmark in FrontPage is very easy and does not require that you work with HTML. Simply select the place, word, or phrase that you want to bookmark, and on the Insert menu, click

Bookmark. You will be prompted to name your bookmark; you can choose a logical name for it (such as naming a link to the word *Plants* as **Plants**), or you might prefer to develop a numeric or alphabetical coding system of your own.

Hyperlinking to a bookmark is also simple: Insert a hyperlink as you normally would. Then in the Insert Hyperlink dialog box, click the page on which the bookmark appears, and then click the Bookmark button to show a list of all the available bookmarks on that page. Hyperlinks to bookmarks are expressed as *filename#bookmark*.

Creating a Frames Page

Instead of using tables to structure a Web page, you can designate that different parts of the page appear in different *frames*. When you lay out a page with frames, the end result looks very similar to a page laid out with tables, but the behind-the-scenes work is much more elaborate.

The concept behind frames is that you create a single shell page, sometimes called a *frameset*, which contains individual frames of information precisely positioned where you want them. Each frame can display either static information that has been entered directly in the frame or the content of another file. The beauty of using frames to organize your data is that you can display the information from one file in multiple locations. When you need to make a change that affects every page in your site (for instance, adding a page to the table of contents), you make the change in only one place.

FrontPage makes the process of creating frames pages quite simple by providing several frames-page templates that you can open, save, and complete with very little fuss.

In this exercise, you will create a frames page using a template.

USE the *tgclogo_sm* file in the practice file folder for this topic. This practice file is located in the *My Documents\Microsoft Press\FrontPage 2003 SBS\PageLayout\Frames* folder and can also be accessed by clicking *Start/All Programs/Microsoft Press/FrontPage 2003 Step By Step*.
BE SURE TO start FrontPage before beginning this exercise.

1   On the **File** menu, click **New** to open the **New** task pane.

2   In the **New page** area, click **More page templates** to open the **Page Templates** dialog box.

3   Click the **Frames Pages** tab.

FrontPage provides ten simple templates for creating frame-based Web pages.

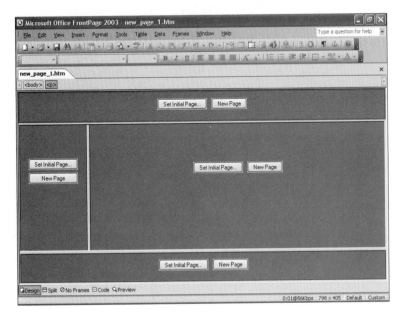

4 Click each template to view the corresponding description and preview the page layout.

5 Click the **Header, Footer and Contents** template, and then click **OK** to close the dialog box and create a page based on the template.

FrontPage creates a new page with four delineated frames, each containing two buttons.

You can click the Set Initial Page button to link existing content to a frame, or you can click the New Page button to create a new content page linked to the frame.

6   In the top frame, click **New Page**.

A blank page opens within the frame. You have actually created an entirely new file, the contents of which are being displayed in the selected frame.

7   On the **Insert** menu, point to **Picture**, and then click **From File**.

The Picture dialog box appears.

8   Browse to the *My Documents\Microsoft Press\FrontPage 2003 SBS\PageLayout \Frames* folder, click the **tgclogo_sm** file, and then click **Insert**.

FrontPage inserts The Garden Company's small logo in the frame. The logo appears to be larger than the space allotted.

9   Move the pointer over the bottom border of the top frame. When the pointer changes to a double-headed arrow, drag the border down until the entire logo is visible.

Save

10   To save the new file that you've created in the frame, click inside the frame, and then on the Standard toolbar, click the **Save** button.

The Save As dialog box appears with the selected frame highlighted.

11   In the **File name** box, type header.

12   Click the **Change title** button to open the **Set Page Title** dialog box.

13 In the **Page title** box, type Header Frame, and then click **OK**.

14 Click **Save** to close the **Save As** dialog box and apply your changes. Save the embedded logo graphic in the images folder when prompted to do so.

To save the frame, you must also save the frameset. FrontPage prompts you to save the frameset page by opening a new Save As dialog box.

15 On the **Places** bar, click **My Documents**, and then click the **My Web Sites** folder.

16 In the **File name** box, type frames_template.

17 Click the **Change title** button, change the page title to Frames Template, and then click **OK**.

18 Click **Save** to close the **Save As** dialog box.

The Folder List opens, displaying the contents of your My Web Sites folder.

CLOSE the Folder List, the *frames_template* file, and the Web site.

Splitting and Deleting Frames

You can split a frame into multiple frames or delete extraneous frames from a frames page.

To split one frame into two frames:

1 Click in the frame you want to split.

2 On the **Frames** menu, click **Split Frame**.

3 In the **Split Frame** dialog box, select the **Split into columns** or **Split into rows** option, and then click **OK**.

FrontPage splits the frame horizontally or vertically as directed. The newly created frame contains Set Initial Page and New Page buttons.

To delete an extraneous frame:

1 Click in the frame you want to delete to select it.

2 On the **Frames** menu, click **Delete Frame**.

Laying Out Web Pages with Frames

When you first start creating Web sites, most of your pages will probably be *static*, which means that the content will be part of each individual page. After you have a pretty good understanding of how to build pages, you will begin to explore more complex page layout techniques, and the question then becomes how to convert all the static pages you have already created to take advantage of the new capabilities of your pages.

In this exercise, you will link existing content to a frames page to convert existing static pages to a frame-based template.

You will work with a sample Web site consisting of the home page (index.htm) and four second-level pages: Products, Class Offerings, Press Releases, and Contact Us. A rudimentary set of links to the other pages appears at the top of each page, and an e-mail link appears at the bottom. The Table of Contents page contains only the TOC with links to the pages and bookmarks of the site.

USE the *GardenCo* Web site in the practice file folder for this topic. This practice file is located in the *My Documents\Microsoft Press\FrontPage 2003 SBS\PageLayout\LayOutFrame* folder and can also be accessed by clicking *Start/All Programs/Microsoft Press/FrontPage 2003 Step By Step.*
OPEN the *GardenCo* Web site.

1   In the **Folder List**, double-click the **frames_template.htm** file to open it in the Page view editing window.

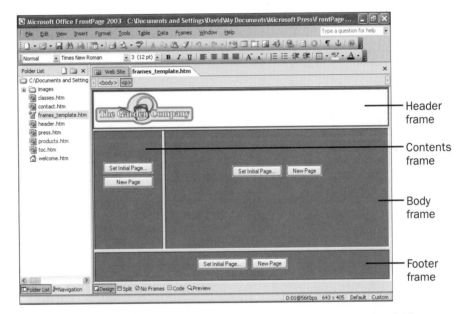

2   To link the contents of the toc.htm file to the contents frame, start by clicking **Set Initial Page** in the contents frame.

The Insert Hyperlink dialog box appears with the current folder visible.

3   In the file list, click **toc**, and then click **OK**.

FrontPage displays the table of contents from the toc.htm file in the contents frame. The table of contents has not actually been inserted in the frame; it is linked to the frame. You can use the vertical scroll bar to see the entire page.

4   To define the starting page of the Web site, in the body frame, click **Set Initial Page**.

5   In the **Insert Hyperlink** dialog box, scroll down, click **welcome**, and then click **OK**.

FrontPage displays the home page in the body frame. Again, you can use the vertical scroll bar to see the entire page.

6   In the footer frame, click the **New Page** button.

A blank page opens within the frame.

7 Type E-mail the Webmaster with questions or comments about this Web site.

Tip You can make changes to the content of a frames page in the source file or in the frame.

Decrease
Font Size

8 Press ⌃+Ⓐ to select the entire contents of the frame, and then on the Formatting toolbar, click the **Decrease Font Size** button.

Insert Hyperlink

9 Select the word *Webmaster*, and on the Standard toolbar, click the **Insert Hyperlink** button.

10 In the **Insert Hyperlink** dialog box, do the following:

▪ On the **Link to** bar, click **E-mail Address**.

Tip If you formatted the Webmaster hyperlink in "Assembling a Web Site from a Page Template" earlier in this chapter, you can click the e-mail link created in that exercise, which is visible in the "Recently used e-mail addresses" box.

▪ In the **E-mail address** box, type Webmaster@gardenco.msn.com.

The word *mailto:* is inserted at the beginning of the line as you type.

▪ In the **Subject** box, type Web site feedback to set the subject line of each e-mail message generated from the link so that you can easily identify the source of these messages.

▪ Click the **ScreenTip** button, type E-mail the Webmaster! in the **ScreenTip text** box, and then click **OK** to set the ScreenTip text.

▪ In the **Insert Hyperlink** dialog box, click **OK** to insert the e-mail link and close the dialog box.

11 Drag the top border of the bottom frame down to resize the bottom frame so that the amount of visible white space is minimized.

12 Save the new page created in the bottom frame as footer, and change the page title to **Footer Frame**.

Tip For step-by-step instructions on how to save a new page created in a frame, refer to "Creating a Frames Page" earlier in this chapter.

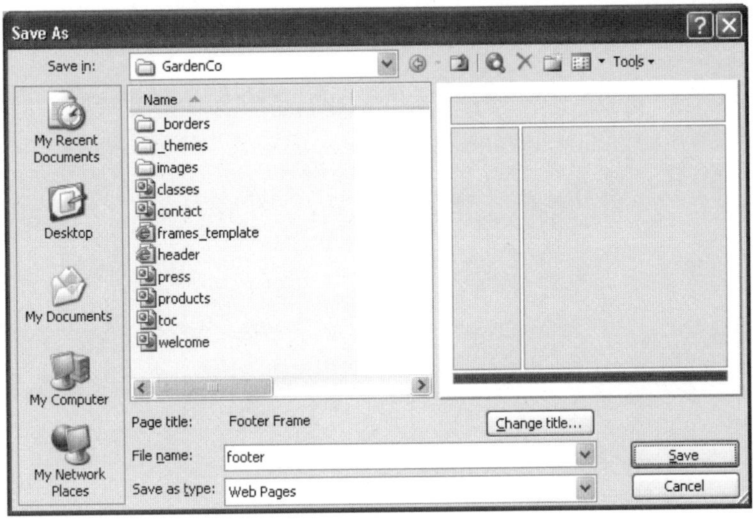

13 On the **File** menu, click **Save As** to open the **Save As** dialog box.

14 Ensure that the entire frames template is displayed in the preview window, change the page title to The Garden Company, and save the file as index.

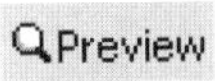

Q Preview
Show
Preview View

15 At the bottom of the Page view editing window, click the **Show Preview View** button.

Depending on the size of the window, the contents and body frames might display scroll bars. The frame borders are visible, which gives a chunky look to the page.

Tip   Some Web browsers don't support frames. To see what your Web page will look like to a visitor whose browser doesn't support frames, click the Show No Frames View button at the bottom of the Page view window.

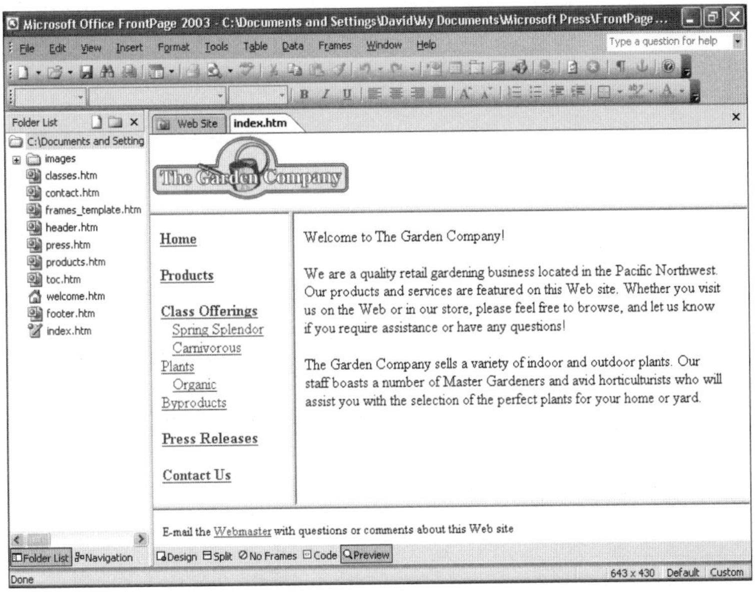

16 At the bottom of the Page view editing window, click the **Show Design View** button to continue editing the **index.htm** file.

17 Right-click the header frame, and click **Frame Properties** on the shortcut menu.

A Frame Properties dialog box appears.

Frame Properties

Name:	top
Initial page:	header.htm	Browse...
Long Description:		Browse...
Title:	

Frame size

Column width: 1 Relative

Height: 80 Pixels

Margins

Width: 0

Height: 0

Options

☐ Resizable in browser Frames Page...

Show scrollbars: Never

Style... | OK | Cancel

18 In the **Options** area, click the **Frames Page** button.

The Page Properties dialog box appears, with the Frames tab visible.

Page Properties

General | Advanced | Custom | Language | Frames | Workgroup

Frame Spacing: 2

☑ Show Borders

OK | Cancel

The options set here affect all the frames on the page.

19 Clear the **Show Borders** check box.

The Frame Spacing measurement is reset to 0.

20 Click **OK** to close the **Page Properties** dialog box, and click **OK** again to close the **Frame Properties** dialog box.

The frame borders are no longer visible.

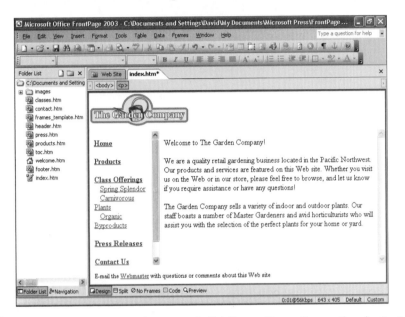

21 Right-click the contents frame, and click **Frame Properties** on the shortcut menu to open the **Frame Properties** dialog box.

22 In the **Show scrollbars** drop-down list, click **Never**, and then click **OK**.

This looks much better, but when viewed at a screen area of 640 by 480 pixels, the table of contents extends beyond the bottom of its frame.

23 Click in the contents frame, and then press ⌃+A to select the text in it. Then on the **Format** menu, click **Paragraph**.

The Paragraph dialog box appears.

24 In the **Spacing** area, set **Before** and **After** to 0, and then click **OK**.

25 Click the **Save** button.

The changes to the toc.htm file are saved.

26 On the Standard toolbar, click the **Preview in Browser** button.

Save

Preview in
Browser

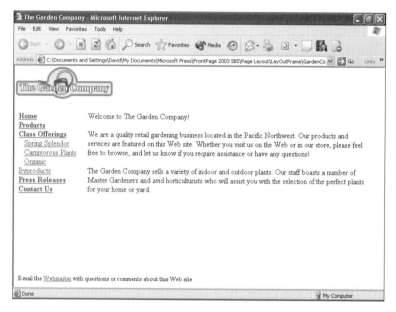

27   Test the site by clicking the links in the contents frame to verify that the content in the body frame is updated appropriately.

> **Tip**   You can use your browser's Back and Forward buttons to move between the pages you have viewed.

28   At the bottom of the page, click the **Webmaster** e-mail link.

If you have an e-mail program installed, a new e-mail message opens in your e-mail program with the To and Subject lines completed.

CLOSE the e-mail message, your browser, and the Web site. If you are not continuing on to the next chapter, quit FrontPage.

Key Points

- The new Layout Tables and Cells task pane makes it easy to lay out and govern the dimensions of your Web page.

- When creating a page template, you should include all the information that is common to every page in the site in the template. You can keep any areas in which information will change on every page separate from the static areas by designating separate cells for the changing information.

- After you have created your basic page template, you can create each page of your Web site from the template.

- In addition to using tables to structure a Web page, you can designate that different parts of the page appear in different frames.

- You can link existing content to a frames page to convert existing static pages to a frame-based template.

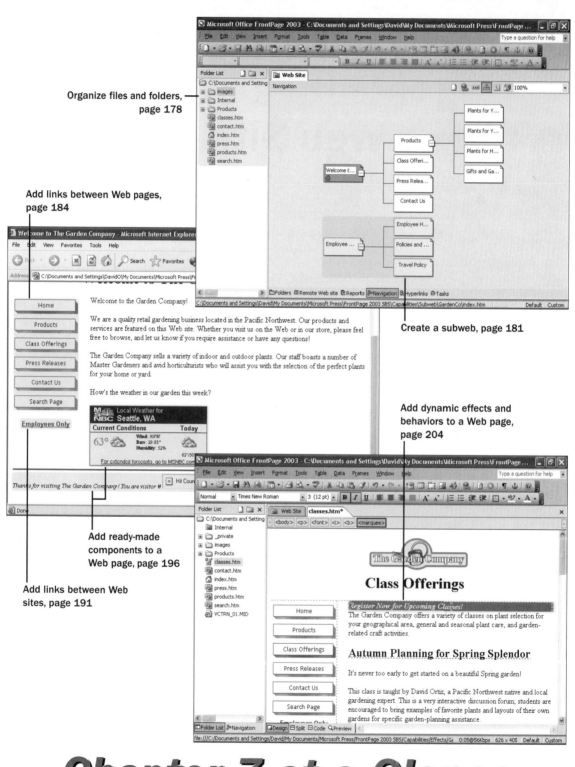

Organize files and folders, page 178

Add links between Web pages, page 184

Create a subweb, page 181

Add dynamic effects and behaviors to a Web page, page 204

Add ready-made components to a Web page, page 196

Add links between Web sites, page 191

Chapter 7 at a Glance

7 Enhancing the Capabilities of Your Web Site

In this chapter you will learn to:

✔ Organize files and folders.

✔ Create a subweb.

✔ Add links between Web pages.

✔ Add links between Web sites.

✔ Add ready-made components to a Web page.

✔ Add dynamic effects and behaviors to a Web page.

In the early days of its existence, the Internet was used primarily as a way of making large volumes of information available to government agencies and universities around the world. This information was plain text, and it was of interest only to researchers and people who needed it for their jobs. When the World Wide Web was developed, it added graphics and interactivity, and the ability to jump from one item of information to another. Static pages of text are a thing of the past. These days, to create an effective Web site you have to be able to enhance it with dynamic elements that set it apart from the competition.

There is no point in building a site if your visitors can't easily move among its pages to find the information that interests them. If you have organized your site into a logical system of files and folders, FrontPage can intuit the hierarchy of the site and add navigational tools so that your Web visitors can easily find their way around using elements such as shared borders and link bars. You can also use graphic elements such as image maps to visually show visitors what's available and how to access it. If your Web site must serve the needs of several different groups of visitors, it might be appropriate to divide your site into a main Web site and one or more linked *subwebs* so that particular categories of visitors aren't distracted by information they don't need. For example, if The Garden Company wants its Web site to cater to both customers and employees, it might create a subweb that is accessible only to employees with a user name and password, and then use the subweb to communicate information of internal interest.

In addition to enhancing the navigational capabilities of your site, you will want to explore the categories of Web components and dynamic elements that come with FrontPage. These ready-made components add a professional touch to your Web site by inserting special-purpose mini-programs that perform such tasks as counting the number of visitors or scrolling banners across the page.

In this chapter, you will organize files and folders within a Web site in a way that makes it easier to enhance the site. You will then refine the navigational structure of the Web site by adding shared borders, link bars, hyperlinks, and image maps. You will also create a subweb and link it to the main Web site. Then you'll take a look at some of the dynamic elements that you can add to a page, including the Web components that come with FrontPage.

See Also   Do you need only a quick refresher on the topics in this chapter? See the Quick Reference entries on pages xxx-xxxii.

 Important   Before you can use the practice files in this chapter, you need to install them from the book's companion CD to their default location. See "Using the Book's CD-ROM" on page xiii for more information.

Organizing Files and Folders

Being able to effectively organize your files into a system of folders is a fundamental computer skill that makes it easier to find things quickly and easily. When it comes to FrontPage, however, this skill is important for another reason. FrontPage can automate some of the processes involved in creating a sophisticated navigation system for your Web site, and organizing the elements of the site into a logical set of folders makes it easier to identify the structure of the site.

In this exercise, you will organize a Web site consisting of many pages and graphics into a useful folder structure.

USE the *GardenCo* Web site in the practice file folder for this topic. This practice file is located in the *My Documents\Microsoft Press\FrontPage 2003 SBS\Capabilities\Organize* folder and can also be accessed by clicking *Start/All Programs/Microsoft Press/FrontPage 2003 Step By Step*.
BE SURE TO start FrontPage before beginning this exercise.
OPEN the *GardenCo* Web site.

Tip   If the Folder List is not already open, on the Standard toolbar, click the Toggle Pane button to open it.

1   At the bottom of the Page view window, click the **Navigation View** button.

🎇 Navigation
Navigation
View

Portrait/
Landscape

2 At the top of the Navigation view window, click the **Portrait/Landscape** button to change the orientation so the site navigation fits better on the screen.

In Navigation view, you can see that the site consists of a home page with four second-level pages. The Products page has four third-level pages, and a separate employee site is at the same level as the home page.

3 Switch to Folders view, and notice the long list of HTML files and graphics files that make up this Web site.

The most obvious way you can impose some organization on this mess is to move the graphic files into a separate folder.

New Folder

4   At the top of the **Folder List**, click the **New Folder** button.

5   When the new folder appears at the bottom of the **Folder List**, type Images, and then press [Enter].

You have created a new folder within the Web site structure.

6   Click the **Type** heading to sort the files by type.

> **Tip**   If the Folders pane displays the contents of the new folder, click the top-level folder in the Folder List to show its contents.

7   Click **custrel1.gif**, press [Shift], and click **tgclogo_sm.gif**.

All four images are now selected.

8   Drag the selected images into the *Images* folder.

FrontPage moves the graphic files and simultaneously updates the links within the content files to reflect the new location of the graphic files.

9   Select the five JPG images, and drag them into the *Images* folder.

10   In the **Folder List**, click the top-level folder to display its contents in the **Folders** pane.

11   Click the **New Folder** button, and name the new folder Internal.

12   Drag the *employee_info.htm*, *handbook.htm*, *policies.htm*, and *travel_policy.htm* files to the *Internal* folder.

As you saw in Navigation view, these files are part of the separate employee information site. Again, FrontPage moves the files and simultaneously updates the links within all the content files to reflect the new location of the files.

Ideally, the only files that should be located at the root level are the home page and any second-level pages that don't have sub-pages.

13   Return to the main folder, and create a new folder called Products.

14   Move the *carnivorous_plants.htm*, *gifts.htm*, *plants_garden.htm*, and *plants_home.htm* files into the new folder.

15   In the **Folders** pane, click the **Name** heading to sort the folders and files alphabetically.

CLOSE the open GardenCo Web site.

Creating a Subweb

A *subweb* is a Web site that is nested inside another Web site. A site that contains a subweb is called a *root Web*. If you think of a Web site as a set of folders, a subweb would be a subfolder containing a stand-alone Web site.

Subwebs are commonly used to display information that requires special access permission or information that is pertinent to only one group of people. For example, The Garden Company might use a subweb so that members of a garden society that the company sponsors can access information about society activities through the company's public Web site.

In this exercise, you will use pages that have already been created and stored in a folder of the *GardenCo* Web site to create a subweb that is accessible only by employees.

USE the *GardenCo* Web site in the practice file folder for this topic. This practice file is located in the *My Documents\Microsoft Press\FrontPage 2003 SBS\Capabilities\Subweb* folder and can also be accessed by clicking *Start/All Programs/Microsoft Press/FrontPage 2003 Step By Step*.
OPEN the *GardenCo* Web site.

1   Switch to Navigation view, and familiarize yourself with the structure of the site. (Click the **Portrait/Landscape** button to change the orientation, if necessary.)

Portrait/
Landscape

Note that there are actually two separate Web sites here.

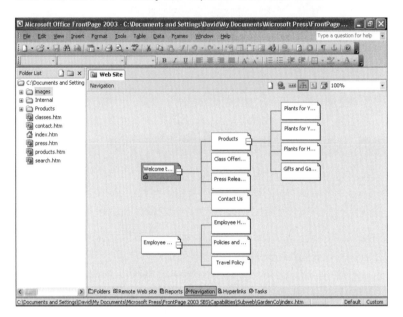

2 In the **Folder List**, expand the *Internal* folder.

The files that make up the Employee Information site are contained in this folder.

3 Right-click the **Internal** folder, and on the shortcut menu, click **Convert to Web**.

A warning appears.

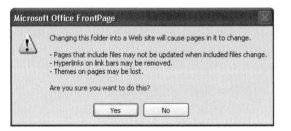

4 Click **Yes**.

FrontPage converts the Internal folder to a Web site that is a subweb of the GardenCo site. This is indicated in the Folder List by the Web site icon on the folder.

Important You can assign specific permissions that prevent unauthorized access to a subweb, or that allow one group of people to view the subweb but only certain people to administer or change it. These permissions are administered through The Web Site Administration page for the subweb.

5 Open Windows Explorer, and browse to the *My Documents\Microsoft Press \FrontPage 2003 SBS\Capabilities\Subweb\GardenCo\Internal* folder.

FrontPage modified the contents of this folder when you converted it to a subweb. The Internal folder icon has been replaced with a Web site icon here as well, but more importantly, the supporting structure for the new subweb is in place.

6   Close Windows Explorer to return to FrontPage.

The Employee Information Web site is no longer visible in Navigation view.

7   In the **Folder List**, double-click the **Internal** subweb folder.

The Employee Information Web site opens in its own instance of FrontPage. To convert this to a fully functioning site, you must set a home page and re-create the navigational structure.

CLOSE the second instance of FrontPage, and then close the GardenCo Web site.

Adding Links Between Web Pages

When you use a wizard to create a Web site, the site's navigation system is created for you. You can quickly move from page to page without needing to understand the underlying mechanisms that make this instant navigation possible. When you create a Web site by hand, however, you need to know how to create a system of navigation from the ground up. And if you ever need to make changes to an existing site—no matter how it was created—you need to understand the basics of navigation to avoid breaking things.

You are already familiar with the *hyperlinks* used to move among pages and items of information on a page. You might even have created a few. But with FrontPage, you can create much more sophisticated navigation systems that add both functionality and visual appeal to your pages.

The primary method of moving around a FrontPage-based Web site is by the one or more *link bars* that appear in a prominent location on each page. A well-designed link bar on the home page acts as a map to the site's major locations, providing easy access to all the important second-level pages that the site contains. These second-level pages in turn have link bars that can point back to the home page, to other second-level pages, and to their own third-level pages. (When a page has its own sub-pages, those pages are known as *child pages*.)

Another popular navigation technique is to use *image maps*, which are graphics that contain one or more *hot spots*. A hot spot is a specific region on a graphic that is associated with a hyperlink. When visitors click anywhere in this region, the hyperlink displays the target page or information. Image maps provide an attractive way to link from one central graphic (usually an overview graphic) to multiple individual pages, sites, or graphics. You can even configure a hotspot to generate an e-mail message when clicked.

In this exercise, you will create the navigation system for a Web site whose pages have already been created. You will use a link bar to navigate to the first-level and second-level files, and hyperlinks to navigate to the third-level files. You will also create an image map that links the company logo to the home page.

USE the *GardenCo* Web site in the practice file folder for this topic. This practice file is located in the *My Documents\Microsoft Press\FrontPage 2003 SBS\Capabilities\LinkPages* folder and can also be accessed by clicking *Start/All Programs/Microsoft Press/FrontPage 2003 Step By Step.*
OPEN the *GardenCo* Web site.

Portrait/
Landscape

1 Switch to Navigation view, and familiarize yourself with the structure of the site. (Click the **Portrait/Landscape** button to change the orientation, if necessary.)

2 Open **index.htm** in Design view.

3 Click the comment in the left shared border to select it, and press ⌦.

The contents area becomes very small.

4 On the **Insert** menu, click **Navigation**.

The Insert Web Component dialog box appears with Link Bars selected in the Component type list.

5 In the **Choose a bar type** box, click **Bar based on navigation structure**, and then click **Next**.

The Choose a bar style list includes about 50 choices, ranging from simple to fancy. Many of them correspond to the built-in FrontPage themes.

6 Scroll to the **Nature** bar style.

Nature bar style

Tip You can position the mouse pointer over any style to display its name in a ScreenTip.

7 Click the **Nature** bar style, and click **Next**.

8 In the **Choose an orientation** box, click **Vertical**.

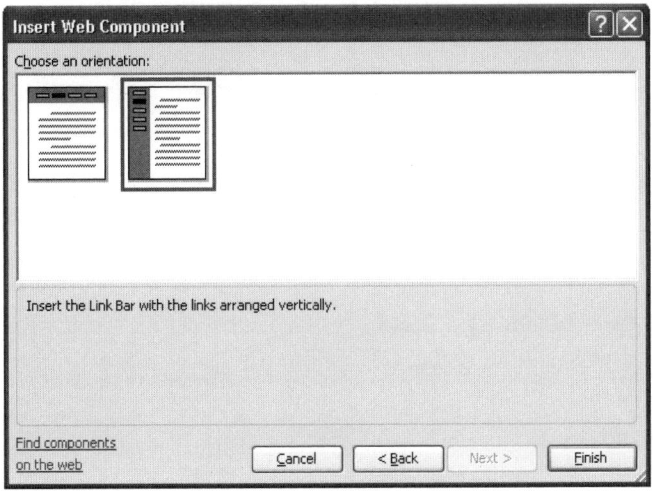

9 Click **Finish**.

The Link Bar Properties dialog box appears so you can select the pages to link to. You can select different options to see the selection reflected in the graphic in the upper-left corner of the General tab. Refer to the key under the graphic for the meaning of each page designation.

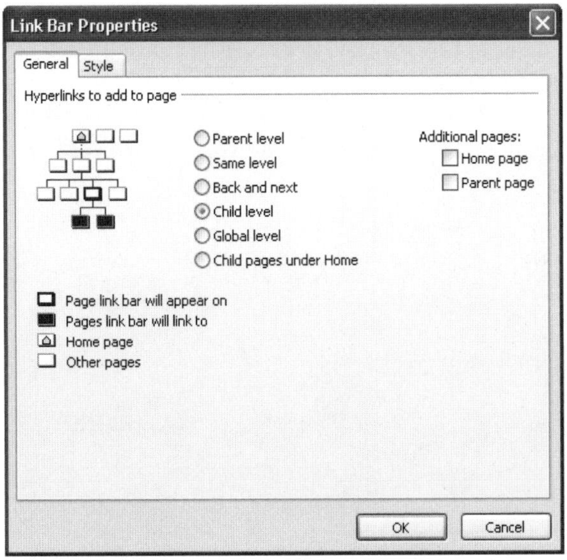

10 To set the link bar to show the home page and second-level pages, select the **Child pages under Home** option, select the **Home page** check box, and then click **OK**.

The vertical link bar is added to the home page.

11 Click the **Web Site** tab, make sure you're in Navigation view, and verify that the Products, Class Offerings, Press Releases, and Contact Us pages shown on the link bar are all child pages of the home page.

12 The search.htm file has not yet been added to Navigation view. Drag **search.htm** from the **Folder List** to the Navigation view window as a second-level page, after *Contact Us*.

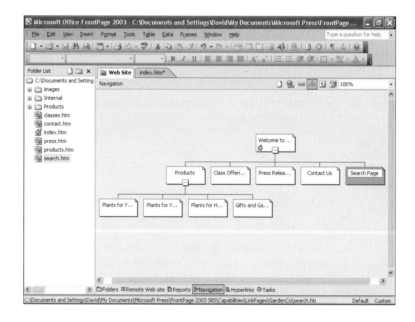

13 Click the **index.htm** tab to switch to Page view.

The Search Page has been added to the link bar.

14 Open **products.htm** in Design view.

The link bar is already present on this page, because it is located in a shared border.

15 In the **Folder List**, click the plus sign next to the **Products** folder to expand the folder.

There are four files in this folder, corresponding to the four subheadings of the Products page. Because the link bar displays only the first-level and second-level files of this Web site, the product detail pages are not currently accessible by means of the link bar. You need to add another type of navigational device—a simple hyperlink—to enable visitors to find these pages.

16 On the Products page, select the **Plants for your home!** heading.

17 On the Standard toolbar, click the **Insert Hyperlink** button. On the **Link to** bar, click **Existing File or Web Page** to list the pages of the Web site.

Insert Hyperlink

> **Tip**   If you prefer to use keyboard shortcuts to quickly access dialog boxes, press $\boxed{\text{Ctrl}}$+$\boxed{\text{K}}$ to open the Insert Hyperlink dialog box.

18 In the **Look in** box, click **Current Folder**, and then double-click the **Products** folder to open it.

19 In the file list, click **plants_home**, and click **OK** to insert a hyperlink from the selected heading to the file.

20 Repeat steps 16, 17, and 19 for the remaining three headings, linking them as indicated in the following table.

Heading	File
Plants for your garden!	plants_garden
Plants for hobbyists!	carnivorous_plants
Gifts and gadgets!	gifts

21 In the top shared border, click the company logo to select it.

22 If the Pictures toolbar is not visible, right-click the toolbar area, and click **Pictures** on the shortcut menu.

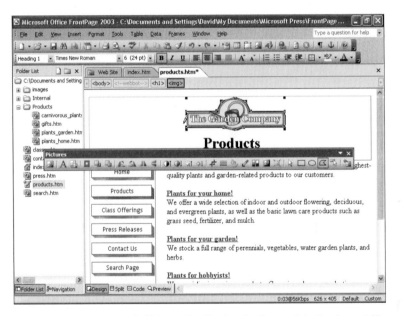

Polygonal Hotspot

23 On the Pictures toolbar, click the **Polygonal Hotspot** button.

24 Move the pencil pointer to one corner of The Garden Company's logo, and click to start a line. Then follow along the border of the logo, clicking each time you want to change the line's direction.

When you return to and click on the line's starting point, the Insert Hyperlink dialog box appears.

Up One Folder

25 In the **Insert Hyperlink** dialog box, click the **Up One Folder** button to browse to the main GardenCo site folder.

26 Click the **index** file, and then click **OK** to insert a hyperlink from the logo to the home page.

Highlight
Hotspots

Tip To identify the hotspots on a Web page, on the Pictures toolbar, click the Highlight Hotspots button.

To change a hotspot link, right-click the hotspot, and click Picture Hotspot Properties on the shortcut menu to open the Edit Hyperlink dialog box. Select a new target page, and then click OK.

Preview in
Browser

27 On the Standard toolbar, click the **Preview in Browser** button.

28 When prompted to save your changes, click **Yes**.

The Web page is displayed in your default Web browser.

29 Click the links on the links bar and on the Products page to move between pages. Then click the company logo to return to the home page.

CLOSE the Pictures toolbar, the browser, and the open GardenCo Web site, saving your changes if you want.

Adding Links Between Web Sites

You will often want to have links from your Web site to other Web sites, usually to point visitors to external information and resources. For example, the GardenCo Web site might contain links to garden society sites or to specific pages of the Web site maintained by the United States Department of Agriculture.

One of the great things about the Web is that it quickly builds communities around special interests. If you know of other compatible, but not competitive, Web sites in your general area of specialty, you can often arrange to put a link to those sites on your Web site in exchange for a similar link on their sites to yours. This is a great way to build traffic to your site and to get the word out about your products and services.

The most common method of linking to another Web site is to insert a hyperlink from the site name or description to the URL of the site's home page or a particular page file.

Important Other people's Web sites are beyond your control. Nothing makes your site look old and poorly maintained as much as inactive hyperlinks. Test any external links regularly to confirm that their target sites are still active and that they still display the information you think they do.

In this exercise, you will insert hyperlinks to a subweb and to an external Web site. You will then look at how FrontPage automatically recalculates links from your site to ensure that they are all working.

USE the *GardenCo* Web site in the practice file folder for this topic. This practice file is located in the *My Documents\Microsoft Press\FrontPage 2003 SBS\Capabilities\LinkSites* folder and can also be accessed by clicking *Start/All Programs/Microsoft Press/FrontPage 2003 Step By Step*.
OPEN the *GardenCo* Web site.

Portrait/
Landscape

1 Switch to Navigation view. If the entire site doesn't appear in the window, click the **Portrait/Landscape** button to change to Portrait mode.

Notice that the GardenCo Web site includes an Internal subweb, which is indicated in the Folder List by the Web site icon, and in Navigation view by its gray color.

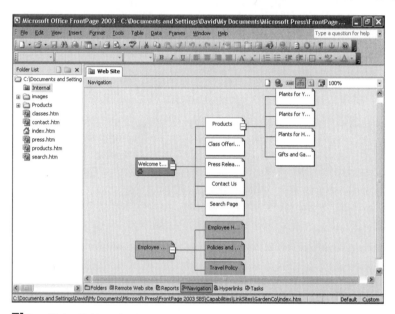

Toggle Pane

Tip If the Folder List is not already open, on the Standard toolbar, click the Toggle Pane button to open it.

2 In the **Folder List**, double-click **index.htm** to open that page in Design view.

3 In the left shared border of the page, click the link bar to select it, and then press `End` and `Enter` to insert a new, blank paragraph after the link bar.

4 Type Employees Only, and then select the text and format it to match the preceding buttons as follows:

Times New Roman
Font

■ In the **Font** drop-down list, click **Trebuchet MS**.

Center

■ Click the **Center** button to center the text within the shared border.

Decrease
Font Size

■ Click the **Decrease Font Size** button to match the font size used on the buttons.

B

Bold

5 To make the text stand out, click the **Bold** button.

6 On the **Format** menu, click **Paragraph**. Then in the **Spacing** area of the **Paragraph** dialog box, type **6** in the **Before** box and **3** in the **After** box, and click **OK**.

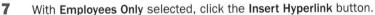

Insert
Hyperlink

7 With **Employees Only** selected, click the **Insert Hyperlink** button.

8 On the **Link to** bar, click **Existing File or Web Page**.

9 Double-click the **Internal** folder, and then double-click the **employee_info** file to insert a link from *Employees Only* to the home page of the subweb.

Preview in
Browser

10 On the Standard toolbar, click the **Preview in Browser** button, and save your changes when prompted.

11 When the Web site opens in your browser, click the **Employees Only** link to test it.

The home page of the Internal subweb appears in your browser.

12 Close the browser to return to FrontPage.

13 In the **Folder List**, expand the Products folder, and double-click **carnivorous_plants.htm** to open it in Design view.

14 Scroll to the bottom of the page.

Under Other Resources, two resources are listed along with their URLs.

Copy

15 Select **http://www.omnisterra.com/bot/cp_home.cgi** (the URL for the Carnivorous Plant Database), and on the Standard toolbar, click the **Copy** button to copy the URL to the Office Clipboard.

16   In the bulleted list, select the words *Carnivorous Plant Database*, and then click the **Insert Hyperlink** button.

17   In the **Insert Hyperlink** dialog box, click the **Address** box, and then press Ctrl+V to paste the copied URL into it.

18   Click **Target Frame** to open the **Target Frame** dialog box.

19   In the **Common targets** box, click **New Window**.

This tells FrontPage to configure the hyperlink to open the target page in a new window instead of replacing the content of the current window with the new content. The main reason for doing this is so that visitors don't lose track of your site while they go off on this side trip.

Tip   When you click New Window, the Target setting box is automatically filled in with the name *_blank*. The Target setting name is primarily used with frame-based sites, where each frame has a name, but you can also use this box to assign a name to a target browser window.

20   Select the **Set as page default** check box to indicate that any hyperlinks opened from this page should open in a new window.

21   Click **OK** to close the **Target Frame** dialog box, and then click **OK** to close the **Insert Hyperlink** dialog box and insert the hyperlink.

22   Repeat steps 15 through 17 to link the words *International Carnivorous Plant Society* to the accompanying URL (*http://www.carnivorousplants.org*).

Save

23 On the Standard toolbar, click the **Save** button to save your changes to the page, and then click the **Preview in Browser** button to open the page in your browser.

24 In the browser, click the **Carnivorous Plant Database** link.

The Carnivorous Plant Database Web site opens in a new browser window.

Troubleshooting You must have an Internet connection to complete this step.

25 Close the second instance of the browser window, and click the **International Carnivorous Plant Society** link.

The International Carnivorous Plant Society Web site opens in a separate browser window.

26 Close the browser to return to FrontPage.

27 Click the **Web Site** tab, and then switch to Hyperlinks view.

The active file, carnivorous_plants.htm, is shown at the center with all hyperlinks to and from the page radiating from it.

Troubleshooting If another file is shown at the center, in the Folder List, click the carnivorous_plants.htm file to move it to the center.

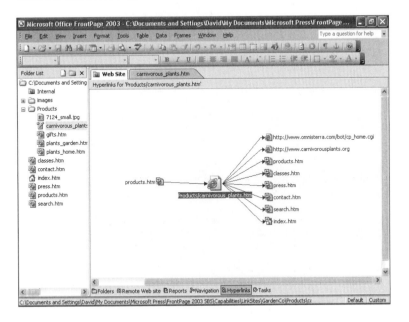

CLOSE the open *GardenCo* Web site.

Adding Ready-Made Components to a Web Page

In the old days, if you wanted to add fancy effects such as scrolling banners or functional elements such as hit counters to your Web site, you needed to be a programmer. These days, many types of elements are available as ready-made *Web components*. FrontPage provides the following Web components that you can simply drop into your Web pages to give your site a professional look and feel:

Component type	Effect
Dynamic Effects	Marquee
	Interactive Button
Web Search	Current Web
Spreadsheets and Charts	Office Spreadsheet
	Office Chart
	Office PivotTable
Hit Counter	Five styles to choose from
Photo Gallery	Horizontal Layout
	Vertical Layout
	Montage Layout
	Slideshow Layout
Included Content	Substitution
	Page
	Page Based On Schedule
	Picture Based On Schedule
	Page Banner
Link Bars	Bar with custom links
	Bar with back and next links
	Bar based on navigation structure
Table of Contents	For This Web Site
	Based on Page Category
Top 10 List	Visited Pages
	Referring Domains
	Referring URLs
	Search Strings
	Visiting Users
	Operating Systems
	Browser

Component type	Effect
List View	(available only for SharePoint team Web sites)
Document Library View	(available only for SharePoint team Web sites)
Expedia Components	Link to a map
	Static map
MSN Components	Search the Web with MSN
	Stock quote
MSNBC Components	Business Headlines
	Living and Travel Headlines
	News Headlines
	Sports Headlines
	Technology Headlines
	Weather Forecast
Advanced Controls	HTML
	Java Applet
	Plug-In
	Confirmation Field
	ActiveX Control
	Design-Time Control
	Movie in Flash Format

Important Most of the Web components available with FrontPage are simple to insert and use. However, some work only in SharePoint team Web sites, and others require that special controls be installed on your system before they can be used.

Some of these ready-made Web components are new in FrontPage 2003:

New in
Office 2003
Interactive
Buttons

■ Interactive Buttons: You can choose from over 220 styles and colors of buttons, each with a corresponding rollover effect. This is a simple way to add great-looking buttons without adding a link bar.

New in
Office 2003
Macromedia
Flash support

■ Movie in Flash Format: You can insert Macromedia Flash content on your Web page and control whether it plays once when a visitor opens the page, or loops continuously.

In this exercise, you will insert two of the more common Web components: a weather forecast and a hit counter. You will also add components that enable people to search both your site and the Web.

USE the *GardenCo* Web site in the practice file folder for this topic. This practice file is located in the *My Documents\Microsoft Press\FrontPage 2003 SBS\Capabilities\Components* folder and can also be accessed by clicking *Start/All Programs/Microsoft Press/FrontPage 2003 Step By Step*.
OPEN the GardenCo Web site.

1 Open the **index.htm** file in Design view.

2 Press Ctrl+End to position the insertion point at the end of the body of the page, and then press Enter to insert a new, blank paragraph.

3 Type How's the weather in our garden this week? and then press Enter.

Web Component

4 On the Standard toolbar, click the **Web Component** button to display the **Insert Web Component** dialog box.

Tip Take a few minutes to explore all the Web components that are available in this dialog box, making a note of any that you might want to try out on your own later.

5 In the **Component type** list, click **MSNBC Components**, in the **Choose a MSNBC component** box, click **Weather forecast from MSNBC**, and then click **Finish**.

6 In the **Weather forecast from MSNBC Properties** dialog box, type Seattle in the **Search for a city by name or U.S. ZIP code** box, and then click **Next**.

Troubleshooting You must have an Internet connection to complete this step.

Troubleshooting   If you see a message telling you that it might be possible for people to see information that you send over the Internet and asking if you want to continue, click Yes.

Seattle, WA appears below the box as the selected option.

7   Click **Finish** to close the dialog box and insert the weather forecast component.

A placeholder appears on your page.

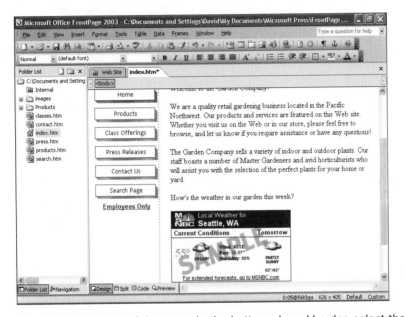

8   Scroll to the bottom of the page. In the bottom shared border, select the words *Insert hit counter here*, and type Thanks for visiting The Garden Company! You are visitor #, followed by a space.

Tip   Hit counters are generally inserted only on the home page of a site, not on every page. In the site used in this exercise, the bottom shared border is shown only on the index.htm page. If this border is shared across all pages, you will want to move the hit counter to the body of the page.

9   On the **Insert** menu, click **Web Component** to display the **Insert Web Component** dialog box.

10   In the **Component type** box, click **Hit Counter**. Then click the last style in the **Choose a counter style** box, and click **Finish**.

The Hit Counter Properties dialog box appears.

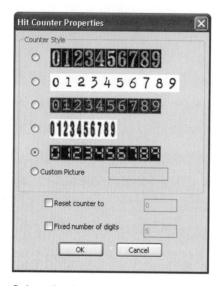

11 Select the **Reset counter to** check box, and enter 100 in the adjacent text box.

For a site that has been up and running for a while, you will want to guess the number of visitors who might already have visited your site and enter that number here.

12 Select the **Fixed number of digits** check box, and enter 4 in the adjacent box.

When the hit counter nears 1000, you can reset the number of digits to 5. In the meantime, four digits will give the illusion of a larger number (because the number of visitors is preceded by fewer zeros).

13 Click **OK** to close the dialog box and insert the hit counter.

14 On the Standard toolbar, click the **Save** button to save your changes.

Save

15 If FrontPage displays a message that you need to publish the site or preview it in a browser to see the hit counter, click **OK**.

Preview in
Browser

16 On the Standard toolbar, click the **Preview in Browser** button, and scroll to the bottom of the displayed page.

At the bottom of the page, you see a placeholder for the hit counter.

Important Hit counters work only on server-based Web sites stored on servers that have FrontPage Server Extensions or SharePoint Team Services installed. Disk-based Web sites don't display the hit counter graphic properly or count the visits, but you can check the placement on a disk-based Web site.

If your Internet connection is active, the weather component connects to the MSNBC Web site, retrieves current weather conditions for Seattle, and displays the information on your page.

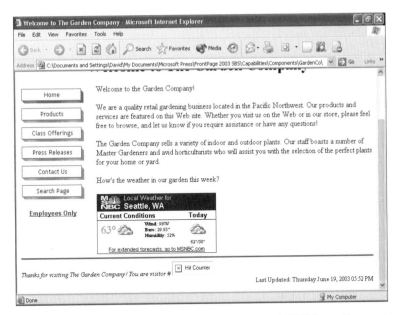

17   Click the extended forecast link to connect to the MSNBC weather page on the Web.

18   Close the browser to return to FrontPage.

19   Open the **search.htm** file in Design view.

20   Select the words *Insert search component here*, and click the **Web Component** button.

21   In the **Component type** box, click **Web Search**, and then click **Finish** to accept the *Current Web* option in the **Choose a type of search** box.

The Search Form Properties dialog box appears.

22 The Search Form Properties dialog box specifies the settings for the presentation of the search form and the search results.

23 Look at the information on both tabs of the dialog box, and then click **OK** to accept the default options.

24 Press ⌐Enter¬ to insert a new, blank paragraph after the search component. Type If you can't find it on our site, search the Web!, and press ⌐Enter¬.

25 Click the **Web Component** button to display the **Insert Web Component** dialog box.

26 In the **Component type** box, click **MSN Components**, and then click Finish to accept the *Search the Web with MSN* option.

FrontPage inserts the MSN Search component.

27 On the Standard toolbar, click the **Save** button, and then click the **Preview in Browser** button to test the search components.

Your page is displayed in the browser.

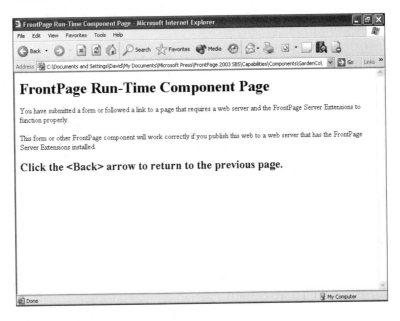

28 In the **Search for** box, type carnivorous, and click **Start Search** to start the search.

Because this site has not yet been published to a Web server, the search is unsuccessful.

29 Click the browser's **Back** button to return to the Search page.

30 In the **Search the Web for** box, type **carnivorous**, and click **Search** to start the search.

If your Internet connection is active, you are redirected to the MSN Search page, with the results of your search shown.

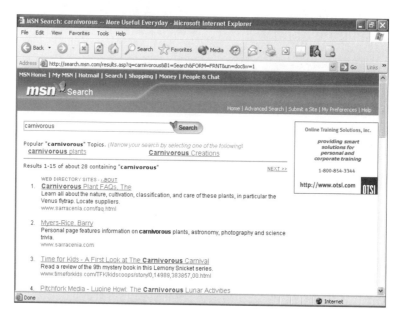

CLOSE the browser and the open *GardenCo* Web site, saving your changes if you want.

Adding Dynamic Effects and Behaviors to a Web Page

You can add a class of Web components called *dynamic effects* to your pages to create an illusion of movement. With a few simple commands, you can create elements that flash on and off, change when your visitor positions the mouse pointer over them, or scroll across the screen.

*New in
Office 2003*
Behaviors

Behaviors are a new feature of FrontPage 2003 that you use to insert professional scripting options on a Web page without doing any programming. These scripted behaviors include such things as changing the font, position, or border of a page element, moving to another page, playing a sound, displaying a message in a popup window, displaying text in the status bar, and exchanging images for other images. Depending on the tag element selected, these behaviors can occur when a page opens, when the visitor clicks or moves the mouse pointer over an element, when an error occurs, when a key is pressed, or when other events occur.

New in
Office 2003
Quick Tag
Selector

When applying behaviors to a Web page or Web page element, the new Quick Tag Selector is very useful. This toolbar is displayed at the top of each open page in Design view, Code view, and Split view. When you position the insertion point on the page, all the HTML tags that apply to that page are shown, in order, on the Quick Tag Selector. To select any element, simply click the corresponding tag.

In this exercise, you will insert a scrolling marquee on a Web page, and make a sound play each time a visitor loads a Web page.

USE the *GardenCo* Web site and the *tada* sound clip in the practice file folder for this topic. These practice files are located in the *My Documents\Microsoft Press\FrontPage 2003 SBS\Capabilities\Effects* folder and can also be accessed by clicking *Start/All Programs/Microsoft Press/FrontPage 2003 Step By Step.* OPEN the *GardenCo* Web site.

1 Open **classes.htm** in Design view.

Web
Component

2 With the insertion point at the beginning of the body of the page, on the Standard toolbar, click the **Web Component** button.

The Insert Web Component dialog box appears.

3 With *Dynamic Effects* selected in the **Component type** box and *Marquee* selected in the **Choose an effect** box, click **Finish**.

The Marquee Properties dialog box appears.

4 In the **Text** box, type Register Now for Upcoming Classes!.

5 Retain all the default settings, and click **OK**.

In Design view, your marquee has been inserted as a new line of text—not very exciting!

Show
Preview View

6 At the bottom of the Page view editing window, click the **Show Preview View** button.

The text scrolls across the top of the content pane from right to left, repeating continuously.

7 Switch back to Design view.

8 Right-click the marquee text, and click **Marquee Properties** on the shortcut menu.

The Marquee Properties dialog box appears.

9 In the **Behavior** area, select the **Alternate** option.

10 In the **Background color** drop-down list, click the **Green** square, and then click **OK**.

Bold   Italic

11 With the marquee text still selected, on the Formatting toolbar, click the **Bold** and **Italic** buttons.

Font Color

12 Click the down arrow to the right of the **Font Color** button, and click the **White** square in the **Standard Colors** area.

The marquee text reflects your changes.

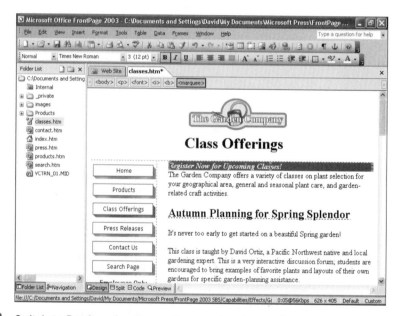

13 Switch to Preview view to see the results of your changes.

14 Open **press.htm** in the Page view editing window.

15 On the **Format** menu, click **Behaviors**.

The Behaviors task pane opens at the right side of the window. The Scripts On Tag area indicates the content on which the behavior will be performed.

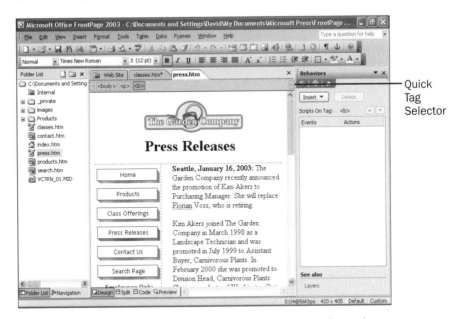

Quick Tag Selector

16 On the **Quick Tag Selector**, click the *<body>* tag to select the entire page.

The Scripts On Tag setting changes to reflect your selection.

17 On the **Behaviors** task pane, click the **Insert** button to display the list of behaviors.

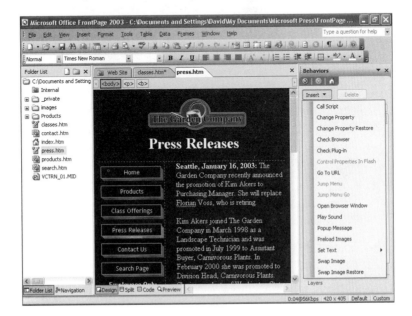

18 In the drop-down list, click **Play Sound**.

The Play Sound dialog box appears.

19 In the **Play Sound** box, type tada.wav, and then click **OK**.

The sound file is located in the GardenCo folder.

20 In the **Events** list, position the mouse pointer over the onload event, and click the down arrow that appears to the right.

FrontPage displays a list of events that pertain to the <body> tag. Read through the list and think about what each of these events is, and when it might occur.

21 Press [Esc] to close the events list and retain the onload setting.

The sound is now set to play when the Press Releases page loads.

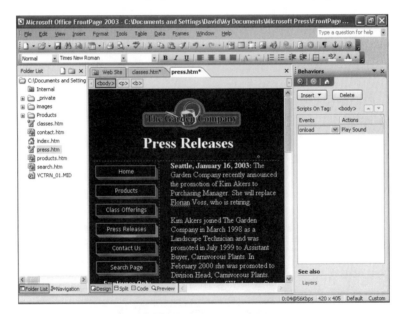

22 On the **File** menu, click **Save All** to save the open files.

23 Click the **Preview in Browser** button.

Preview in Browser

When the Press Releases page opens, the trumpet call sounds.

Troubleshooting You need to have an audio card and speakers installed on your computer to hear this sound.

24 On the link bar, click the **Class Offerings** link to see the marquee.

25 Return to the **Press Releases** page to hear the sound again.

CLOSE the browser and the *GardenCo* Web site. If you are not continuing on to the next chapter, quit FrontPage.

Key Points

- FrontPage can automate much of the process of creating a sophisticated navigation system for your Web site.

- Organizing the elements of a Web site into a logical set of folders makes it easier to identify the structure of the site.

- You can create a subweb (a Web site that is nested inside another Web site) inside your FrontPage-based Web site.

- You can add links to other pages of your FrontPage-based Web site, and add links from your Web site to other Web sites.

- You can easily add fancy effects such as scrolling banners or functional elements such as hit counters to your Web site.

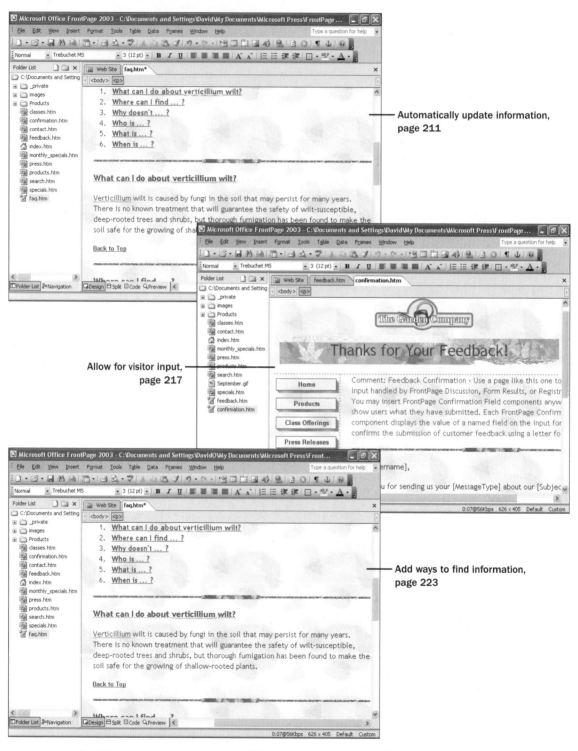

Automatically update information, page 211

Allow for visitor input, page 217

Add ways to find information, page 223

Chapter 8 at a Glance

Communicating with Your Visitors

In this chapter you will learn to:

✔ Automatically update information.

✔ Allow for visitor input.

✔ Add ways to find information.

Very few people create a Web site with the expectation that no one will ever see it. Web sites are designed to be published and viewed by other people. The number of visitors, or *hits*, a Web site receives is a common benchmark of its success. In fact, in the late 90s a lot of dot-com companies made money not by selling products or services, but by selling advertising space based on the number of visitors that passed through their sites. Assuming that you are interested in developing a loyal group of visitors who will associate your site positively with your company or organization, you need to spend some time thinking about how you will communicate with those visitors.

Communication is a two-way process: you give your visitors information, and if your Web site meets their needs, they give information back to you. You can attract repeat traffic by ensuring that your information is timely and easy to find. You can solicit information from your visitors by providing a simple mechanism for giving feedback.

In this chapter, you will first insert information that is to be displayed on a Web page for only one month. Then you will create a feedback form so that visitors can give you specific information you want, as well as suggestions and requests. Finally, you will look at a simple way to enable your visitors to search for information on your site.

See Also   Do you need only a quick refresher on the topics in this chapter? See the Quick Reference entries on pages xxxii–xxxiv.

Important   Before you can use the practice files in this chapter, you need to install them from the book's companion CD to their default location. See "Using the Book's CD-ROM" on page xiii for more information.

Automatically Updating Information

Microsoft Office FrontPage 2003 includes a set of Web components, called *Included Content components*, that you can use to create links to the text or graphics you want to display on a Web page, rather than inserting them directly. Why would you want to do that? Suppose The Garden Company frequently updates the document in which it maintains its calendar of classes and other events. If the company also displays the calendar information on its Web site, it has to update not only the document but also the Web page. By displaying the calendar document as included content, the company can maintain the calendar in just one place and know that the Web page always displays the most up-to-date information. Because included content is automatically updated whenever an included page or graphic is updated, a writer or graphic artist can make changes to Web site content without having to open or edit any Web pages. Included content simplifies the process of reusing content across multiple pages or sites.

FrontPage offers five types of included content:

- The *Substitution component* associates names, called *variables*, with text. In the Web Settings dialog box, you can assign a variable to a block of text and then insert the variable on a Web page instead of inserting the text itself. For example, you might assign a variable named Disclaimer to a block of text that consists of a 200-word legal disclaimer, and then insert the variable in a Substitution component on every page of your Web site. If you need to change the wording of the disclaimer, you change it once in the Web Settings dialog box, and it is instantly updated on every Web page.

- The *Page component* displays the contents of a file wherever it is inserted.

- The *Page Based On Schedule component* displays the contents of a file for a limited period of time. You can stipulate the beginning and end dates or times of the period during which the file should be displayed. You can also specify alternate content that should be displayed outside of the scheduled time period.

- The *Picture Based On Schedule component* has the same function as the Page Based On Schedule component, but it works with graphics files.

The *Page Banner component* is used to create a page title consisting of either text or graphics that appears on every page where the component is inserted. This is the equivalent of inserting a page banner from the Insert menu. In this exercise, you will include a page and a scheduled picture in an existing Web site.

USE the *GardenCo* Web site in the practice file folder for this topic. This practice file is located in the *My Documents\Microsoft Press\FrontPage 2003 SBS\Communicate\AutoUpdate* folder and can also be accessed by clicking *Start/All Programs/Microsoft Press/FrontPage 2003 Step By Step*.
BE SURE TO start FrontPage before beginning this exercise.
OPEN the *GardenCo* Web site.

1 In the **Folder List**, double-click **specials.htm** to open the file in the Page view editing window.

The page is currently empty.

2 On the **Insert** menu, click **Web Component** to open the **Insert Web Component** dialog box.

3 In the **Component type** list, click **Included Content**.

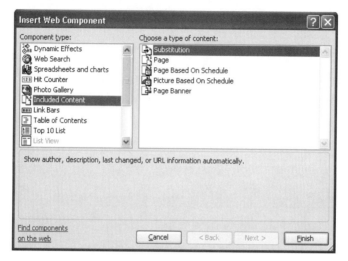

4 In the **Choose a type of content** list, click **Page**, and then click **Finish**.

The Include Page Properties dialog box appears.

5 Click the **Browse** button.

Tip Unlike most Browse dialog boxes, this one limits you to browsing the current Web site.

6 Click **monthly_specials.htm**, and then click **OK** to return to the **Include Page Properties** dialog box.

FrontPage enters the file name in the "Page to include" box.

7 Click **OK** to close the **Include Page Properties** dialog box and insert the included component.

The content of the Monthly Specials page is inserted in the Specials page.

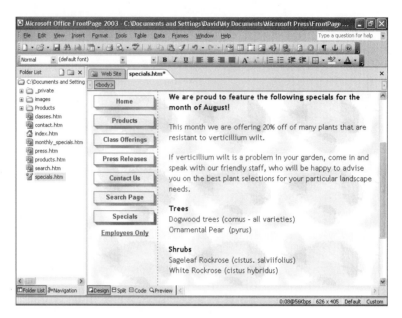

8   Click anywhere on the page.

The included content is selected as a single block and cannot be edited from the Specials page.

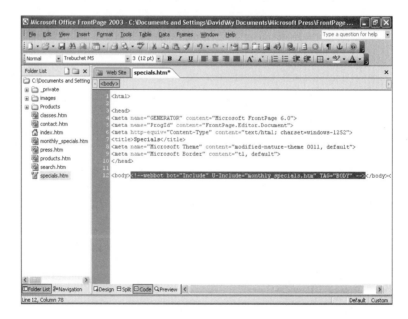

9   At the bottom of the Page view editing window, click the **Show Code View** button to view the HTML code that makes up this page.

Instead of displaying the page content within the <body> tags, you will see the following code, which specifies where the contents of the monthly_specials.htm file should be displayed.

Show
Design View

10 At the bottom of the Page view editing window, click the **Show Design View** button to return to Design view.

Save

11 On the Standard toolbar, click the **Save** button to save your change to the Specials page.

12 Open the **monthly_specials.htm** file in Design view.

The file itself contains no special formatting. The formatting of the host page is applied to the file content when it is displayed there.

13 Select the word **August**, and replace it with September.

14 Save the file and then click the **specials.htm** page tab to switch back to the Specials page.

The Specials page reflects the changes you made to the included content.

15 Open **products.htm** in Design view.

16 Press Ctrl+End to move the insertion point to the end of the page.

Web
Component

17 On the Standard toolbar, click the **Web Component** button to display the **Insert Web Component** dialog box.

18 In the **Component type** list, click **Included Content**.

19 In the **Choose a type of content** list, click **Picture Based On Schedule**, and then click **Finish**.

Scheduled Picture Properties ☒

Picture to display

During the scheduled time:

[   ] [Browse...]

Before and after the scheduled time (optional):

[   ] [Browse...]

Alternative text

During the scheduled time:

[   ]

Before and after the scheduled time:

[   ]

Starting: [2003 ▾] [Jul ▾] [02 ▾] [04:33:50 PM ▴▾]
Wednesday, July 02, 2003

Ending: [2003 ▾] [Aug ▾] [01 ▾] [04:33:50 PM ▴▾]
Friday, August 01, 2003

[OK] [Cancel]

The Scheduled Picture Properties dialog box appears.

20 In the **Picture to display** area at the top of the dialog box, click the **Browse** button to the right of the **During the scheduled time** box.

Again, browsing is limited to the current FrontPage-based Web site, but you can enter file paths and URLs manually in the URL box.

21 Double-click the **images** folder, click **september.bmp**, and then click **OK**.

This file is a picture that advertises The Garden Company's September Savings advertisement. The file's path is displayed in relation to your current location.

22 In the **Before and after the scheduled time** box, type images/everyday.bmp.

This file is the one you want to display at all times other than during the month of September.

23 To schedule the *september*.bmp file to appear for the entire month of September, set the **Starting** date and time to Sep 01 at 12:00:00 AM, and the **Ending** date and time to Sep 30 at 11:59:59 PM.

Tip To change the times, click each time segment and then click the up and down arrows to scroll that segment.

24 Click **OK** to insert the Web component.

If your system date is currently set to any date in September, you will see a graphic titled *September Savings*. Otherwise, you will see a graphic titled *We Love Great Prices!*

25 Click the **Scheduled Picture** component to select it, and then on the Standard toolbar, click the **Align Right** button.

Align Right

The graphic is aligned with the right edge of the page.

26 Right-click the component, and click **Scheduled Picture Properties** on the shortcut menu.

27 Set the **Starting** and **Ending** dates for today's date, leave the times as they are, and click **OK**.

The September Savings advertisement is now visible and will be displayed for the entire day.

CLOSE the *GardenCo* Web site, saving your changes if you want.

Allowing for Visitor Input

Providing visitors with information is probably the most common reason for building a Web site. But after you've attracted visitors' attention, you would be missing a prime opportunity if you did not also provide a mechanism for visitors to send information back to you.

The value of the information you receive from your visitors depends to a large extent on the way you present your request. Visitors are unlikely to fill out surveys and provide personal information that might be sold to mailing-list vendors without some significant reward. To get them to take the time and the risk of giving you information, you have to appeal to their best interests. They are more likely to be willing to help you gather information if they have an interest in your specialty area and if your Web site makes an effort to provide them with useful information that goes beyond your money-making endeavors.

Only you can decide how you want to present your request for information to your visitors, and only you can ensure that your Web site offers plenty of value in return. But FrontPage can help by providing ready-made templates for a feedback form and confirmation page that you can use as is or customize to meet your needs.

In this exercise, you will create and personalize a feedback form and its accompanying confirmation form for the GardenCo Web site, and you will position them appropriately within the site's navigational structure.

USE the *GardenCo* Web site in the practice file folder for this topic. This practice file is located in the *My Documents\Microsoft Press\FrontPage 2003 SBS\Communicate\VisitorInput* folder and can also be accessed by clicking *Start/All Programs/Microsoft Press/FrontPage 2003 Step By Step*.
OPEN the *GardenCo* Web site.

1 Familiarize yourself with the site in Navigation view. If the site doesn't fit on your screen, change the zoom level or switch to Portrait orientation.

2 On the **File** menu, click **New**.

The New task pane appears.

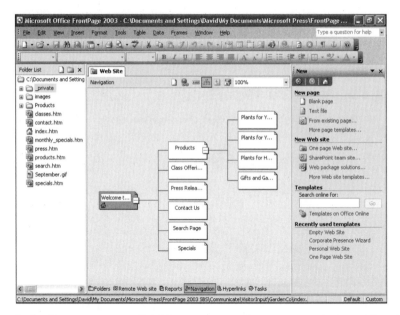

3 In the **New page** area, click **More page templates** to open the **Page Templates** dialog box.

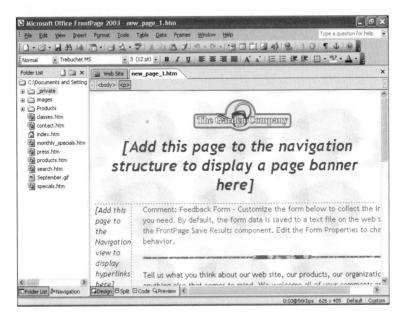

4 On the **General** tab, click **Feedback Form**, and then click **OK**.

FrontPage creates a new page containing a general feedback form. Because the page hasn't yet been added to the navigation structure of the site, the page banner and link bar are not operational.

Save

5 On the Standard toolbar, click the **Save** button to display the **Save As** dialog box.

6 In the **File name** box, type feedback.

7 Click the **Change title** button. In the **Set Page Title** dialog box, change the page title to **Feedback**.

8 Click **OK** to close the **Set Page Title** dialog box, and then click **Save** to close the **Save As** dialog box and save your file.

The file appears in the Folder List.

9 Click the **Web Site** tab to return to Navigation view.

10 Drag the **feedback.htm** file from the **Folder List** to the navigation structure at the same level as the home page.

In this position, the feedback form is not a child page of any other page, and will not show up on the current navigation link bars.

11 Click the **feedback.htm** page tab to return to Design view.

The page title and navigation link bars are now shown correctly on the Feedback page.

12   Review the content of the Feedback page, and then near the middle of the page, double-click the box that is currently set to **Web Site**.

The Drop-Down Box Properties dialog box appears.

13   Click the **Add** button.

14   In the **Add Choice** dialog box, type choose one... in the **Choice** box.

15   In the **Initial state** area, select the **Selected** option, and then click **OK**.

Your new entry is added to the Choice list in the Drop-Down Box Properties dialog box.

16   Click **choose one...** in the list, and then click the **Move Up** button until it is the first choice.

17   Use the **Move Up** and **Move Down** buttons to arrange the other items on the list in alphabetical order, with the exception of the **(Other)** choice, which should remain last.

18   Click the **Validate** button.

19   In the **Drop-Down Box Validation** dialog box, select the **Disallow first choice** check box to indicate that the form cannot be submitted with **choose one...** selected. Then click **OK**.

20   Click **OK** again to close the **Drop-Down Box Properties** dialog box, and then click the **Show Preview View** button to preview the page.

Q Preview
Show
Preview View

21   Scroll down to the drop-down box, and then click the down arrow to display the list of choices and view the results of your work.

22 Return to Design view, and save the page.

23 On the **View** menu, click **Task Pane** to open the **New** task pane.

24 In the **New page** area, click **More page templates** to open the **Page Templates** dialog box.

25 On the **General** tab, click **Confirmation Form**, and then click **OK**.

FrontPage creates a standard confirmation form. Visitors will see this acknowledgement after submitting their feedback forms. Information such as the name and contact information of the person submitting the feedback is pulled from the feedback form to this page.

26 Save the page as confirmation, with a page title of Thanks for Your Feedback!

27 Click the **Web Site** tab to switch to Navigation view, and drag the confirmation page to the navigation structure at the same level as the Feedback page.

28 Click the **confirmation.htm** page tab to return to Design view to see the results.

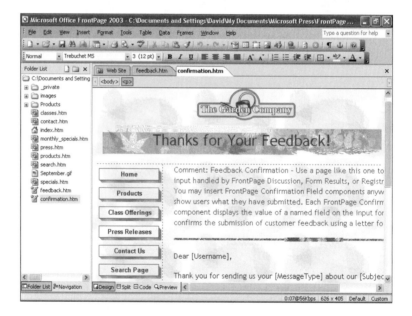

CLOSE the *GardenCo* Web site.

Adding Ways to Find Information

Visitors will come to your Web site for many reasons, but the most common is to search for information. A good Web site presents pertinent information on each page in a concise, readable, organized format. Most sites follow a basic structure in the presentation of general information, and many include a specific page that addresses the questions that are most often asked by visitors. The information on this page can cover all aspects of a business or organization, and this page is often an opportunity to present information that doesn't fit elsewhere.

To simplify the process of finding information on a Web site, especially on a large site consisting of many pages or several levels of pages, it is a good idea to provide a search page through which visitors can locate specific information. FrontPage includes two simple methods of incorporating site search functionality into your Web site: the Current Web Search component and the Search Page template.

In this exercise, you will create freestanding Frequently Asked Questions and Search pages using page templates included with FrontPage. You will experiment with personalizing the template's text, and you will also replace an existing file within the navigational structure of a FrontPage-based Web site.

USE the *GardenCo* Web site in the practice file folder for this topic. This practice file is located in the
My Documents\Microsoft Press\FrontPage 2003 SBS\Communicate\FindInfo folder and can also be
accessed by clicking *Start/All Programs/Microsoft Press/FrontPage 2003 Step By Step.*
BE SURE TO start FrontPage before beginning this exercise.
OPEN the *GardenCo* Web site.

Portrait/
Landscape

1 Switch to Navigation view, and if the entire site is not visible on your screen, click the **Portrait/Landscape** button to switch to Portrait orientation.

2 Open the **New** task pane.

3 In the **New page** area, click **More page templates** to open the **Page Templates** dialog box.

4 Click **Frequently Asked Questions**, and then click **OK** to generate the new page.

5 On the **File** menu, click **Save As**.

6 In the **Save As** dialog box, in the **File name** box, type faq.

7 Click **Change title**, change the page title to Common Questions, and click **OK** to close the dialog box.

8 Click **Save** to apply your changes.

9 Click the **Web Site** tab to return to Navigation view.

10 Drag the **faq.htm** file from the **Folder List** to the navigation structure, as a child page of the existing search page.

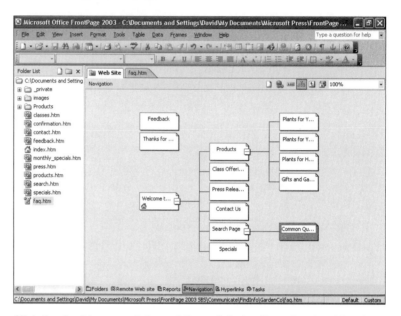

Show
Preview View

11 Click the **faq.htm** page tab, and then click the **Show Preview View** button to preview the page.

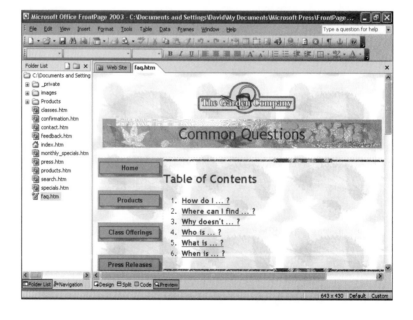

12 Return to Design view. Scroll down, select the phrase *How do I...?*, and then type **What can I do about verticillium wilt?**

You have replaced the first question. Now you need to replace the bookmarked answer. This is one of the few cases in FrontPage in which you will want to go behind the scenes and work in the HTML code. This is because the questions and answers are linked with bookmarks, and it can be difficult to replace bookmarked text in Design view without losing the code. Also, the template page was generated with a series of named bookmarks that will not correspond to your new questions.

☐ Split
Show
Split View

13 At the bottom of the Page view editing window, click the **Show Split View** button to simultaneously view the page and the underlying HTML code.

14 Scroll one-third of the way down the code pane so you can see both the questions and the answers.

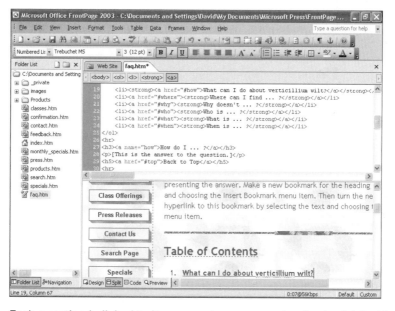

Each question is linked to its answer by an *anchor* tag (<a href>) that jumps to an inserted bookmark tag (<a name>). The question you just replaced is coded like this:

```
<a href="#how">What can I do about verticillium wilt?</a>
```

The number sign (#) indicates that the anchor tag is linked to a bookmark, rather than to a file. The text following the number sign is the bookmark that identifies the corresponding answer. The beginning of the answer is coded like this:

```
<a name="how">How do I ... ?</a>
```

The FrontPage-generated bookmarks reflect the placeholder questions. When you update the questions, the bookmarks no longer reflect the text of the questions, even though they still link the questions to their answers.

Tip   You can leave the bookmarks as they are, update the bookmarks to reflect the new questions, or use an alternative naming convention, such as numbers, dates, keywords, department codes, author initials, or any other combination of characters (without spaces). Some Web designers are uncomfortable using numbered bookmarks because they feel constrained to present the questions in order. However, the questions and answers do not have to appear in the same order; each question is linked to its matching answer as long as the bookmarks match.

Copy

15   In the code pane, select **What can I do about verticillium wilt?** (the new question), and on the Standard toolbar, click the **Copy** button to copy the phrase to the Office Clipboard.

Paste

16   In the code pane, select **How do I ... ?** (the linked answer), and on the Standard toolbar, click **Paste** to replace it with the new question.

Tip   To avoid errors, it is always best to cut or copy and paste text such as bookmarks rather than retype them.

17   In the bookmarks for both the question and the answer, select *how*, and replace it with `verticillium_wilt`.

The text of the bookmark now corresponds to the question.

18   Return to Design view, and select *[This is the answer to the question.]* (the bracketed phrase in the first answer block).

19   Type the following to replace the selected text:

Verticillium wilt is caused by fungi in the soil that may persist for many years. There is no known treatment that will guarantee the safety of wilt-susceptible, deep-rooted trees and shrubs, but thorough fumigation has been found to make the soil safe for the growing of shallow-rooted plants.

If you want, you can complete this Frequently Asked Questions page by replacing the FrontPage-generated questions, answers, and bookmarks with your own.

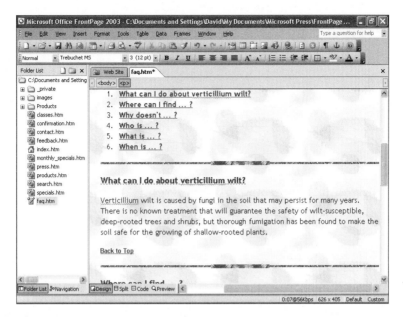

Tip   To include more questions and answers than the six included in the page template, copy and paste an existing question and answer and customize the copy. To include fewer questions and answers, simply delete the unused items.

20   Open the **New** task pane, and in the **New page** area, click **More page templates** to open the **Page Templates** dialog box.

21   On the **General** tab, click **Search Page**, and then click **OK**.

The Search Page template creates a freestanding page from which users can search for keywords across all the documents in a Web site using *Boolean queries*.

22   On the **File** menu, click **Save As** to open the **Save As** dialog box.

23   In the file list, double-click **search**.

A message box warns you that the file already exists.

24   Click **Yes** to replace the existing page.

Because you saved the file by overwriting an existing file, the new page inherited the old file's page title and location in the navigational structure of the Web site.

25   On the **View** menu, click **Refresh** to refresh the page title and link bar.

Your visitors can now search the contents of your Web site.

CLOSE the *GardenCo* Web site, saving your changes if you want. If you are not continuing on to the next chapter, quit FrontPage.

Office Proofing Tools

Common to all the Microsoft Office System 2003 applications are the proofing tools—including spelling and grammar checkers, thesauruses, and AutoCorrect lists—that help you create and edit Office documents. These tools are especially helpful when you are entering large amounts of text. In FrontPage, the Spelling and Thesaurus commands can be run individually from the Tools menu, or you can configure FrontPage to check your spelling automatically.

To turn the automatic spell-checking feature on or off:

1   On the **Tools** menu, click **Page Options**.

2   In the **Page Options** dialog box, on the **General** tab, select or clear the **Check spelling as you type** check box, and then click **OK**.

When automatic spell checking is turned on, words that don't appear in the Office dictionary are underlined with wavy red lines. Right-clicking a word flagged in this way presents a list of replacement suggestions, as well as the options to ignore the word or add it to the dictionary. Similarly, grammatically incorrect phrases are underlined with a wavy green line, and replacement suggestions are presented on the shortcut menu.

In Page view, the spelling and grammar tools are available only in Design view and Split view, and not in Code view or Preview view.

The different language versions of Office come with the proofing tools that are most likely to be used in those languages. For example, the English version of The Microsoft Office System includes proofing tools for the English, Spanish, and French languages. If you require a broader selection of language resources, you can install the Microsoft Office 2003 Proofing Tools add-in, which contains resources for over 30 languages.

For more information about proofing tools, see the Microsoft Office Web site at *office.microsoft.com*.

Key Points

■ Using Included Content components simplifies the process of reusing content across multiple pages or sites.

■ You can provide pages that invite your Web site visitors to give you feedback about your Web site.

■ Visitors to your Web site are often looking for specific information. It is a good idea to provide a search page or search engine to assist them in finding what they are looking for.

■ A Frequently Asked Questions page is a good way of answering common questions your visitors might have, and other questions they haven't yet thought of!

Use a Web site to track a project, page 232

Use a Web site to discuss a topic, page 236

Create a SharePoint team Web site, page 245

Customize a SharePoint team Web site, page 248

Maintain the security of Web site files, page 252

Chapter 9 at a Glance

9 Creating a Web Site to Support Team Projects

In this chapter you will learn to:

✔ Use a Web site to track a project.

✔ Use a Web site to discuss a topic.

✔ Create a SharePoint team Web site.

✔ Customize a SharePoint team Web site.

✔ Maintain the security of Web site files.

These days, very few people work in isolation. The ability to work in *teams* so that whatever needs to get accomplished is done on time and on budget is a valued skill. To facilitate team *collaboration*, Microsoft Office FrontPage 2003 includes a number of templates to help you create Web sites that keep everyone informed, facilitate information sharing, and include a central repository for all the information people need to do their jobs successfully.

Important   All the sites discussed in this chapter are server-based. For them to be accessible to a team of people, they must be hosted on a Web server running Microsoft Windows NT 4 or later and the FrontPage Server Extensions or Windows SharePoint Services. For more information, search for the specific type of site in the Microsoft Office FrontPage Help file.

This chapter shows you how to create a Project Web site, a Discussion Web site, and a SharePoint team Web site. It offers insights into how you might use these Web sites to support the work of your company. For those times when the focus of a team is the creation of a Web site, the chapter also shows you how to use FrontPage's *source control* feature to prevent more than one person from working on the same file at the same time.

See Also   Do you need only a quick refresher on the topics in this chapter? See the Quick Reference entries on pages xxxiv–xxxv.

Important   Before you can use the practice files in this chapter, you need to install them from the book's companion CD to their default location. See "Using the Book's CD-ROM" on page xiii for more information.

Using a Web Site to Track a Project

One of the hardest parts of project management is making sure that at any given point in time, everyone knows the project's goals, schedule, and status. It is also important for everyone to be kept informed about known problems and their solutions.

For example, suppose The Garden Company has invested a lot of money to register as an exhibitor at the annual Pacific Northwest Flower and Garden Show. The Garden Company's staff members need to design the company's exhibit, determine and obtain the plants and accessories for the exhibit, and work out the logistics of shipping soil and plants and keeping the plants alive for the five days of the show.

The FrontPage Project Web Site template can help you to quickly build a Web site to track such a project. When hosted on an *intranet*, the Web site serves as a central location for project management and helps everyone involved to see at a glance where the project stands.

In addition to the home page, where the overall project, recent updates, and key milestones are outlined, a FrontPage Project Web site contains six *second-level* pages:

- The *Members* page lists all the project team members. Members' names are linked to a description area, which can include personal captions, photographs, job titles, and contact information.

- The *Schedule* page lists the full timeline of project milestones and includes space to talk about upcoming tasks.

- The *Archive* page contains links to archived documents that team members or other interested parties might want to access.

- The *Search* page contains a basic site search feature, created using one of the ready-made FrontPage Web components.

See Also   For more information about Web components, refer to "Adding Ready-Made Components to a Web Page" in Chapter 7, "Enhancing the Capabilities of Your Web Site."

- The *Discussions* page contains links to any public project discussions that might be available to this project team. These discussions are hosted in discussion Web sites that are created with another of FrontPage's templates.

- The *Contact Information* page contains contact information for this specific project.

In this exercise, you will use the Project Web Site template to create a new project-management Web site that you can customize to fit the needs of The Garden Company.

BE SURE TO start FrontPage before beginning this exercise.

1 If the **New** task pane is not open, on the **File** menu, click **New**.

2 In the **New Web site** area, click **More Web site templates** to open the **Web Site Templates** dialog box.

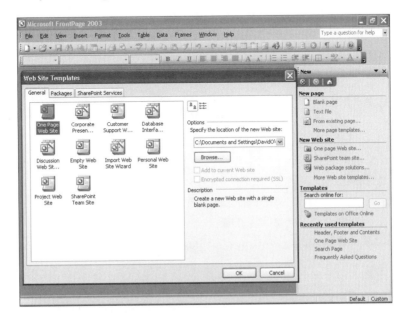

3 On the **General** tab, click (don't double-click) the **Project Web Site** icon.

4 In the **Options** area, click the **Browse** button.

The New Web Site Location dialog box appears.

5 On the **Places** bar, click **My Documents**.

6 In the folder list, double-click **My Web Sites**.

7 On the toolbar, click the **Create New Folder** button.

Create
New Folder

8 In the **New Folder** dialog box, type **ProjectWeb**, and then click **OK**.

9 In the **New Web Site Location** dialog box, click **Open**.

The full path to the location you browsed to is entered in the "Specify the location of the new Web site" box.

10 In the **Web Site Templates** dialog box, click **OK**.

The new project Web site is created at the specified location. In Folders view, you can see the extensive list of files that FrontPage creates for this type of Web site.

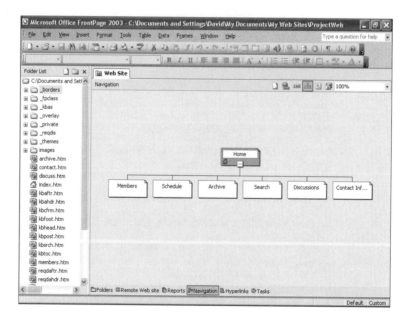

11 Scroll to the bottom of the list.

The Title column indicates that many of the files are merely headers and footers, and not actual Web pages.

12 To better understand the actual structure of the Web site, click the **Navigation View** button.

The best way to experience a site of this size is to view it as visitors to the site will.

Preview in
Browser

13 On the Standard toolbar, click the **Preview in Browser** button.

Troubleshooting If the Preview in Browser button isn't active, click the Home page box in Navigation view, and then click the Preview in Browser button.

The project Web site opens.

Maximize

14 If the browser window is not already maximized, on the browser window title bar, click the **Maximize** button for a better view of the home page.

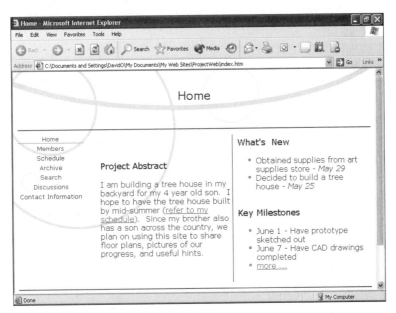

15 Click the links on the navigation link bar to browse through the site, and notice the pages and text FrontPage has supplied.

16 Close the browser window to return to FrontPage.

17 To give this site the same look as The Garden Company's main Web site, on the **Format** menu, click **Theme** to display the **Theme** task pane.

18 In the **Select a theme** box, scroll down to the **Nature** theme. Hold the mouse pointer over the theme preview, click the down arrow that appears, and then click **Apply as default theme**.

A message box appears, warning you that previous formatting will be overwritten.

19 Click **Yes** to apply the Nature theme to the site.

20 To see the results of your change, click the **Preview in Browser** button. When you finish previewing the site, close the browser window.

21 On the **File** menu, click **Close Site** to close the open Web site.

Using a Web Site to Discuss a Topic

One of the advantages of the World Wide Web is that it enables people who might otherwise never interact to form a virtual community around a topic of interest. Whether the topic is general enough to be of public interest or specific to a particular project or a particular team, FrontPage can help you create a forum that facilitates communication.

Using the FrontPage Discussion Web Site template, you can create a Web site where people communicate by submitting, or *posting*, messages or articles. Discussion Web sites include the following features:

- The *Contents* page lists all the articles submitted to date.

- The *Welcome* page includes an overview of the site and how it works.

■ The *Post Article* form is a required form that visitors can use to post articles consisting of a subject line, author line, and comments.

■ The *Search* form is a standard site search form that visitors can use to search the articles posted to the current discussion.

■ The *Confirmation* page, which appears after a visitor submits an article, prompts the visitor to refresh the main page to see the submission.

In this exercise, you will use a FrontPage Web site template to create a new discussion Web site. You will then publish the Discussion Web site to a Web server to test it.

Important   To complete this exercise, you need access to a Web server running Windows SharePoint Services. Note the name of the Web server before beginning this exercise.

BE SURE TO start FrontPage before beginning this exercise.

1 In the open task pane, click the down arrow to the right of the task pane name, and then click **New**.

> **Tip**   If the task pane is not already open, on the View menu, click Task Pane.

2 In the **New Web site** area, click **More Web site templates** to open the **Web Site Templates** dialog box.

3 On the **General** tab, click the **Discussion Web Site Wizard** icon.

4 In the **Options** area, click the **Browse** button.

The New Web Site Location dialog box appears.

5 On the **Places** bar, click **My Documents**.

6 In the folder list, double-click **My Web Sites**.

7 On the toolbar, click the **Create New Folder** button.

Create
New Folder

8 In the **New Folder** dialog box, type DiscussionWeb, and then click **OK**.

9 In the **New Web Site Location** dialog box, click **Open**.

The full path to the location you browsed to is entered in the "Specify the location of the new Web site" box.

10 In the **Web Site Templates** dialog box, click **OK**.

The Discussion Web Site Wizard starts.

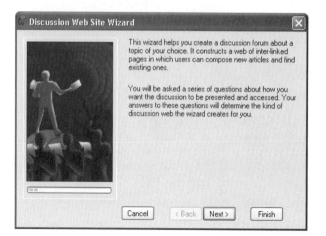

11 Click **Next**.

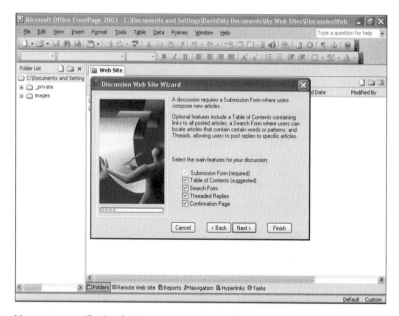

You can specify the features you want to have available in your discussion Web.

12 Leave all the check boxes selected, and click **Next**.

You need to supply a title for the discussion and the name of the discussion folder. A discussion can be created for a very specific issue (such as *Indigestion Problems of Venus Flytraps*) or a very general subject (such as *Herbs*).

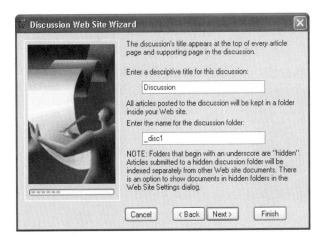

13 For the purposes of this exercise, type **Soil-Borne Diseases** as the discussion title, type `disc_sbd` as the folder name, and then click **Next**.

Troubleshooting Discussion folders whose names begin with an underscore (_) character will be hidden in the Folder List and will be visible only when you select the option to show documents in hidden folders in the Web Settings dialog box.

You can choose from these submission form input fields:

14 For now, accept the default selection of **Subject, Comments** by clicking **Next**.

The choices you make here are not permanent; you can update them later.

The next page of the wizard appears, including the option to allow access to the discussion Web site only to registered users.

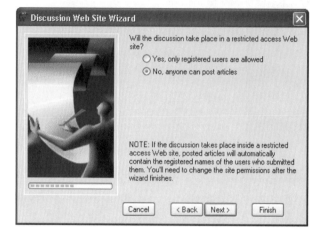

15 Because this discussion will take place on your public Web site, accept the default selection of **No, anyone can post articles** by clicking **Next**.

You are prompted to choose the sort order of articles as they are posted in the table of contents.

You see this page only if you chose to include a table of contents in this discussion Web site.

16 To make the most recent information available first, select the **Newest to oldest option**, and then click **Next**.

FrontPage can create a welcome page with links to your discussion site, or you can incorporate the table of contents into the welcome page. (Again, you see this page only if you chose to include a table of contents.)

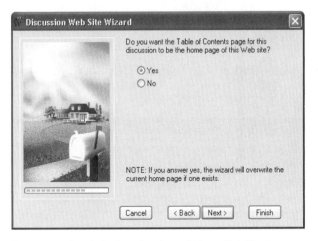

17 To accept the default selection of **Yes**, click **Next**.

You can direct the Search form to report a variety of data when locating documents.

18 Select the **Subject, Size, Date, Score** option, and then click **Next**.

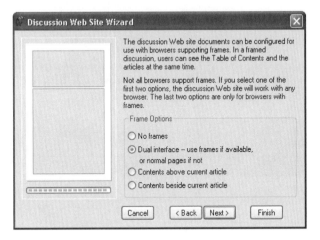

You can select options for the way the discussion Web site frames are presented.

If you know that your visitors will be working in an environment that does not support frames—for example, on a corporate server that uses Netscape Navigator 3.0—you should select the **No frames** option.

19 Because your discussion group will be Internet-based and open to all users, accept the default **Dual interface – use frames if available, or normal pages if not** option by clicking **Next**.

FrontPage generates all the necessary files for the discussion Web site.

20 On the wizard's final page, click **Finish**.

21 On the **File** menu, click **Publish Site**.

The Remote Web Site Properties dialog box appears.

22 In the **Remote Web site location** box, type http://<server>/Discussion, substituting the name of your Web server for <*server*>, and then click **OK**.

23 When prompted to create a new Web site at the specified location, click **Yes**.

The files and folders to be published are indicated in the Local Web site pane.

Right-facing blue arrows indicate files to be
published from the local site to the remote site.

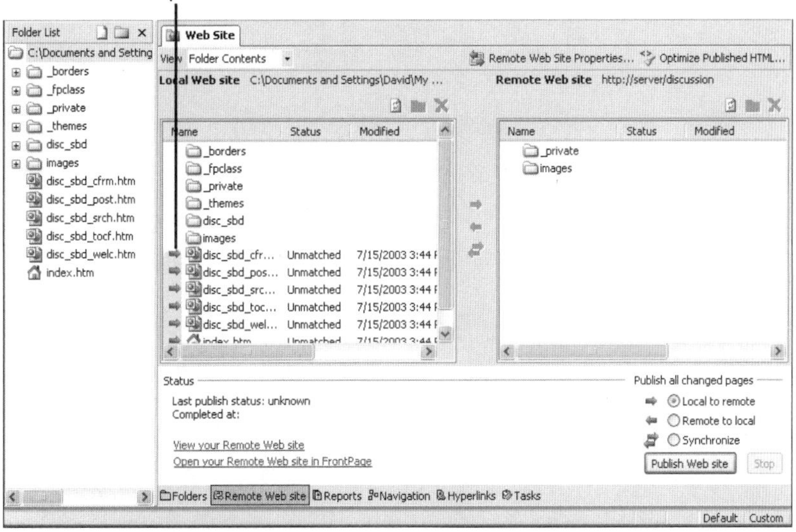

24 Click the **Publish Web site** button to complete the publication of the site.

When the process is finished, a message appears below the Local Web site pane.

Published files

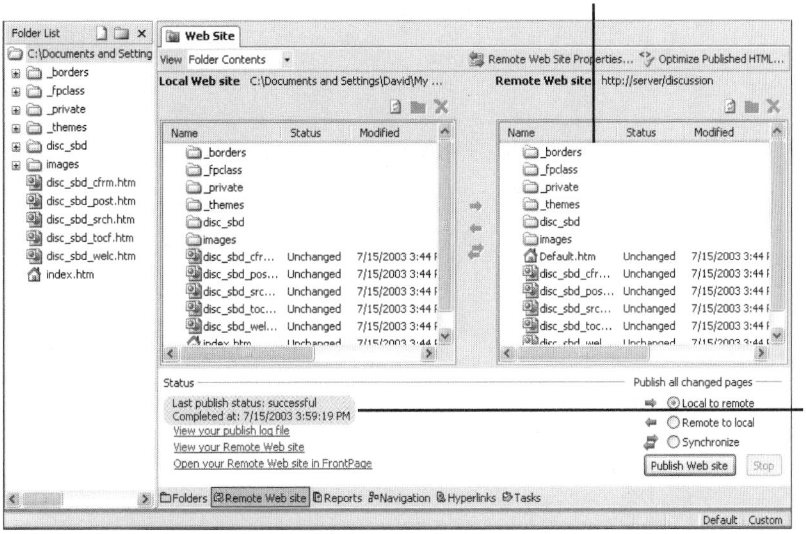

25   Click the **View your Remote Web site** link to view your published Web site.

The discussion Web site opens in your browser at the specified location.

26   On the welcome page, click **Post a new article** to open the **Submission** form.

27   In the **Subject** box, type Test message, in the **From** box, type your name, and in the **Comments** box, type This is a message to test the discussion Web site.

28   Click the **Post Article** button.

Depending on your Web server's security settings, you might see a warning about sending information to your local intranet or the Internet.

29   If you see the warning, click **In the future, do not show this message**, and then click **Yes** to continue.

The Confirmation page is displayed.

30   Click **refresh the main page** to see your message.

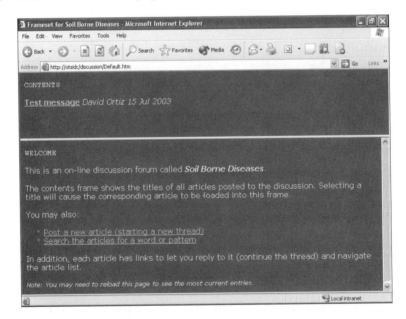

CLOSE the Web browser window to return to FrontPage, and then close the *Discussion* Web site.

Creating a SharePoint Team Web Site

An exciting feature in FrontPage is the ability to quickly create *SharePoint team Web sites*, which are full-scale team *collaboration sites*. The default SharePoint team Web site consists of the following pages:

■ The *Home* page features announcements and events, links to favorite sites, and Quick Launch links to other team Web site elements. You can easily add new announcements, events, and links to this page.

■ The *Documents and Lists* page includes links to libraries of shared documents or pictures, and to five ready-made lists: Announcements, Contacts, Events, Links, and Tasks. Lists can be included on the home page, and their information can be sorted in a variety of ways to find items quickly. You can create new document libraries, picture libraries, and lists from this page.

■ The *Create Page* page makes it easy to create new team Web site elements, including custom lists, document libraries, surveys, discussion boards, links lists, announcements lists, contacts lists, events lists, and tasks lists. You can also create new lists based on information that you import from a spreadsheet.

■ The *Site Settings* page is where the Web site administrator can set the name and description of the site, change the permissions that control who can use it, edit and view user information, customize the site content, or create new content.

Depending on your installation, FrontPage may provide additional SharePoint Services site templates on the SharePoint Services tab of the Web Site Templates dialog box.

The Microsoft Office FrontPage online Help file includes extensive information and instructions for creating and using SharePoint team Web sites.

In this exercise, you will create a SharePoint team Web site by using a simple template.

Important   To complete this exercise, you need access to a Web server running Windows SharePoint Services. Note the name of the Web server before beginning this exercise.

BE SURE TO start FrontPage before beginning this exercise.

Create a new
normal page

1   On the Standard toolbar, click the down arrow to the right of the **Create a new normal page** button to expand the list of elements that can be created.

2   In the drop-down list, click **Web Site** to open the **Web Site Templates** dialog box.

3   On the **General** tab, click (don't double-click) the **SharePoint Team Site** icon.

4   In the **Specify the location of the new Web site** box, type http://<server>/TeamSite, where <server> is the name of your Web server. Then click **OK**.

FrontPage creates a new team Web site at the specified location. This process takes significantly longer than the creation of other FrontPage- created Web sites.

5   When the Web site creation process is complete, expand the folders in the **Folder List** to see all the files.

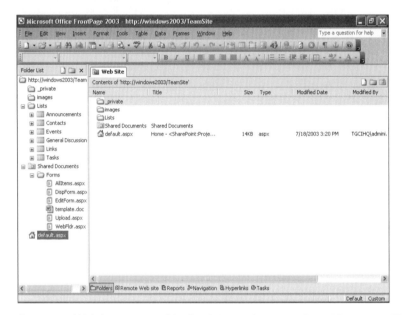

6   Open your Web browser, and in the **Address** box, type http://<server>/TeamSite, where <server> is the name of your Web server, and then press [Enter].

Your SharePoint team Web site opens.

Quick Launch area   Navigation links

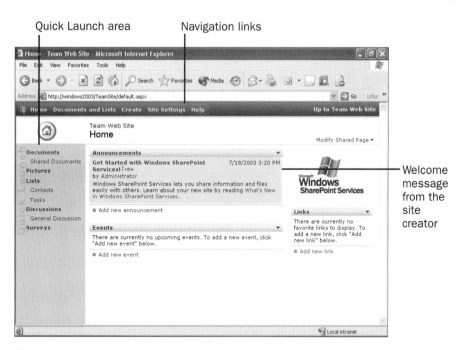

Welcome
message
from the
site
creator

Tip   You can apply a theme to your team Web site in the usual manner, but the easiest way to do so is through the SharePoint Site Settings page.

Maximize

7   If your Web browser window is not maximized, click the **Maximize** button.

8   Click each of the navigation links across the top—**Documents and Lists**, **Create**, **Site Settings**, and **Help**—pausing to look at the contents of each page.

9   Close the Help window, and then click the **Home** link in the upper-left corner of the page.

10   In the Quick Launch area at the left side of the Home page, click **Documents**.

The existing types of pages in the default team site are listed at the left side of the page.

CLOSE the Web browser window, and then close the SharePoint team Web site.

Customizing a SharePoint Team Web Site

SharePoint team Web sites can be created only as server-based sites on Web servers running Windows SharePoint Services. With this set of powerful team collaboration features, you can open up new collaboration possibilities, including the following:

- You can edit SharePoint team Web site content, upload documents, and participate in threaded discussions directly from your Internet browser. Multiple users can contribute to and interact with your team Web site, and receive automatic notifications when pages or discussions are modified.

- You can use FrontPage to customize SharePoint team Web sites; apply themes; insert graphics, link bars, and automatic live content; and insert lists such as Announcements, Events, Contacts, Surveys, and Links on the Web site for the entire team to view.

- You can add a document library to your team Web site so that documents can be stored centrally with either general or restricted access.

In this exercise, you will work with a few of the available options to customize an existing SharePoint team site.

Important To complete this exercise, you must have already created a SharePoint team site as described in the previous exercise.

USE the *Landscape* document in the practice file folder for this topic. This practice file is located in the *My Documents\Microsoft Press\FrontPage 2003 SBS\TeamWeb\Customize* folder and can also be accessed by clicking *Start/All Programs/Microsoft Press/FrontPage 2003 Step By Step*.
OPEN your Web browser and display the SharePoint team site you created in the previous exercise.

1 At the top of the page, click **Create**.

   The Create Page page opens.

2 To add a new document library to the site, click **Document Library**.

   The New Document Library page opens.

3 In the **Name** box, type Pacific NW Landscaping.

4 In the **Description** box, type General landscaping information for the greater Pacific Northwest region of the United States.

5 Leave the **Navigation** and **Document Versions** options. In the **Document Template** drop-down list, click **Microsoft Office FrontPage Web page** to indicate that the default document type is a Web page.

Troubleshooting　If the Microsoft Office FrontPage Web page menu item is not available, click Blank Microsoft FrontPage Document.

6　Click the **Create** button to create the new document library.

7　On the **Pacific NW Landscaping** link bar, click **Upload Document**.

8　To the right of the **Name** box, click the **Browse** button.

9　Browse to the *My Documents\Microsoft Press\FrontPage 2003 SBS\TeamWeb \Customize* folder, click the **Landscape** document, and then click **Open**.

10　Click the **Save and Close** link to return to the Pacific NW Landscaping page, which now features the new addition.

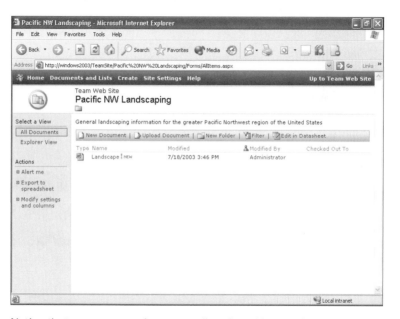

Notice that you can sort documents listed on this page by the *Type*, *Name*, *Modified*, *Modified By*, and *Checked Out To* columns.

11　At the top of the page, click **Documents and Lists**.

You return to the Documents and Lists page. Notice that the Pacific NW Landscaping library is now shown here.

12　In the **Lists** area, click **Contacts**.

13　On the Contacts page, click **New Item**.

14　On the Contacts: New Item page, create a new entry for the owner of The Garden Company, as shown in the following table.

In this box	Enter this
Last Name	Berg
First Name	Karen
E-mail Address	Karen@gardenco.msn.com
Company	The Garden Company
Job Title	Owner
Business Phone	(206) 555-0100, ext. 101
Fax Number	(206) 555-0101
Address	1234 Oak Street
City	Seattle
State	WA
Postal Code	10101
Web Page	www.gardenco.msn.com

15 At the top of the page, click **Save and Close** to save the new contact in the team site **Contacts** list.

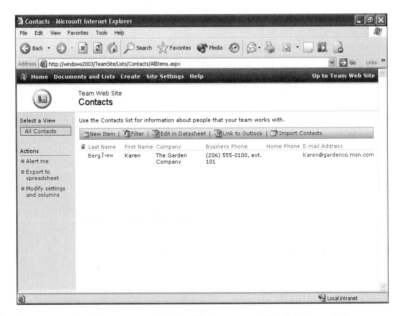

16 Return to the Home page. In the **Links** area, click **Add new link**.

17 On the Links: New Item page, press the ⌨End⌨ key to move the insertion point in the **URL** box to the end of *http://*. Then type **www.omnisterra.com/bot/cp_home.cgi**.

18 In the **Type the description** box, type Carnivorous Plant Database, and then click **Save and Close** to save the Web site link to your **Links** list.

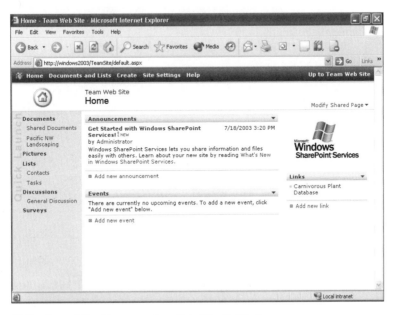

19 At the top of the Home page, click **Site Settings**.

20 On the Site Settings page, click **Change site title and description**.

21 In the **Title** box, type The Garden Company Team Web Site.

22 In the **Description** box, type This is where we can all come together to pool ideas and resources!

23 Click **OK** to return to the Site Settings page.

24 In the **Customization** area, click **Apply theme to site**.

25 On the **Apply Theme to Web site** page, click each of the listed themes to preview it in the **Preview** area. Then click **Sonora**, and at the bottom of the page, click **Apply**.

You return to the Site Settings page, with the new theme applied.

26 Click the **Home** link to return to the Home page, where you can see the results of your work.

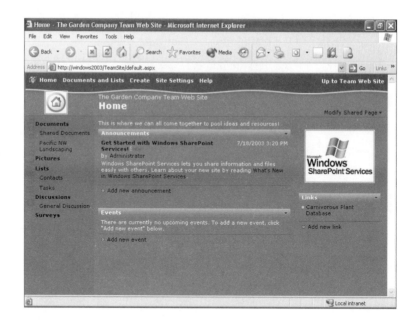

CLOSE the Web browser window.

Maintaining the Security of Web Site Files

Most small business or personal Web sites have only one developer working on them at any given time. In some cases, however, especially with larger corporate sites, multiple developers need to work on a single site at the same time. In such situations, you can use FrontPage's *source control* feature to protect the integrity of your Web site's files. The source control feature ensures that only one person at a time can edit a particular file. This avoids the frustration and anguish of having your changes overwritten by someone else.

FrontPage's source control works like a library that has only one copy of everything. You can check a file out, work with it, and then check it back in. While you have the file, no one else can check it out. Other people can open the file as *read-only* and look at it, but any changes they make to the file will be lost unless they save the file with a different name.

Tip FrontPage's source control feature is adequate for small projects, but if you need more rigorous source control, you might want to use Microsoft Visual SourceSafe (VSS). You can integrate a VSS project with a FrontPage project and have FrontPage act as a front end to the VSS project.

Source control options are disabled in the default installation of FrontPage. Unless you need source control, you will probably be happier leaving this feature disabled. It will be simpler to open and edit files, and you will not run the risk of losing changes made to a read-only file.

In this exercise, you will turn on source control and then check a file in and out.

USE the *GardenCo* Web site in the practice file folder for this topic. This practice file is located in the *My Documents\Microsoft Press\FrontPage 2003 SBS\TeamWeb\Source* folder and can also be accessed by clicking *Start/All Programs/Microsoft Press/FrontPage 2003 Step By Step*.
BE SURE TO start FrontPage before beginning this exercise.
OPEN the *GardenCo* Web site.

1 On the **Tools** menu, click **Site Settings** to open the **Site Settings** dialog box.

2 On the **General** tab, select the **Use document check-in and check-out** check box, and then click **OK**.

3 If a message box appears, warning you that there will be a delay while FrontPage recalculates the Web site, click **Yes** to proceed.

Troubleshooting   Source control must be enabled for each individual Web site; the setting does not apply across sites.

4 Right-click any file name in the **Folder List**, and click **Check Out** on the shortcut menu.

A green check mark appears in front of the file name to indicate that the file is checked out to you. You can now open the file in the Page view editing window, but no one else can.

5 Open the file, change a word or two on the page, save the page, and close it. (Save any embedded files if prompted to do so.)

6 In the **Folder List**, right-click the file name, and click **Check In** on the shortcut menu to check the file back in with your changes.

You can click Undo Check Out to discard the changes you made since you last checked out the file.

Troubleshooting   If you attempt to open a file in the Page view editing window without checking it out, a message box warns you that the file is under source control, and asks whether you want to check it out. If you don't check out the file, you can still make changes to your local copy.

CLOSE the *GardenCo* Web site, and if you are not continuing on to the next chapter, quit FrontPage.

Key Points

- FrontPage provides numerous templates and wizards to help you quickly create useful Web sites.

- You can share information, including files and photos, with your co-workers through a SharePoint team site.

- You can use FrontPage's built-in source control feature to ensure that only one person works on a Web site file at a time.

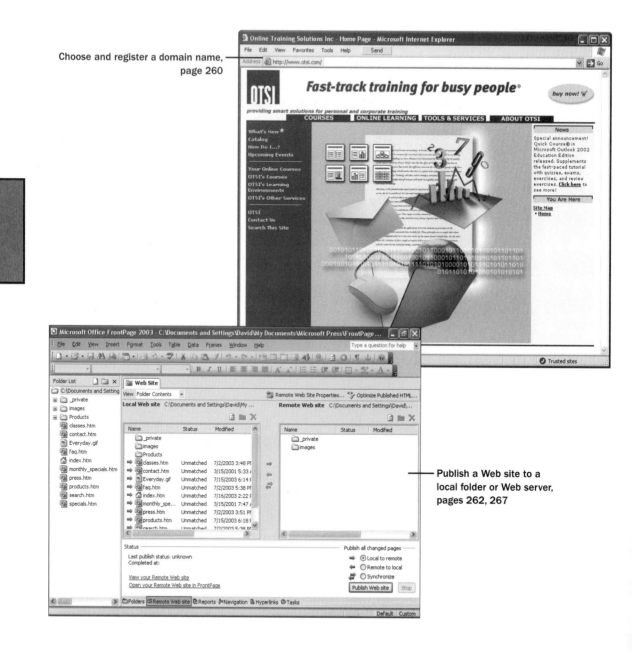

Choose and register a domain name, page 260

Publish a Web site to a local folder or Web server, pages 262, 267

10 Publishing Your Web Site

In this chapter you will learn to:

✔ Find a suitable host for your Web site.

✔ Choose and register a domain name.

✔ Publish a Web site to a local folder.

✔ Publish a Web site to a Web server.

There is no point in going to all the trouble of building an attractive, informative, creative Web site if no one is going to look at it. The culmination of all your work is the moment when you make your Web site available to the outside world by publishing it either to an intranet or to the Internet. Publishing a Web site for the first time is also known as *launching* the site.

In Web site terms, *publishing* means copying all your Web site files to a *Web server*. After the site is published, it is considered "live," that is, the intended private group of people (in the case of an intranet) or the general public (in the case of the Internet) can view the site in their Web browsers.

You can publish a Web site in three ways:

■ You can use *Hypertext Transfer Protocol (HTTP)* to publish to a Web server that has Windows SharePoint Services or FrontPage Server Extensions installed.

■ You can use *File Transfer Protocol (FTP)* to publish to a Web server that does not have Windows SharePoint Services or FrontPage Server Extensions installed. To use FTP, you need to know the name of the FTP server that will receive your files, and have a valid user name and password.

■ You can copy your Web site to a folder on your own computer. With a FrontPage-based Web site, it is advisable to publish the Web folder rather than simply copying the files, to ensure that the structure and integrity of the site is maintained.

See Also   Do you need only a quick refresher on the topics in this chapter? See the Quick Reference entries on page xxxvi.

Important   Before you can use the practice files in this chapter, you need to install them from the book's companion CD to their default location. See "Using the Book's CD-ROM" on page xiii for more information.

Finding a Suitable Host for Your Web Site

Web sites fall into two categories: *disk-based Web sites* and *server-based Web sites*. When you are developing a Web site, it's important to understand the difference.

Disk-based Web sites can be run on any kind of computer, or even from a floppy disk or CD-ROM. They support basic HTML functionality, and that's all. Most of the Web components included with FrontPage won't work in disk-based sites.

Server-based Web sites are run on a Web server—a computer that is specifically configured to host Web sites. On a small scale, a local computer such as your own might be designated as a Web server, or the server that hosts your company's intranet can serve this function. Personal Web sites are often hosted on the servers of *Internet service providers (ISPs)*. On a larger scale, Web servers that host corporate Web sites are usually located at professional *Web hosting companies*.

A bewildering number of Web hosting companies are available to choose from, each offering different rate plans and different levels of support. As is the case when choosing any kind of a service provider—from cellular phones to hairdressers—it can be difficult to evaluate all the choices and determine which one will best fit your needs.

The Web hosting industry is large and worldwide. Several paper-based and online magazines are dedicated to reviewing and reporting on the field of Web hosting, such as *The Web Host Industry Review*, which you can browse on the Internet at *www.thewhir.com*.

The best way to start your search for a Web hosting company is to do a search on the World Wide Web for *Web hosting*. You will find a variety of Web sites representing individual Web hosting companies. You can also find sites that collate and categorize hosting companies. Good resources you might want to check out include TopHosts at *www.tophosts.com*, HostSearch at *www.hostsearch.com*, and Web Host Directory at *www.webhostdir.com*. These sites help you sort through the choices based on different criteria.

Some Web hosting companies offer free or very inexpensive hosting services; be wary of these offers, though, because this is one of those times when you really do get what you pay for. Reliable, high-speed servers and reliable, high-speed technicians are neither free nor inexpensive! Changing Web hosting services can be difficult (although not impossible), so it is a good idea to make an informed decision from the beginning rather than learning from your mistakes.

Geographic location should not be a factor in your choice of Web hosting companies, other than choosing a Web host located in your own country to avoid any potential problems if there is a disagreement over payment. You will never need to physically visit your hosting company's office, and almost all companies have toll-free numbers in the event that you need to telephone them.

One good way to make a decision, or at least to narrow the field to fewer choices, is to talk to people who have established businesses and ISP-hosted corporate Web sites, and ask for their positive and negative impressions of any ISPs they have used. Most of the professional ISPs offer very good information on their own Web sites that should also help you to decide.

As the developer of a FrontPage-based Web site, your choices are limited because if you use any of the special FrontPage functionality, your ISP must support Windows SharePoint Services or FrontPage Server Extensions. Web hosting companies that support Windows SharePoint Services or FrontPage Server Extensions will advertise this fact on their Web sites. You can use many of the previously listed resources to search specifically for FrontPage-enabled hosting services.

Microsoft also maintains a list of registered Web Presence Providers—ISPs that have agreed to offer full support of FrontPage-based Web sites. A list of Web Presence Providers around the world is available at *www.microsoftwpp.com/default.asp*.

What is Windows SharePoint Services?

Windows SharePoint Services is a set of *server-side applications*—programs that are run on the Web server rather than on the Web visitor's own computer. You can use these applications to run specialized Web components using code stored and executed on the Web server, rather than on the Web visitor's computer. This saves time for the Web visitor and provides an element of security for the Web site owner, because your code is not directly exposed.

Windows SharePoint Services has been specially designed to enable information sharing and document collaboration.

Because the programs are run on the server, Web designers don't need to write the code and scripting that would be necessary to embed the functionality of these types of elements in the Web pages themselves. Instead, the code is "called" from the page and run on the Web server.

Previous versions of FrontPage were dependent on FrontPage Server Extensions, which similarly enabled certain server-side capabilities. Much of the FrontPage 2003 functionality will work on a Web server running FrontPage Server Extensions. The exceptions to this are the new data-driven Web site features such as XML Support, Web Package Templates, and Web Parts, which are beyond the scope of this book.

Windows SharePoint Services or FrontPage Server Extensions are not necessary to host Web sites created in FrontPage; however, they extend what the Web site is capable of doing. Link bars, top 10 lists, form handlers, discussions, full text searches, hit counters, and categories all require either Windows SharePoint Services or FrontPage Server Extensions to be fully functional.

Choosing and Registering a Domain Name

Before launching a commercial Web site on the Internet, you will need to choose and register a *domain name*. The domain name is the base of the alphanumeric address, called the *uniform resource locator (URL)*, where visitors locate your Web site on the World Wide Web. For example, *www.microsoft.com* is Microsoft Corporation's URL, and *microsoft.com* is its domain name. Your domain name might be your name, the name of your company, a word or phrase that represents what your company does, or any string of letters and numbers you desire.

When choosing a domain name, it is prudent to look for a name that will be easy for people to remember and easy for people to spell. Domain names that spell common words are good choices. Your domain name might be made up of more than one word, in which case you must decide to run the words together as one string, or to separate them with other characters; underscores are common word separators. Remember, though, that if you need to spell the name out over the phone, you will appreciate something short and simple!

Choose a name that means something to your company; if you have a registered trademark, consider using that. Domain names are not case-sensitive. You can use uppercase and lowercase letters in your written material to separate and differentiate between words, but visitors do not need to follow your capitalization to get to your site.

Part of your choice of a domain name is the extension. Depending on the type of Web site you are registering, you might choose an extension of .com, .org, .net, .edu, or one of the new extensions that have recently been made available in order to handle the increasing numbers of new Web site registrations. Each of these extensions has a meaning: *.com* is for companies, *.org* is for non-profit organizations, *.net* is for networks, and *.edu* is for educational institutions.

Some examples of domain names tied to product lines include *QuickCourse.com* and *eclecticClassroom.com*. You can use humor or wit in your choice of a domain name, such as *eFishinSea.com*, which is owned by a witty boat enthusiast. (When you pronounce the name it sounds like "efficiency.")

Obviously, for URLs to work, each domain name must be unique. To avoid duplication, all domain names are registered. You can register a domain name through many Web hosting companies; some of them will even help you with your search for the right name. Network Solutions (*www.networksolutions.com*) is a good one-stop shop for researching and registering domain name/extension combinations. You can also go directly to *www.internic.com*, the Internet Corporation for Assigned Names and Numbers (ICANN) domain registry Web site, for more information.

Configuring Your Own Computer to Host a Web Site

Most Web sites are initially developed as disk-based sites; that is, the site is developed and tested on a local computer. Only after a site is finished is it published to a Web server that is maintained either by the organization that owns the Web site or by a Web hosting company. And only at that point does it become a server-based site. The drawback to this strategy is that the server-specific components of the site won't work until the site is published to the server.

If you're going to do a significant amount of Web site development, you might consider configuring your own computer as a server for testing. For FrontPage 2003, Microsoft recommends the following configuration for a Web server:

- Windows Server 2003

- Internet Information Services 6.0 or later

- Windows SharePoint Services

If your computer does not meet these requirements, or if you do not want to run a full-blown Web server on your computer, you can set up your Windows 2000, Windows NT, or UNIX computer as a personal Web server, using the following configuration:

- Windows 2000

- Internet Information Services 5.0 or later

- FrontPage Server Extensions 2002

FrontPage Server Extensions 2002 do not support Windows 9x operating systems. As a workaround, Windows 98 users can install FrontPage 2000 Server Extensions from the Microsoft Web site.

Publishing a Web Site to a Local Folder

If you have developed a FrontPage-based Web site on your local machine and you want to move the Web site files to a different location or create a copy of the Web site, it is prudent to publish the site to the new location rather than simply moving or copying the files in Windows Explorer. This guarantees that the underlying structure of the site will be updated as necessary to maintain the integrity of the links.

New in Office 2003
Remote Web Site view

When you publish your Web site from FrontPage 2003, you work in the new Remote Web Site view. Remote Web Site view is similar to many FTP programs. It displays the contents of the local folder from which you are publishing, and the local or remote folder to which you are publishing. In Remote Web Site view, you select the local or remote files you want, and then simply click a button to transfer files in either direction, or to synchronize the files in the two locations. You can also access the log file created during the most recent publishing process and open your remote Web site in your default Web browser or in FrontPage.

In this exercise, you will publish a disk-based Web site to a local folder.

USE the *GardenCo* Web site in the practice file folder for this topic. This practice file is located in the *My Documents\Microsoft Press\FrontPage 2003 SBS\PublishWeb* folder and can also be accessed by clicking *Start/All Programs/Microsoft Press/FrontPage 2003 Step By Step*.
BE SURE TO start FrontPage before beginning this exercise.
OPEN the *GardenCo* Web site.

1 On the **File** menu, click **Publish Site**.

The Remote Web Site Properties dialog box appears.

Important   If you have previously published this Web site, FrontPage skips the Remote Web Site Properties dialog box and takes you directly to Remote Web site view, as shown in step 7. On the File menu, click Publish Site again to display the Remote Web Site Properties dialog box.

2   Select the **File System** option to indicate that you are publishing to a local folder.

3   Click the **Browse** button to open the **New Publish Location** dialog box, and browse to the *My Documents\My Web Sites* folder.

4   On the dialog box's toolbar, click the **Create New Folder** button to open the **New Folder** dialog box.

Create
New Folder

5   In the **Name** box, type PublishLocal, and then click **OK** to return to the **New Publish Location** dialog box with your newly created folder selected.

6   Click **Open** to return to the Remote Web Site Properties dialog box.

FrontPage has entered the specified name and path in the Remote Web site location box.

7   Click **OK**. When prompted to create a new site at that location, click **Yes**.

The files that will be transferred are indicated in the "Local Web site" list.

Blue arrows indicate files to be published.

8 Click **Publish Web site** to create the new Web site at the specified location.

The Publishing FrontPage Components dialog box appears, listing components that will not work unless they are published to a Web server running SharePoint Services or FrontPage Server Extensions.

Publishing FrontPage Components

⚠ The following pages in your Web site contain dynamic FrontPage components, such as a Search Form or a FrontPage form handler. They will not work unless they are published to a Web server running the FrontPage Server Extensions or SharePoint Services.

_borders/bottom.htm
index.htm
search.htm

To enable these components, publish your Web site to a server running the latest version of the FrontPage Server Extensions or Windows SharePoint Services.

[Ignore and Continue] [Cancel]

9 Click **Ignore and Continue**.

The Publishing FrontPage Components dialog box informs you of files that exist in the _private folder, which is normally hidden, but might be visible in the local folder.

Publishing FrontPage Components

⚠ The following files in your web site exist in the _private folder. The _private folder may be viewable on the destination Web server.

_private/feedback.txt

To better protect the safety of these files, you should publish your site to a Web server running SharePoint Services from Microsoft. Are you sure you want to publish these files?

[Ignore and Continue] [Cancel]

10 Click **Ignore and Continue**.

FrontPage displays a progress bar in the Status area while publishing the selected files, and when the publishing process is finished, displays the publish status information.

Original files   Published files

The newly published files are now visible in the Remote Web site list.

11   Click the **View your publish log file** link.

Because the Publish Log is an HTML file, it opens in your default Web browser. It contains the date, time, and description of each transaction involved in the publishing process.

12   Scroll through the file, and review the publishing process that just finished.

FrontPage first creates the required folder structure, copies each individual file, and then copies the navigation structure. The entire process takes approximately one minute. (The publishing time depends on the size and complexity of the individual Web site.)

Tip   By using the "Show only" box, you can filter this report to display only certain types of transactions: Publish Starts, Folder Creations, File Copies, File Renames, File Deletions, Confirmations, Warnings, or HTML Optimizations. The default is to display all the transactions.

13 Close the browser window to return to FrontPage.

14 Click the **View your Remote Web site** link.

The folder structure of the newly published Web site is displayed.

15 Scroll down, and double-click the **index** file to open The Garden Company's home page.

16 Click the navigation links to browse around the site, testing its functionality.

Notice that FrontPage Web components, such as the hit counter on the home page and the search engine on the search page, do not work properly.

17 Close the browser window and the PublishLocal window.

Back in FrontPage, the original disk-based Web site is still open, as shown in the Folder List.

CLOSE the *GardenCo* Web site.

Optimizing Published HTML

*New in
Office 2003*
Optimize HTML

FrontPage 2003 offers the option of cleaning up and "optimizing" the HTML code that makes up each Web page, at the time you publish the Web page or site. The new Optimize HTML feature gives you the option of removing some or all of the comments, some or all of the whitespace (such as extra paragraph marks that make it easier for you to read the code), and unnecessary HTML code generated by FrontPage. While these elements are certainly useful to the programmer or Web designer working on the site, they are not required for the site to function as designed. Optimizing the HTML will not affect the site performance, except perhaps to decrease the time it takes to load a page in your Web visitor's browser.

To use the Optimize HTML feature:

1 In Remote Web Site view, click the **Optimize Published HTML** button.

2 On the **Optimize HTML** tab of the **Remote Web Site Properties** dialog box, select the **When publishing, optimize HTML by removing the following elements** check box.

3 Select the check boxes of the HTML elements you would like to remove.

4 If you want to optimize the HTML for every Web page or site you publish, click the **Set as default** button.

5 Click **OK** to close the **Remote Web Site Properties** dialog box, and then publish your Web page or site as you normally would.

Publishing a Web Site to a Web Server

Developing a Web site is an iterative process. You work on a few pages, and you publish them to see whether they work as intended. Then you make corrections, work on a few more pages, and publish again. Gradually the pages evolve into a full-fledged Web site that you are ready to present to its intended audience.

While you are working on the site, you will want to publish it to a development server, not to one that is accessible to outsiders. Depending on your resources, this development server might be another computer, or it might be a personal Web server hosted on your own computer. When you are finally ready to launch the site, you will need to publish it again, this time to a Web server that is capable of supporting the many visitors you hope will come to take a look.

With FrontPage 2003, you can publish only the files that you want, rather than the entire Web site. You can even publish a single Web page by right-clicking the file name in the Folder List or in Folders view and clicking Publish Selected Files on the shortcut menu.

You can also mark specific files for exclusion from the publishing process by right-clicking the file name in the Folder List or in Folders view and clicking Don't Publish on the shortcut menu.

In this exercise, you will publish a disk-based Web site to a Web server.

Important To complete this exercise, you must have access to a Web server running either Windows SharePoint Services or FrontPage Server Extensions.

USE the *GardenCo* Web site in the practice file folder for this topic. This practice file is located in the *My Documents\Microsoft Press\FrontPage 2003 SBS\PublishWeb* folder and can also be accessed by clicking *Start/All Programs/Microsoft Press/FrontPage 2003 Step By Step.*
BE SURE TO start FrontPage before beginning this exercise.
OPEN the *GardenCo* Web site.

1 On the **File** menu, click **Publish Site**.

The Remote Web Site Properties dialog box appears.

Troubleshooting If you published this Web site in the previous exercise, FrontPage switches to Remote Web site view. On the File menu, click Publish Site again to display the Remote Web Site Properties dialog box.

2 Select the **FrontPage or SharePoint Services** option.

3 In the **Remote Web site location** box, type http://<server>PublishRemote, where *<server>* is the name of your Web server, and then click **OK**.

4 When prompted to create a new site at that location, click **Yes**.

5 Click **Publish Web site**.

FrontPage displays a progress bar while copying files and folders to the Web server, and displays the word "successful" in the Status area when the procedure has been successfully completed.

6 Click the **View your Remote Web site** link to view the Web site in your browser, testing its functionality.

Notice that the hit counter is fully functional.

7 Click the **View your publish log file** link to see the transactions included in the publishing process.

8 Close the Publish Log window to return to FrontPage.

CLOSE the *GardenCo* Web site, and if you are not continuing on to the next chapter, quit FrontPage.

Publishing a Web Site from a
Remote Web Server to a Local Computer

With FrontPage, you can publish any Web site to which you have access to any location. The publishing process goes both ways—in addition to publishing from a local computer to a remote server, you can do the opposite: publish a Web site from the Internet to your computer.

To publish from the Web to your computer:

- The remote server must have Windows SharePoint Services or FrontPage Server Extensions installed.

- You must have a valid user name and password for the remote server.

- You must have a working Internet connection.

To publish a FrontPage Web site from a remote server to a local folder or to your personal Web server:

1   If necessary, start your Internet connection.

2   On the **File** menu, click **Open Site**. In the **Site name** box, type the URL or IP address of the remote Web site preceding it with *http://* to indicate that it is a server-based site (for example, http://www.microsoft.com/frontpage/ or http://207.46.131.13 /frontpage/), and then click **Open**.

3   If the remote server requires a user name and password, it will prompt you for them. Supply a valid user name and password, and click **OK**.

    The remote Web site opens in FrontPage.

4   Publish the Web site to your local folder as directed in the earlier exercise.

Key Points

- You can host a server-based Web site at your own organization or through an Internet service provider or Web hosting company.

- If your Web site will be publicly available on the Internet, you will need to select and register a domain name.

- Many FrontPage Web components require Windows SharePoint Services or FrontPage Server Extensions to be functional. All the new data-driven Web site features in FrontPage 2003 require Windows SharePoint Services.

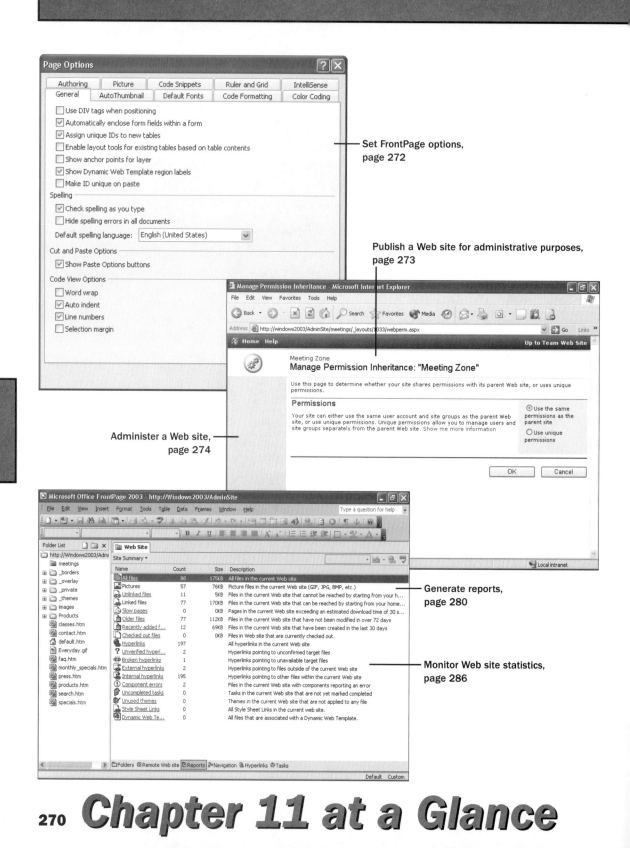

Set FrontPage options,
page 272

Publish a Web site for administrative purposes,
page 273

Administer a Web site,
page 274

Generate reports,
page 280

Monitor Web site statistics,
page 286

11 Managing Your Web Site

In this chapter you will learn to:

✔ Set FrontPage options.

✔ Publish a Web site for administrative purposes.

✔ Administer a Web site.

✔ Generate reports.

✔ Monitor Web site statistics.

Many of the administrative tasks associated with ongoing site maintenance don't apply to newly published sites, and the administrator of your Web server will handle many of the more difficult site administration tasks. However, as you work your way through this chapter, you will get a broad overview of the administrative tasks you are likely to want to carry out when developing a FrontPage-based Web site, and where to look for the settings needed for a particular task.

Administrative tasks fall into three major categories: working with Microsoft Office FrontPage 2003 so that future development efforts are efficient; assigning roles and permissions to the people who will have access to your Web site, with the goal of controlling who can do what to the site; and generating reports that tell you whether everything is running correctly and how your site is being used.

Important In the second exercise in this chapter, you publish a Web site to a Web server. You cannot do the third and subsequent exercises without having done the second. For this reason it is important to follow along sequentially rather than completing the exercises out of order.

See Also Do you need only a quick refresher on the topics in this chapter? See the Quick Reference entries on pages xxxvi–xxxvii.

Important Before you can use the practice files in this chapter, you need to install them from the book's companion CD to their default location. See "Using the Book's CD-ROM" on page xiii for more information.

Setting FrontPage Options

Setting up your FrontPage environment is not, strictly speaking, a management task. However, as you learn how to create a Web site, you gain a better understanding of the development environment's impact on your efficiency, and you will probably want to customize your FrontPage settings to ensure that future development tasks go as smoothly as possible.

Most of the options you use to set up FrontPage are available on the tabs of the Options and Page Options dialog boxes. You have several choices in the Options dialog box, including the following:

- You can set startup options that determine what tools are available each time you start FrontPage.

- You can tell FrontPage to alert you when a Web site needs to be updated or when you might inadvertently override individual page formatting with a theme.

- You can connect to your browser's Properties dialog box.

New in Office 2003
Improving quality for the customer

- You can participate in the Customer Experience Improvement Program, a program that sends anonymous information about the way you use FrontPage to Microsoft, to provide input into the next version of the application.

- You can turn the status bar on and off.

- You can specify which programs should be used to edit specific types of files so that double-clicking the file name opens the file in the correct application.

- You can define the age of recent files and old files, the download speed of slow pages, and the number of months of usage polled so that your usage reports contain exactly the information you want.

- You can specify types of files to transfer through FTP as ASCII files, and types of files to transfer as binary files.

These choices are available in the Page Options dialog box:

- You can specify various HTML coding and code viewing options, set the spelling options, and stipulate whether the Paste Options button is shown each time you paste text or graphics into a Web page.

- You can specify the default size, border thickness, and bevel width for thumbnails created using FrontPage's Auto Thumbnail command.

- You can specify different default proportional and fixed-width fonts, as well as a code font and size, for each of the 24 language character sets supported by The Microsoft Office System 2003.

- You can stipulate specific code formatting options that control the way code appears in Code View or Split View.

- When viewing a Web page in Code View or Split View, you can stipulate the colors in which different types of elements such as HTML tags, attributes, comments, and scripts should be displayed. FrontPage uses a variety of colors by default, but you can adjust these based on your preferences or needs.

- You can specify the browsers, browser versions, and server applications that you want your FrontPage-based Web site to work with. FrontPage will warn you if you include functionality in your Web site that is not supported by the configurations you select.

- You can specify the format in which different types of images are saved when converted or pasted into FrontPage.

New In Office 2003
Code snippets

- You can save frequently used blocks of code, and then insert them by simply typing a keyword and pressing Ctrl+Enter.

New In Office 2003
Page rulers and layout grid

- You can control the units (pixels, inches, centimeters, or points) and spacing that are used in the ruler and grid, as well as the style and color of the gridlines.

New In Office 2003
IntelliSense

- You can use IntelliSense technology to automatically complete or insert elements when working in Code View or the Split View code pane.

Take the time to explore the Options and Page Options dialog boxes, both of which are available from the Tools menu in FrontPage.

Publishing a Web Site for Administrative Purposes

Many server administration tasks can be carried out only on server-based Web sites; that is, Web sites that have been published to a Web server with FrontPage Server Extensions installed. Some of the FrontPage reports will work with a disk-based Web site, but you will need access to a Web server to complete most of the exercises in this chapter.

See Also   For more information about publishing Web sites, refer to "Publishing a Web Site to a Local Folder" and "Publishing a Web Site to a Web Server" in Chapter 10, "Publishing Your Web Site."

In this exercise, you will publish a disk-based Web site to your Web server so that you have something to work with in the following exercises.

USE the *GardenCo* Web site in the practice file folder for this topic. This practice file is located in the *My Documents\Microsoft Press\FrontPage 2003 SBS\ManageSite* folder and can also be accessed by clicking *Start/All Programs/Microsoft Press/FrontPage 2003 Step By Step*.
BE SURE TO start FrontPage before beginning this exercise.
OPEN the *GardenCo* Web site.

1   On the **File** menu, click **Publish Site** to open the **Remote Web Site Properties** dialog box.

2   Select the **FrontPage or SharePoint Services** option if your server supports one of these, or the **FTP** option if it doesn't.

3   In the **Remote Web site location** box, type http://<server>/AdminSite, where *<server>* is the name of your FrontPage Server Extension-enabled Web server, and then click **OK**.

4   When prompted to create a new Web site at the specified location, click **Yes**.

5   On the **Web Site** tab, click **Publish Web site** to publish the site to your Web server.

    When the publishing process is complete, the Status area reflects this and the files are visible in the Remote Web site list.

CLOSE the *GardenCo* Web site.

Administering a Web Site

If you are creating and publishing full-fledged Web sites, you are most likely using the services of either your own company's Information Technology (IT) department or a professional Web hosting company. In either case, someone else will be taking care of the site's administration.

If you don't have an IT department (or if you are the IT department) and you have published a Web site on a local server, you will need to take care of the site's administration yourself. Provided your Web server has the FrontPage Server Extensions installed, you can carry out the following administration tasks on the site's Web Site Administration page:

■   As the Web site's administrator, you can create new *subwebs* within the *root Web* site and specify whether the subweb will be a blank Web site or a SharePoint site. For example, The Garden Company might want to set up a For Members Only subweb of the main GardenCo Web site, where members of a special-interest club can meet online.

■ You can allow anyone to have access to your site and assign them to a specific group so you can control what they can see and do. These groups are called *roles*. Members of the general public who view your site are known as *anonymous users*. You can allow specific people to have specific access rights by assigning them to other roles. The default roles are Administrator, Advanced author, Author, Contributor, and Browser. Each role carries with it particular rights, or *privileges*, enabling or restricting access to view or modify the site. As the Web site's administrator, you can add, modify, and delete roles and privileges.

■ When you create a subweb, you can specify who can access it, and if necessary, designate a different administrator for the subweb. You can stipulate that subwebs should use the same permissions as their root Web site, or that they should have their own unique permissions.

■ For a *discussion Web site*, you can turn discussions on and off, allow local or remote discussions, and choose to automatically delete discussion items after a certain number of days. You can view and manage all discussions maintained on the Web server. If your Web server is also configured to send e-mail messages, you can view and manage all Web subscriptions maintained on the Web server.

In this exercise, you will open a server-based Web site and explore the server administration options offered by FrontPage 2003. Then you will create a subweb and take a look at how you would go about setting its permissions.

Important   The Web server used in this exercise is running Windows SharePoint Services. If your Web server is running FrontPage Server Extensions, your experience will be different from that shown here.

BE SURE TO have access to the *AdminSite* Web site that you published to your Web server in the previous exercise.

Open

1   On the Standard toolbar, click the down arrow to the right of the **Open** button, and then click **Open Site**.

The Open Site dialog box appears.

2   In the **Site name** box, type http://<server>/AdminSite, where *<server>* is the name of your Web server, and then click **Open**.

The server-based Web site opens in FrontPage.

3   On the **Tools** menu, point to **Server**, and then click **Administration Home**.

The SharePoint Site Settings page opens in your default Web browser.

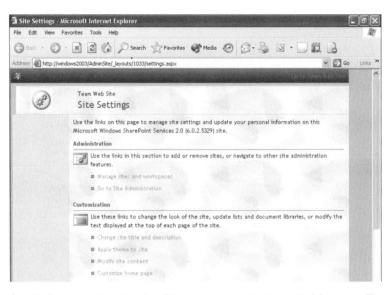

4   Scroll down, and notice the things you can do through this page. Then in the **Administration** area, click **Manage sites and workspaces**.

The Sites and Workspaces page shows all the sites below this one to which you have access.

5   To create a new subweb, click **Create**.

The New SharePoint Site page opens.

6   In the **Title** box, type Meeting Zone.

7   In the **URL name** box, type meetings.

Notice that this is appended to the end of the current Web site URL.

8 At the bottom of the page, click the **Create** button.

The Template Selection page opens, in which you can choose from a variety of SharePoint site templates (or you can create a blank site).

9 In the **Template** list, click **Basic Meeting Workspace**, and then at the bottom of the page, click **OK**.

Your new meeting workspace opens. A link to the original site is in the upper-right corner.

10 Click the **Up to Team Web Site** link to view the original site you posted in the previous exercise.

Notice there is no link to the administration features on the site itself.

11 Click the browser window's **Back** button to return to the Meeting Zone page.

12 In the upper-right corner of the page, click **Modify This Workspace**, and then click **Site Settings**.

The Site Settings page for the subweb opens.

13 In the **Administration** area, click **Go to Site Administration**.

The Site Administration page opens.

Tip The administration pages describe a lot of useful features. It's worth checking them out to see how they can help you administer your site.

14 Scroll down, and notice the things you can do through this page. Then in the **Users and Permissions** area, click **Manage permission inheritance**.

This site was originally set up to use the same permissions as its parent site, but you can change that setting here.

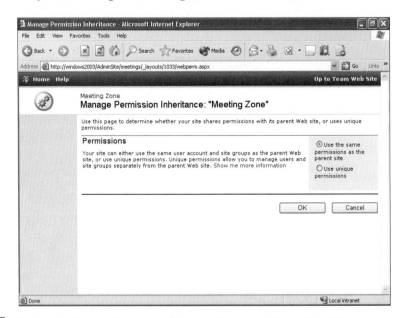

15 Select the **Use unique permissions** option, and then click **OK**.

You return to the Site Settings page. The links in the Administration section have changed to reflect that this site has its own set of permissions.

16 In the **Administration** area, click **Manage users**.

The people who have permission to work on this site are listed on the Manage Users page.

17 Click **Add Users** to open the Add Users page.

18 In the **Users** box, type the e-mail address of a person who has permission to access the server on which the SharePoint site is hosted.

For the purposes of this exercise, we typed *Kim@gardenco.msn.com*.

Troubleshooting The users you enter must have permission to access the server on which the site is hosted.

19 In the **Site groups** area, select the **Contributor** check box, and then click **Next**.

There are four types of Site groups to which users can belong: *Reader*, *Contributor*, *Web Designer*, and *Administrator*. Each has its own set of permissions, allowing group members to interact with the site in different ways.

20 For the purposes of this exercise, clear the **Send the following e-mail** check box.

Tip When assigning SharePoint site permissions to another person, it is a good idea to send this e-mail so he or she has a record of the site location and their access level.

21 Click **Finish**.

22 In the **Users** list, click the additional user you added.

For the purposes of this exercise, we clicked *Kim Akers*.

The Edit Site Group Membership page for this site opens, displaying the selected person's permissions.

23 In the **Site Group Membership** area, select the **Reader** check box, clear the **Contributor** check box, and then click **OK**.

You return to the Manage Users page, where the selected permissions have been changed.

CLOSE the Web browser window and the *GardenCo* Web site.

Generating Reports

You can easily generate a wide variety of *reports* about the condition of a FrontPage-based Web site. The FrontPage 2003 reporting options range from interesting to useful, depending on the size of your Web site and the size of your organization.

After you have published a Web site to a Web server that is running FrontPage Server Extensions, you can generate five types of reports: Site Summary, Files, Problems, Workflow, and Usage. Each of these categories of reports has several options. In this exercise, you will look at the first four types of reports, starting with the *Site Summary report*. This report does just what it says it does: it summarizes statistics for the entire site. Many of the statistical groupings are linked to more complete reports, and you can click any hyperlinked group name to see a more specific report.

FrontPage can produce *Files reports* about all the files in the Web site or about these specific groups of files:

■ If your Web site has been running well for some time, you might want to see a report that includes only the files you have added recently. By default, any file that was added to the Web site fewer than 30 days ago is considered a recently added file.

■ You can also see a report that includes only files you have recently changed. Again, the timeframe for a file to be considered recently changed is 30 days.

■ FrontPage can identify the older files in the site. By default, any file that is more than 72 days old is considered an older file.

The definitions of *recently added*, *recently changed*, and *older* can be changed on the Reports View tab of the Options dialog box.

Whether your Web site is having problems or not, you should consider running *Problems reports* at regular intervals. FrontPage can report on the following types of problems:

■ Unlinked files and broken hyperlinks.

■ Pages that are slow to download and that might cause frustration for your visitors. By default, any page that takes at least 30 seconds to download over a 56-kbps (kilobits per second) connection is considered a slow page. This option can be changed on the Reports View tab of the Options dialog box.

■ Components inserted in your pages that produce errors.

Workflow reports give you an idea of the current status of a site that is under development. (Some people think Web sites are always under development, and in fact, to stay current and appealing to repeat visitors, a Web site should be changed frequently.) You are able to review the status of files, see to whom their development is assigned, see whether or not files have been published, and see whether files are currently checked out to anyone. (This report is available only when *source control* has been turned on.)

In this exercise, you will open a server-based Web site, generate a series of reports about the Web site, and make changes to the site based on the reported information.

BE SURE TO have access to the *AdminSite* Web site that you published to your Web server previously in this chapter.

1   Close the **Folder List** if it is open.

2   On the Standard toolbar, click the **Open Site** button.

Open Site

> **Tip**   On the Standard toolbar, the Open and Open Site buttons toggle back and forth depending on which one you last used.

3   In the **Site name** box, type **http://<server>/AdminSite**, where *<server>* is the name of your Web server, and then click **Open**.

4   On the **View** menu, point to **Reports**, and then click **Site Summary**.

FrontPage switches to Reports view, displays the Reporting toolbar, and generates a Site Summary report.

This report contains statistics on the entire site. You can click the links in the Name list to look at each of the individual reports that make up the Site Summary report.

5   On the Reporting toolbar, click **Site Summary** to display the list of available reports, point to **Files**, and then click **All Files**.

FrontPage generates a report that includes every file in the site.

6 Click the **Type** column heading to sort the files alphabetically by type, and then click the **Type** column heading again to reverse the sort order.

7 Click the down arrow to the right of the **Type** column heading to display a list of the **Type** options.

8 In the drop-down list, click **htm** to filter the report information so that it displays only the static HTML pages.

9 On the Reporting toolbar, click **All Files** to display the list of available reports, point to **Problems**, and click **Unlinked Files**.

FrontPage generates a report of every file contained within the Web site folder that can't be reached by a direct link.

Tip You can delete files from within Reports view.

10 In the list of unlinked files, click **custrel1.gif**.

11 Hold down the [Shift] key, and press the [↓] key twice to select all three *custrel* images. Then on the **Edit** menu, click **Delete**.

12 In the **Confirm Delete** dialog box, click **Yes to All** to delete these three unused images.

FrontPage deletes the images and updates the Unlinked Files report.

Tip If the view of the report is not automatically updated, or if it is not updated correctly, press the [F5] key to refresh the screen.

13 On the Reporting toolbar, click **Unlinked Files** to display the list of available reports, point to **Workflow**, and click **Categories** to generate a Categories report.

The Category column is blank because none of the Web site files are currently assigned to a category.

14 Right-click the selected row containing *7124.jpg*, click **Properties** on the shortcut menu to open the file's **Properties** dialog box, and then click the **Workgroup** tab.

Troubleshooting   If the 7124.jpg file is not already selected, you can sort the list by name or scroll through the list to find the file and then select it yourself.

Using categories makes it simple to easily identify a group of files for later use. You can assign categories to all of your documents. A number of categories are set up automatically: Business, Competition, Expense Report, Goals/Objectives, Ideas, In Process, Miscellaneous, Planning, Schedule, Travel, VIP, and Waiting. If you don't like these categories, you can create your own.

15 Click the **Categories** button to display the **Master Category List** dialog box, type Carnivorous Plants, and then click **Add**.

The new category appears in the list.

16 In the **New category** box, type Thumbnails, click **Add** to add that category to the list, and then click **OK** to close the **Master Category List** dialog box.

FrontPage updates the "Available categories" list on the Workgroup tab to include the two new categories.

17 In the **Available categories** list, select the **Carnivorous Plants** check box to assign the 7124.jpg file to that category.

The category appears in the "Item(s) belong to these categories" box.

18 In the **Assigned to** area of the **Workgroup** tab, click **Names**.

The Usernames Master List dialog box appears so that you can designate the person assigned to work on the 7124.jpg file.

19 In the **New username** box, type Graphic Artist, and then click **Add** to add that name to the list of user names. Repeat this step to add Web Author to the list, and then click **OK** to close the **Usernames Master List** dialog box.

20 In the **Assigned to** drop-down list, click **Graphic Artist** to assign that person to work on the 7124.jpg file.

21 In the **Review status** drop-down list, click **Pending Review**.

You can add additional review status options by clicking the Statuses button and adding the options to the Review Status Master List.

22 Click **OK** to close the dialog box and apply your changes.

23 Right-click the row containing 7124_small.jpg, and click **Properties** on the shortcut menu to open the file's **Properties** dialog box.

24 On the **Workgroup** tab, select the **Carnivorous Plants** and **Thumbnails** check boxes to assign the file to those categories, and then click **OK**.

25 Click the down arrow to the right of the **Category** button to see the filter options, and click (**Custom...**) in the drop-down list to open the **Custom AutoFilter** dialog box.

26 Specify that you want to show only the files that have been assigned to the **Thumbnails** category by clicking **contains** (scroll the list if necessary) in the first drop-down list and typing Thumbnails in the second drop-down list.

27 Click **OK** to close the dialog box and apply your selections.

FrontPage regenerates the Categories report and this time shows only the 7124_small.jpg file.

28 Click the down arrow to the right of the **Category** button again, and click (**All**) to regenerate the report for all the files.

CLOSE the open Web site.

Monitoring Web Site Statistics

After you've published your Web site, it is likely that you will want to know something about the people who come to take a look at it. Armed with information about how your Web visitors use your site, how often they visit it, how they found it, and what operating systems they used, you can make better decisions about the effectiveness of certain elements of your site and how to modify and improve it. With FrontPage, you can have all this information at your fingertips to analyze, compare, and study.

You can track the usage of your site by having FrontPage maintain usage analysis logs. You can set the frequency of recurring usage analysis, delete stored usage data after a certain number of months, process log files for full days only, and (if your Web server has also been configured for e-mail) send e-mail confirmations to specified server or site administrators when the usage analysis processes have been run.

FrontPage can generate the following types of *usage reports*:

- Usage Summary, Monthly Summary, Weekly Summary, and Daily Summary reports include information about the activity on your Web site. These reports summarize all the other types of reports.

- Monthly Page Hits, Weekly Page Hits, and Daily Page Hits reports tell you how many times each page of your site was visited during the specified time period. You might decide to eliminate pages that no one seems to be visiting, or you might want to investigate whether they are simply too hard to find.

- Visiting Users, Operating Systems, and Browsers reports tell you how many different people visited your site during a specific period of time and what operating systems and browsers they used. When you know what kinds of browsers your visitors are using, you can make informed decision about the types of functionality to include on your site. For example, if you find that 95 percent of your visitors are using Microsoft Internet Explorer 4.0 or later, you can safely implement frames on your site without alienating your visitors.

- Referring Domains, Referring URLs, and Search Strings reports tell you how visitors found your site. For example, if a visitor found you through a search engine such as MSN Search, Dogpile, or Yahoo!, this statistic will be indicated along with the exact search string that was used. You will also know if a visitor clicked a banner ad on another site to link through to your site. These reports help you measure the usefulness of different marketing efforts.

In this exercise, you will open a server-based Web site and investigate the types of visitor information that FrontPage can monitor and report on, including browsers and operating systems. You will also see how to find out where your visitors come from by identifying the referring domains and URLs, and the search strings used by visitors to find your site. Finally, you will identify the most popular pages of your Web site, based on the number of times visitors come to each page.

BE SURE TO have access to the *AdminSite* Web site that you published to your Web server in the previous exercise.

Open Site

1 On the Standard toolbar, click the **Open Site** button.

2 In the **Site name** box, type http://<server>/AdminSite, where *<server>* is the name of your Web server, and then click **Open**.

The server-based Web site opens.

📄 Reports

Reports View

3   If necessary, click the **Reports View** button to switch to Reports view.

Important   Usage reports are available only for root Web sites (not subwebs) hosted on Web servers running Windows SharePoint Services, Microsoft SharePoint Team Services, or Microsoft FrontPage Server Extensions 2002. To display the full range of options explored in this exercise, the *AdminSite* Web site must be designated as a root Web site. Ask your Web server's administrator to take care of this task for you.

4   On the **View** menu, point to **Reports**, point to **Usage**, and then click **Usage Summary**.

FrontPage generates a Usage Summary report.

This report contains usage statistics on the entire site. Many of the groupings are linked to more complete reports, which you can see by clicking any hyperlinked group name.

5   On the Reporting toolbar, click **Usage Summary**, point to **Usage**, and then click **Monthly Page Hits**.

The Monthly Page Hits report appears.

6   Scroll across the page to see the information included in the report.

Each month is tracked in its own column. (You specify the number of months on the Reports View tab of the Options dialog box.)

7   On the Reporting toolbar, click **Monthly Page Hits**, point to **Usage**, and then click **Browsers**.

8   Browse through the other reporting options.

Because your site is newly published, there won't be much data available to look at right now, but you can see the options offered for the future.

CLOSE the *GardenCo* Web site, and quit FrontPage.

Key Points

■   You can change many aspects of your Web site from the Windows SharePoint Services administration site that is automatically created when you publish your site to a Web server running Windows SharePoint Services.

■   You can generate a variety of reports that help you improve your Web site and find out useful information about your Web site visitors.

Glossary

absolute path   A designation of the location of a file including the root directory and the descending series of subdirectories leading to the end file. See also *relative path*.

access violation   A type of error caused by attempting to access a page or site that is not allowed.

alias   An alternate name used for identification. Using a generic e-mail alias that automatically forwards received e-mail messages to one or more individuals ensures that messages are always received by the appropriate person.

anchor tag   Code in an HTML document that defines a bookmark or a link to a bookmark, Web page, Web site, or e-mail address.

anonymous users   Members of the general public who view a Web site.

article   A message posted to a Discussion Web site.

bookmark   An anchor tag that defines a specific location in an HTML document.

Boolean query   A True or False query that utilizes logical operators including AND, OR, IF THEN, EXCEPT, and NOT.

border   The edge or visible frame surrounding a workspace, window, document, table, cell, or graphic.

browser sniffer   A program that detects the Web browser and version used by each Web visitor.

bulleted list   An unordered list of concepts, items, or options.

cell   The intersection of a row and a column in a table or spreadsheet. A cell is displayed as a rectangular space that can hold text, a value, or a formula.

cell padding   The space between the borders of a cell and the text inside it.

child page   A Web page that is subordinate to another Web page, known as the parent page.

clip art   A ready-made graphic that can be copied and incorporated into other documents.

Code pane   One of the four panes in Page view. This pane displays the HTML code behind the Web page.

collaboration   The sharing and coordination of information among team members using Web sites created from FrontPage templates.

collaboration site   A Web site for team use. See also *SharePoint team Web sites*.

column   The vertical line of cells in a spreadsheet or table.

comment   A note embedded in a Web page that is not visible in the published version of the Web page.

cropping   Cutting off the top, bottom, or sides of a graphic to trim it to a smaller size.

Design pane   One of the four panes in Page view. This pane displays your page much as it will appear in a Web browser. You work primarily in this pane when creating Web pages.

dimmed   In reference to menu commands, unavailable and displayed in gray font.

discussion Web site   A Web site where people communicate by submitting, or posting, messages or articles.

disk-based Web site   A Web site that is located on a floppy disk, CD-ROM, or a computer that is not configured as a Web server.

docking   Attaching a toolbar to one edge of the window.

domain name   The unique name that identifies an Internet site. A domain name has two or more parts, separated by periods, as in *my.domain.name*.

drawing canvas   The frame in which Office Drawings are created in FrontPage.

dynamic effect   A Web component, such as a banner ad or marquee, that adds motion to a Web page.

e-mail link   A hyperlink that initiates a new e-mail message window.

embedded cascading style sheet   A document embedded within a Web page that defines formats and styles for different page elements.

external cascading style sheet   A document outside of a Web page that defines formats and styles for different page elements. External style sheets can be referenced by multiple documents to provide a consistent look across pages and sites.

file name   The name of a file.

file structure   description of a file or group of files that are to be treated together for some purpose. Such a description includes file layout and location for each file under consideration.

File Transfer Protocol (FTP)   The protocol used for copying files to and from remote computer systems on a network using TCP/IP, such as the Internet.

Files report   A report generated in FrontPage that provides information about all the files in a Web site or about specific groups of files, such as those most recently added or modified.

Folders view   The FrontPage view that displays the visible files and folders that are part of the open Web site.

frame   A division of a Web page that contains either content or a link to content from another source.

frameset   The single shell page of a frames page that contains individual frames of information drawn together from multiple sources.

friendly name   A simple name that translates into a more complex one; friendly names used to identify Web locations are translated by the computer to more complex IP addresses.

FTP   See *File Transfer Protocol*.

Graphics Interchange Format (GIF)   A file format for saving pictures that displays well over the Web.

grouping   Combining several drawing elements together so that they can be moved, sized, or otherwise treated as one.

header column   The column in a table that contains the title of each row.

header row   The row in a table that contains the title of each column.

hit counter   A feature on a Web site, usually on the home page, that counts the number of "visits" to the site.

home page   The starting page for a set of Web pages in a Web site. The home page includes links to other pages and often provides an overview of the entire Web site.

hosting   The process or service of storing a Web site on a configured Web server and serving it to the intended audience.

hotspot   A defined area on an image map that is hyperlinked to a bookmark, Web page, Web site, or e-mail address.

HTML   See *Hypertext Markup Language*.

HTTP   See *Hypertext Transfer Protocol*.

hyperlink   The text or graphic that users click to go to a file, a location in a file, an Internet or intranet site, page, location, and so on. Hyperlinks can also lead to Gopher, telnet, newsgroup, and FTP sites. Hyperlinks usually appear underlined and in color, but sometimes the only indication is that the pointer changes to a hand.

Hyperlinks view   The FrontPage view that displays the hyperlinks to and from any selected page in the open Web site.

Hypertext Markup Language (HTML)   A tagging system used to code documents so that they can be published on the World Wide Web and viewed with a browser.

Hypertext Transfer Protocol (HTTP)   The client/server protocol used to access information on the World Wide Web.

image map   A graphic element containing hotspots.

Included Content components   A set of Web components that you can use to create links to the text or graphics you want to display on a Web page, rather than inserting them directly.

Internet Protocol (IP) address   The number that uniquely identifies a specific computer on the Internet.

Internet service provider (ISP)   A company that provides individuals or organizations with the necessary software and information to get access to the Internet, and with the Internet connection itself. Many ISPs also serve as Web hosts. See also *Web hosting company*.

intranet   A network designed for information processing within a company or organization. Its uses include such services as document distribution, software distribution, access to databases, and training.

IP address   See *Internet Protocol address*.

ISP   See *Internet service provider*.

Joint Photographic Experts Group (JPG)   A graphics format used for photos and other graphics with more than 256 colors.

kerning   The distance between letters in a word.

launching   Publishing a Web site to the Internet for the first time.

link bar   A hyperlinked list of Web pages within a Web site, providing access to the specified pages.

lists   Items of information, either numbered or bulleted, set off from a paragraph.

localhost   An example of a friendly name for an IP address. See also *friendly name*.

media   Graphics, videos, sound effects, or other material that can be inserted into a Web page.

menu   A list of commands a user can select from to perform a desired action.

Microsoft Office System 2003   The Microsoft suite of applications for personal and professional use, updated for 2003.

navigation structure   A hierarchical map of how Web pages are connected within a Web site and what routes the user can take to get from one page to another.

Navigation view   A view of all the files that have been added to the navigational structure of the open Web site.

nesting   Embedding one element inside another.

numbered list   An ordered list of concepts, items, or options.

Office Drawings   The specially formatted lines, shapes, WordArt objects, text boxes, and shadowing that can be incorporated into Microsoft Office documents.

ordered list   The Hypertext Markup Language (HTML) term for a numbered list.

page banner   A textual or graphic image that displays the title of a Web page.

page hits   The number of visits a Web page or site receives. See also *unique users*.

Page Based On Schedule component   A component in FrontPage that displays the contents of a file for a limited period of time.

Page component   A component in FrontPage that displays the contents of a file wherever it is inserted.

page title   The text that is displayed on the page banner of a Web page and in the title bar of a Web browser.

Page view   The FrontPage view from which page creation and editing tasks are done. This view displays the open page or pages in the Page view editing window.

Page view editing window   The FrontPage window in which a Web page is edited.

Personal Web Server (PWS)   An application that transmits information in Hypertext Markup Language (HTML) pages by using the Hypertext Transport Protocol (HTTP). It provides the ability to publish Web pages on the Internet or over a local area network (LAN) on an intranet.

Picture Based On Schedule component   The component that displays the contents of designated graphics files for a specified period of time.

pixel   Short for picture element. One pixel is a measurement representing the smallest amount of information displayed graphically on the screen as a single dot.

posting   Submitting messages or articles for display on a Web site.

Preview pane   The FrontPage window in which Web pages can be viewed before they are published.

privileges   Access rights that enable or restrict a user in viewing or modifying a Web site.

Problems report   A report generated in FrontPage that can analyze and summarize problems such as broken links and slow downloading time.

publishing   Copying your Web site files to a Web server to display the site to the intended audience.

PWS   See *Personal Web Server*.

read-only   The designation of a file that can be viewed but not modified.

relative path   A designation of the location of a file in relation to the current working directory. See also *absolute path*.

Remote Web Site view   A view of information about the published version of your Web site that you use to see the local and remote file structures simultaneously. You can manipulate local and remote files and folders from this view.

report   A detailed account of the workings of aspects of a Web site. Types of reports you can generate include Site Summary, Files, Problems, Workflow, and Usage.

Reports view   The FrontPage view that displays the available reports about the open Web site.

roles   Assignments, to groups, of varying degrees of Web site access rights. Groups include anonymous users (the general public), Adminstrator, Advanced author, Author, Contributor, and Browser.

root Web   A Web site that contains a subweb.

row   A horizontal line of cells in a spreadsheet or table.

screen real estate   A term for the amount of space a designer has in which to present the information in a Web page.

screen resolution   The width and height of a computer monitor display in pixels.

ScreenTip   The small text box that appears when the mouse pointer passes over a button, telling the user the name of the command.

second-level   See *child page*.

server-based Web site   A Web site that is located on a computer that is configured as a Web server. See also *disk-based Web site*.

server farms   Large-scale operations for hosting corporate or organizational Web sites.

Server Health   A FrontPage feature used to detect and repair potential problems with links on a server.

server-side applications   Programs that run on the Web server rather than on a Web visitor's own computer and allow you to post and modify content on a Web site.

shading   Background and foreground colors or pictures the designer places on the Web page.

shared border   The areas at the top, bottom, left, or right of all or some of the pages in a Web site, in which common elements are displayed. Shared borders give the site a consistent look.

SharePoint team Web site   A collaboration site for team use that consists of a Home page, a Document Libraries page, a Discussion Boards page, a Lists page, a Create Page page, and a Site Settings page.

site map   A graphical depiction of the locations of Web pages in a Web site.

Site Summary report   A report generated in FrontPage that collates the results of the other reports.

source control   A FrontPage feature that helps prevent more than one person from working on the same file at the same time.

Split pane   One of the four panes in Page view. This pane simultaneously displays the design view and HTML code.

static page   A Web page with hard-coded content.

Substitution component   A component in FrontPage that associates names, or variables, with text. See also *variables*.

subweb   A stand-alone Web site that is nested inside another Web site; subwebs can have a unique set of permissions.

table   A structured presentation of information consisting of vertical columns and horizontal rows.

table of contents (TOC)   The group of navigation links to each page of a Web site.

table title   The overall name of a table that appears either as a separate paragraph above the body of the table or in the table's top row.

Tasks view   The FrontPage view that displays a list of tasks to be completed in the open Web site.

teams   Groups of users who work in collaboration to accomplish a task.

template   A predefined layout and design for specific types of Web pages and sites.

theme   A predefined package of colors, graphics, fonts, and styles that you can apply to a single Web page or an entire Web site.

thumbnail   A small version of a graphic that is hyperlinked to the full-size version.

TOC   See *Table of contents*.

toolbar   A grouping of commands represented by buttons or icons.

ungrouping   Separating a drawing into its individual elements so that they can be moved, sized, or otherwise edited one at a time. See also *grouping*.

uniform resource locator (URL)   The alphanumeric address that Web visitors use to locate your Web site on the World Wide Web.

unordered list   The Hypertext Markup Language (HTML) term for a bulleted list.

URL   See *uniform resource locator*.

usage report   A report that helps you count, track, analyze, and summarize the activity on your Web site.

variable   A named object that can assume any set of values.

view   One of several ways of focusing on specific aspects of a FrontPage-based Web site.

Web browser   A program used to view Web pages on the World Wide Web.

Web component   A ready-made programmatic element that adds capabilities such as link bars and tables of contents.

Web hosting company   A business that provides server space for Web sites. Many ISPs provide Web hosting. See also *server-based Web site*.

Web page   The document or one of multiple documents that make up a Web site. See also *file name*.

Web server   A computer that is specifically configured to host Web sites.

wizard   A program that creates the layout of a Web page or Web site and leads the user through the process of personalizing the content and the appearance of the final product.

WordArt   Text objects with special formatting applied to add bend, slope, color, or shadow.

WorkFlow report   A FrontPage report that gives site administrators an idea of the current status of a site that is under development. You can review the status of files, see to whom their development is assigned, see whether or not files have been published, and see whether files are currently checked out to anyone.

Workflow report   A FrontPage report that enables review of the status of a Web site under development. You can review the status of files, see to whom their development is assigned, see whether or not files have been published, and see whether files are currently checked out to anyone.

wrapping   The breaking of lines of text to fit the width of the cell or text box.

Index

Numerics

K

L

M

N

Navigation view, 9, 13, 179, 292
adding pages to, 188
orientation, changing, 12
orientation, switching, 13
Portrait mode, vs. Landscape
mode, 13
subtrees in, viewing only, 12
switching to, 11, 160, 178
zooming in, 12
Navigation View button, 160
Navigation View button (Page
view window), 178
nesting, 292
Netscape. *See browsers*
New Folder button (Folder
List), 180
New Page or Web task pane
displaying at startup, 32
opening, 32
opening, by default, 32
numbered lists, 292. *See also
bulleted lists*
adding items to, xxiii
converting paragraphs into, 60, 62
HTML code for, 64
Numbering button (Formatting
toolbar), 62

O

Office Drawings, 293
Office proofing tools, 228
older files report, 280
One Page Web template, xxi, 27
online retailing, 33
opening
Drawing toolbar, 7
files, 10, 19
files, from outside FrontPage, 18
Folder List, 10, 11, 192
FrontPage-based Web sites, xxi, 9,
19, 121
hyperlink target pages in new
windows, 194
New Page or Web task pane, 32
New Page or Web task pane, by
default, 32
Pictures toolbar, 94

subwebs, 184
Tables toolbar, 75
tasks, 17
templates, 155
toolbars, xxi
Web pages, 18
Web pages, blank, 89
Web pages, from outside
FrontPage, 18
Web pages, multiple, 139
Web sites, xxi
Web sites, in Page view, 31
Word documents, 43
operating systems, hits by,
viewing, 287
optimizing
display, 55
HTML, 14
screen display, 55
ordered lists, 64, 293
organizing
clip art (*see Clip Organizer*)
files, 178–180
folders, 178–180
pictures, 180
orientation link bar,
choosing, 186
ovals, drawing, 100
overwriting
formatting, with shared
borders, 135
text, 44
overwriting files, 125

P

padding, border, setting, 131
padding, cell. *See cell padding*
Page Banner Properties dialog
box, 135
page banners, 20, 133–138,
212, 293
centering, 136
customizing, 43
inserting, xxviii, 135, 161
selecting, 136
shared borders and, 134
styles, applying, 136

text, replacing, 43
themes and, 133
updating, 44
Page Based On Schedule
component, 212, 293
Page component, 212, 293
page hits, 211, 293
page layout, tables, 154. *See also
Web page layout*
page loading times, report of, 280
Page Properties dialog box, 4
Formatting tab, 127
page titles. *See titles*
Page view, 18, 293
Code pane, 18, 289
Design pane, 18, 290
editing window, 3, 19, 293
opening Web sites in, 31
Preview pane, 18
Split pane, 18, 295
pages, home. *See home pages*
pages. *See Web pages*
panes
switching between, 22
toggling, 11
paragraphs
aligning, xxii, 48, 114
borders, xxii, 47
centering, xxii, 48, 114
converting into bulleted lists, 60
converting into numbered lists, 62
creating, 38
deleting, 42
formatting, xxii, 48, 114
indenting, xxii, 48
inserting, 131, 192
selecting, 42
spacing, xxii, 48, 173, 193
Paste button (Standard
toolbar), 106
pasting
drawings, 106
options, 40
pictures, 106
text, 44
permissions for subwebs,
assigning, 183
Personal Web Server, 293
Personal Web template, 30

305

Learning solutions for *every*
software user

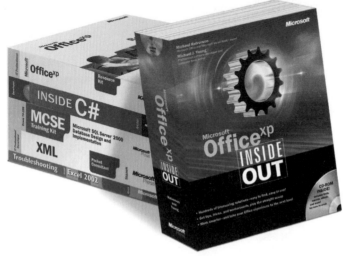

Microsoft Press learning solutions are ideal for every software user—from business users to developers to IT professionals

Microsoft Press® creates comprehensive learning solutions that empower everyone from business professionals and decision makers to software developers and IT professionals to work more productively with Microsoft® software. We design books for every business computer user, from beginners up to tech-savvy power users. We produce in-depth learning and reference titles to help developers work more productively with Microsoft programming tools and technologies. And we give IT professionals the training and technical resources they need to deploy, install, and support Microsoft products during all phases of the software adoption cycle. Whatever technology you're working with and no matter what your skill level, we have a learning tool to help you.

The tools you need to put technology to work.

Microsoft®
microsoft.com/mspress

Get a **Free**
e-mail newsletter, updates,
special offers, links to related books,
and more when you

register online!

Register your Microsoft Press® title on our Web site and you'll get a FREE subscription to our e-mail newsletter, *Microsoft Press Book Connections.* You'll find out about newly released and upcoming books and learning tools, online events, software downloads, special offers and coupons for Microsoft Press customers, and information about major Microsoft® product releases. You can also read useful additional information about all the titles we publish, such as detailed book descriptions, tables of contents and indexes, sample chapters, links to related books and book series, author biographies, and reviews by other customers.

Registration is easy. Just visit this Web page and fill in your information:

http://www.microsoft.com/mspress/register

Microsoft

Proof of Purchase

Use this page as proof of purchase if participating in a promotion or rebate offer on this title. Proof of purchase must be used in conjunction with other proof(s) of payment such as your dated sales receipt—see offer details.

Microsoft® Office FrontPage® 2003 Step by Step
0-7356-1519-5

CUSTOMER NAME

Microsoft Press, PO Box 97017, Redmond, WA 98073-9830